JULES MICHELET

Nature, History, and Language

LINDA ORR is Assistant Professor of French at Yale University, where she received her Ph.D. A graduate of Duke University, she also studied at the University of Montpellier and she has taught at the University of Iowa and Swarthmore College.

JULES MICHELET

Nature, History, and Language

LINDA ORR

Cornell University Press

ITHACA AND LONDON

Cornell University Press gratefully acknowledges
a grant from the Andrew J. Mellon Foundation
that aided in bringing this book to publication.

First published 1976 by Cornell University Press.
Published in the United Kingdom by Cornell University Press Ltd.,
2–4 Brook Street, London W1Y 1AA.

International Standard Book Number 0–8014–0976–4
Library of Congress Catalog Card Number 76–13662
Printed in the United States of America by York Composition Company, Inc.
Librarians: Library of Congress cataloging information
appears on the last page of the book.

To Fanny Albouy and in memory of
Pierre Albouy (1920–1974)

The heroic character, steadfast and unchangeable, excludes the infinite metamorphosis that is art.
—manuscript variant, *La Montagne*

He watches you from the depths of his mystery. . . . I dare not say, from the depths of his guile.
—Michelet on Richelieu in the *Histoire de France*

Contents

Preface

Jules Michelet is an essential figure in modern European historiography, for his lifework is devoted to a continuing attempt to define the task of the historian, or more precisely, the task of any writer of fictions. At the apex of his career and at a turning point in the history of Europe and, indeed, in western romantic literature, Michelet—the author of a study of medieval France and the *Histoire de la Révolution française*, who was slowly filling in the entire *Histoire de France*—turned to writing natural history as if his questions on the nature of time and change required a broader scope for analysis. He wrote four books, *L'Oiseau*, *L'Insecte*, *La Mer*, and *La Montagne*, that form a fundamental counterpoint to the volumes on French history he was still writing; in fact, had he not approached natural history Michelet might not have found the ideological and physical impetus to go on with his larger enterprise. I do not suggest that the "real" Michelet is to be found in any one work, even in the four natural histories; rather, my premise is that a careful look at Michelet through the displaced perspective of the nature books will illuminate the whole, that the difference in the two kinds of texts begets the dialogue of the parts.

My book begins by tracing Michelet's search for patterns of imagined coherence in nature, which has become the exemplary field for history in general. Opening himself up to such a profound revision was potentially dangerous for the historian. It led him into a period of equally intense self-consciousness and repression in which his very notions of the self's identity in history were shaken and the profession of the writer was revealed in its falseness and necessities. It is inevitable that the middle of my book should evoke Michelet's *Journal*, one of the most fascinating documents of nineteenth-century literature and another extension of the historian's psychic and intellectual battleground. The autobiographical texts, adding still more complexity to the masks of Michelet, enter their voice in the polyphonic debate. Finally, the burden of this progressive questioning and subjectivity, of a gradually fragmented self and universe, is shifted to language. Michelet, like many of his contemporaries, both historians and poets, was forced to deal with his craft as an exercise in linguistic action. The last part of my book attempts to follow the influence of language on the writing of (natural) history itself; how the narrative of a sentence, word, or morpheme can, in the end, become the event.

If the naturalist books seem to assume an unwarranted "place" in my book, Michelet himself spoke of the history of nature as the shadow behind man's constrained activities, as the greater contour of the *scienza nuova*. His four nature books were an "eccentric" concentration that brought together the naturalist texts submerged in the *Histoire de France*, the hidden story relating the *Sorcière* to Palissy and Galileo, to Lyell and Darwin. The mere suggestion in *La Mer* and *La Montagne* of the nineteenth century's advances in biology, zoology, and geology shifts, subtly but irreparably, Michelet's entire history that had previously been built around the political Revolution of 1789. Despite the new gravitational pull of nature in Michelet's later works, the prestige of its twin, history, is never lessened. On the contrary, the naturalist works, as my allusions should prove, feed back into the sheer physical vastness of the *Histoire de France*, for natural history is history in its essence and Michelet's naturalist books are a meditation on the limits of history, where it is most productive, that is, aggrandizing. Perhaps more than any discipline, history has had to reckon with its "borderline" status between literature and science. Michelet was one of the first historians to be obsessed with the "unreadable" and "unthinkable" nature of his profession's objects: the mute and lost ones of time, the corpses. His interest in the natural world, where the slippery border of culture is most in jeopardy, was the logical continuation of this obsession. The same concerns have, not ironically, stimulated new historical research in France (and in the United States?). The notion of documents has been amplified to include local history, mentalities, experiences of death, peasant societies, asylums, and other marginal communities: this is what Michelet anticipated. The historian Lucien Febvre, one of the founders of *Annales: Economies, Sociétés, Civilisations*, acknowledged most openly his debt to Michelet; in addition, Jacques Le Goff's work on medieval history, Robert Mandrou's study of the seventeenth-century witch-magistrate dialogue, Fernand Braudel's *longue durée*, Michel de Certeau's theoretical essays on historical writing, and Michel Serres' essay on *La Sorcière* combining psychoanalytic, anthropological, and philosophical threads, are examples of the nineteenth-century historian's lineage.

The naturalist works bare Michelet's primary preoccupations or fabrications since there is less interference from the inlay of event and fact than in his histories, and politics begins to recede so that the essential political nature of the text can surface, for the point of departure is always the present, to which history returns after a fictional voyage into the past and silence. Because the word "ideology" has been so diversely discussed, unloaded and reloaded in English as well as French, particularly in Marxist literature, I use it sparingly though I am constantly suggesting it. Systems, networks, or collages of beliefs, of socioeconomic self-images, of norms and functions, "ideologies" allow for the nuance of unconscious formation, whereas "consciousness," the more common word in critical literature, is perhaps too burdened with the conflicting contexts of German romantic philosophy and Kant. A third notion which I use, blending and blurring the other two, is "myth," a word which the users of "ideology" would shun but which can describe (as in Lévi-Strauss) the same kind of cultural representations. In the naturalist books, Michelet is looking for a suitable myth, personal and social. Certainly that is history's ultimate project: the constant shattering and refabrication of myth, of the "minimal fiction."

Does every text ultimately address itself to smoothing over those symbolic wounds and rifts we are reminded of at every level of discourse? Rifts of whole and part, of referent and sign, of eternity and time, of signifier and signified, of people and social class, of law and politics . . . the endless rifts. Michelet's naturalist books are a textual experiment in rearrangement, realignment. The text is, at the minimum, doubled: one repeats the organizations of tradition, one explores. The second course may contradict the first, yet both are intertwined invisibly in the texture of language. Michelet, like his contemporary romantics, tried to adapt pre-Revolutionary society to the industrial state that enforced its changes. His history houses culture while noting its exits, its deaths and potential recoveries. The ideological conclusions can, therefore, only be numerous, multilayered, at times contradictory though inextricably linked. My book demands its own coherence of object in the naturalist works, but its conclusions can be applied to other "strict" historical texts—Michelet's and probably that of many of his contemporaries. I hope it also provides the appropriate introduction into Michelet's *Histoire de France*, which is traversed and circumscribed without being sullied—still fresh for the pleasure of reading. And the rest of Michelet should be read, not only the claustrophobically monstrous history of the Ancien Régime and the "desperate" *Histoire du XIXe siècle* because they are contemporaneous with the naturalist works, but the bizarre essays on woman, *L'Amour* and *La Femme*, the Blakean *Bible de l'humanité*, the shifty *L'Etudiant*, *Le Peuple*, and *Nos Fils*, the inexhaustible *Sorcière*. They should be read on their own merits and refracted in the biases of the past or at least of the special history of Michelet himself.

Almost immediately following Michelet's death in 1874, the Third French Republic, in search of heroic predecessors, began to assimilate, to domesticate Michelet's *unheimlich* insights, and by the time of the Fifth Republic, when de Gaulle and Malraux proclaimed their approval of the national figure, the case seemed closed. Michelet was a symbol one read for inspiration and style. But even these double-pronged praises of the Général hardly mattered since they descended in a partial vacuum: Michelet's strident anticlerical republicanism assured his dubious role in the educational system of twentieth-century France. Only a faithful few have kept the texts alive and free from oversimplification. For Catholic and traditional France, Michelet is a statue, a bust, the name of a street in Paris, a passage from *Jeanne d'Arc*. He is sometimes associated with writers of "adolescent" literature like Jules Verne and Lewis Carroll.

Historians who read Michelet usually focus their attention on his earlier works, which are less confused by disillusion and polemics, by the intensely personal, even hallucinatory, tone of the later writings. There have always been readers for the *Histoire de la Révolution française* (1847–1853) and the volumes on the Middle Ages (1833–1844). The rest, it was said, was unreadable, unthinkable, whether from passion or senility. In 1852, when Michelet left Paris, the National Archives, and the Collège de France, the spotlight of the ages dimmed and he was abandoned, as a curious creature, to his erotic daydreams, his biological nonsense, and his utopian cities of love. Whether the legends have encrusted or whether after a hundred years of criticism one can finally separate out various misreadings, Michelet keeps returning like his own ghostly *revenants* of the resurrected past. The efforts of his disciple Gabriel Monod, simultaneously aided and thwarted by Madame Michelet, kept the historian's memory alive until both Anglo-Saxon and French critics began to consider his career from a greater distance (Pommier, Guéhenno, Halévy, Cornuz, Gay Wilson Allen, Oscar Haac, and Roland Barthes). Finally, the publications of Paul Viallaneix, the foremost Michelet scholar writing today, ushered in a true renaissance of interest. Viallaneix' thesis, *La Voie royale*, and the edition of the first volume of Michelet's *Journal* both opened in 1959 a Pandora's box whose contents must, at times, have surprised even Viallaneix, as his own evolving interpretations gave rise to a network of "michelétistes." Beyond this professional group, readers of Michelet seemed to be either natural admirers of historical writing, such as Henri Peyre and Geoffrey Hartman, or *hugoliens* undaunted by the shelves of volumes, such as Pierre Albouy, Jean Gaudon, and Jacques Seebacher. Albouy's career, which ended so abruptly and painfully in the summer of 1974, significantly crisscrossed my own, from Montpellier in 1965, to Yale in 1968, and Paris in 1974. We met always at the juncture of our interest in Michelet and such texts that open onto the problems of self-reflexive and socially generated myths.

The year 1974 was also the centennial of Michelet's death and the occasion for colloquia at the Collège de France and the château of Vascoeuil (the former domain of Michelet's son-in-law, recently restored by François Papillard); in 1975, Lionel Gossman transferred the interest in Michelet to The Johns Hopkins University, where a two-day discussion brought participants together from both sides of the Atlantic. The new critical edition of Michelet's *Oeuvres complètes* was, by then, well under way, and Michelet was attracting the diverse revisions he has long deserved. It is important now, however, not to adapt him to fashionable currents, but to see him again, to see where he left off and how he got there.

Michelet's concerns with historiography and writing transgress national and generic borders. Gibbon, Macaulay, Ranke, and Bancroft experienced some of the same crises and investigated the same provisional solutions. Coleridge, Wordsworth, Emerson, Nietzsche, and Thoreau echo in Michelet's aspiration and language. Another genre, which this book could not pursue—nineteenth-century scientific literature, especially popular science—paralleled his publications, yet here again, boundaries blur, for what was vulgarized and serious merged in the nineteenth-century mind. All of these traditions relate to Michelet as he eludes them, since he is most at home with the breed of tireless and fertile romantics who seem Herculean to us in their egos and ambitions, Antaean in their rich and sensuous grounding. Hugo, Goethe, Whitman, Dickens, Balzac—they overwhelm us, they are "*Hénorme*," to quote Flaubert; their incredible capacity for *travail* dismays us who might be more sympathetic to the modern agonies of Baudelaire, Flaubert himself, and Dickinson.

The translations of Michelet into twentieth-century American are mine; what exists in English is partial or sounds too strangely antiquated. But any such metamorphosis seems to be only a betrayal; let the reader simply return to the original to confirm that Michelet is a great writer.

My thanks to Jean Gaudon, with the hope that I can thank him in the future for more books, both his and mine; to the team of Iowa friends, Lois Dahlin, Claire Silvers, Lexie Kirkpatrick, and especially Charles Phillips, a writer who guided the preparation of the manuscript in my absence; to my parents, Marianna and Henry Orr, and to other cherubim and daemons. My gratitude also to the American Philosophical Society for a summer grant in 1972, and to the American

Council of Learned Societies for the centennial year's concentration of effort (1973–1974).

I am grateful to Alfred A. Knopf, Inc., and to Faber and Faber, Ltd., for permission to reprint lines from "The Auroras of Autumn," *The Collected Poems of Wallace Stevens*, copyright 1954 by Wallace Stevens, and to the Viking Penguin, Inc., and to Clive E. Driver, Literary Executor of the Estate of Marianne C. Moore, for permission to reprint lines from "The Spider and the Swallow," *The Fables of La Fontaine*, by Marianne Moore, copyright 1954 by Marianne Moore.

LINDA ORR

New Haven

Part I

THE DIALECTICS OF CONSCIOUSNESS

1 Introduction: Changing Sides

Jules Michelet (1798–1874), more than a historian, was almost the hero he wanted to be. His *Histoire de France* and *Histoire de la Révolution française*, monuments of research and writing, are deceptive; like his epics, political and moral essays, novelistic nonfiction, and rhapsodies in naturalism, history was conceived of by Michelet as a new, dynamic genre he alone would perfect, a genre that would bring converts. He mesmerized his students, and with his fiery, *engagé* presentation he hoped to instill in a new generation the forgotten ideals of 1789.

Nor did his courses fit into the usual curriculum categories. Combining anthropology, political science, and ethics with history, he rendered it personal and vital for his listeners. Victor Cousin had imagined a "more regular" course in history for the position Michelet occupied at the Ecole Normale, so the latter resigned in 1838. That same year, however, he was offered a more appropriate podium at the prestigious Collège de France as professor of "histoire et morale." In 1842, a question of conscience threatened the very institutions he championed; the Jesuits campaigned to recapture their once undisputed claim to the control of French education. With his close friend and colleague Edgar Quinet, Michelet fought for the concept of a less sectarian religion and a free university. Their collaboration culminated in a polemical publication, *Les Jésuites* (1843). Quinet and Michelet became symbols of resistance. When Michelet, flanked by his liberal colleagues, entered the lecture hall, the crowd stood and applauded. In 1846, Quinet lost his chair. In January 1848, Michelet's course was suspended. Considering the motives that could have prompted Louis-Philippe's opposition, Michelet related it to his first journalistic battle against a state of mind he generalized as "le jésuitisme politique et religieux" (*L'Etudiant*, p. 92). Whether Michelet's course on social reunification simply reflected the climate of pre-1848 revolutionary awareness or whether it actually kindled opinion is hard to discern. More was at stake than a job, for fifteen hundred students and well-wishers appeared at the Collège de France to protest the absence of their spokesman and leader.

The historian did not have to run for public office in order to fulfill his ambition. Though deprived of his young following and their encouragement, he maintained the same sense of moral usefulness by creating an imaginary and real dialogue with an astonishingly vast audience of readers, and correspondence became an essential function of his life. His nonhistorical works, a kind of "inspirational literature," regularly met with success, or at least with a heated reception. Rilke, calling him that "child Michelet,"[1] came under his charm and later begrudgingly attributed to *L'Amour* (1858) his decision to marry; Carey Thomas, an emerging American woman educator, wept in rage over Michelet's prescriptions for happiness in *La Femme* (1859).[2]

Still, notoriety and book sales were no substitute for palpable influence. According to the Goncourts' *Journal*, the usually critical Sainte-Beuve explained what he called the *hystérisme* of the historian's books as a reflection of a deep-

[1] *Letters of Rainer Maria Rilke, 1892–1910*, tr. Jane Bannard Greene and M. D. Herter Norton (New York, 1945), p. 61; letter to Gustav Paul, 8 Jan. 1902.

[2] Barbara Cross, *The Educated Woman in America* (New York, 1965), p. 33.

seated "désir de prêtre": Michelet harbored the same desire for power that his Jesuit enemies were guilty of.

Dates are sometimes arbitrary historical divisions, but 1848 was truly a national and personal crisis for those who lived through it, one that altered their ideologies and identities, their visions and their modes of expression. The year 1848 was to affect Michelet as deeply as any man then at the pinnacle of a successful career.

The year found Michelet confronting a most painful topic of historical research: the Terror, that is, the demise of the glorious national Revolution of 1789 and 1791. For him French history was a building toward this Revolution, whether directly or indirectly. Saint Louis, Joan of Arc, Luther were all forerunners, all actual incarnations of what was to come. The initial shock of 1789 could not immediately fulfill all of France's revolutionary potential; that fulfillment became the mission left for the nineteenth century, left for the generation coming of age in 1830, the generation ready in 1848. But the apocalypse failed to materialize; the Revolution was betrayed. On June 23, 1848, the National Guard, after only three months earlier having joined with the uprising in the first heat of republican fervor, turned and fired on the demonstrating workers. Michelet was thunderstruck. And worse, there was nothing he could do: "The unbearable night of June 24th, after February's great light and hope, caused the violent heart contractions I felt. I tried to bring forth out of myself a popular book and could not. Humiliated, sad, and somber, I went back to the impersonal work of historical writing" (*Journal*, II, 23). Before, all his books, not just the "bestsellers" but the *Histoire de France*, had been "popular books," a tradition, according to Michelet, upheld by Vico, Virgil, and Dante in that they reached a profound level of expression merging with the people's own sense of themselves.[3] Now the historian's

[3] Michelet's hierarchy of "livres populaires" is outlined in a project he proposed for himself in his *Journal* (I, 680): "1. Study the great

lifework seemed a gratuitous task. It had lost its pivot and raison d'être: the realization of the Revolution. Nor could 1848 be rationalized away; it was not simply a false start, but an indication of what the future might have in store. And it was not *his* future.

The Popular Book and Language

Michelet wanted to write the book that would subvert its own existence and explode into action. He wanted the writer, reader, and printed page to merge and dissolve at the appropriate moment of *fiat* into a state in which the book would have come true.[4] The orator, Danton, reborn as a historian, would have been the ideal: "In this sublime and sinister moment, Danton was, it must be said, the very voice of the Revolution and of France; in him she found the quick heart, the generous breast, the grandiose gestures able to express her faith. Let it not be said that speech is of little importance in such moments. Word and deed are one and the same. An affirmation that is strong, energetic, and reassures hearts, this is the creation of acts; it produces what it says. Here action is the servant of speech; it follows docilely behind, as on the first day of the world: *He spoke, and the world was.*"[5] There were moments

---

popular books, for and by the people, their formation, their influence. Here Vico: *The People made the people.* 2. Study the semipopular books, though aristocratic, adopted by the people. Examples: Virgil, Dante, Tasso. 3. Study the books written for one particular class, primarily didactic, but later popularized. Examples: the manuals that led to the *Imitation.*"

[4] Although the disappearance of the "deplorable lines" between writer and reader, between articulated desire and realization, represented the ideal, Michelet sometimes seemed to contradict himself because of a shift in emphasis. On the one hand, language and action were considered mutually exclusive: "Books mean nothing next to acts" (*Histoire de France*, IX, 1), and, on the other, language was already itself the action and any immediate results of speech appeared almost anticlimactic: "To say such things is to prepare them" (*Histoire du XIXe siècle*, I, 218).

[5] "Danton fut, il faut le dire, dans ce moment sublime et sinistre, la

when Michelet felt he was approaching his goal. The students demonstrating on his behalf inspired him to think that for the historian anything was possible; his eloquence responded to the audience's tension "And history? . . . Yes! history, nothing more awesome, gentlemen."[6] Awesome, Michelet explained, because it used as its tool: "The fraternal word striking, without intermediary, warm and live at the heart; and the same word written, a new literary movement, a large spirit, neither letter, nor people, but France" (*L'Etudiant*, pp. 93 and 94). The writer and the popular orator moving masses to great deeds would be the same man. But this exalted mood lasted only a few months. In the same set of lectures, all delivered in 1848, Michelet was already aware of being deluded: "I say to you, I did not have many languages, I used the only one I had, unfortunately it was perhaps too abstract, but that is not easy to change; I say to you that popular books are an infinitely rare thing; that the French Revolution, so powerful, so fertile, could not produce a single one" (*L'Etudiant*, p. 56). He expected, erroneously, event to carry language beyond itself.

Yet he was convinced of the reality of popular books, and in addition to the work of Vico, Virgil and Dante, *L'Imitation de Jésus Christ* profoundly intrigued him.[7] It was not simply

---

voix même de la Révolution et de la France; en lui elle trouva le coeur énergique, la poitrine profonde, l'attitude grandiose qui pouvait exprimer sa foi. Qu'on ne dise pas que la parole soit peu de chose en de tels moments. Parole et acte, c'est tout un. La puissante, l'énergique affirmation qui assure les coeurs, c'est une création d'actes; ce qu'elle dit, elle le produit. L'action est ici la servante de la parole; elle vient docilement derrière, comme au premier jour du monde: *Il dit, et le monde fut*" (*Histoire de la Révolution française*, I, 1025).

[6] Points of suspension in quotations that appear in the original text are closely spaced in the French manner. My own ellipsis points, to indicate omission in the quotations, are more widely spaced out.

[7] Michelet describes the experience of reading *L'Imitation* on three different occasions: *Mémorial*, *Le Peuple*, and *Histoire de France, le Moyen Age*. All three passages are discussed in Paul Viallaneix' introduction to the *Ecrits de jeunesse*, p. 21. The *Ecrits de jeunesse* cover

that God spoke directly through the inspired book, but that a reader had the illusion of hearing his own darkest thoughts and most intimate voice: "What emotion the people, women, anyone unhappy (at that time it was everyone) must have felt when for the first time they heard the divine word, no longer as a dead language, but as the *living* word, not as the formula of ritual but as the live voice of the heart, their own voice, the marvelous manifestation of their secret thought" (*Histoire de France*, V, 8). To speak the language of the people was a curious and widespread romantic aspiration (Wordsworth, Herder, Goethe), but simply by collecting folk literature and by creating characters of ordinary, even poor, circumstances, a writer would not produce the effect Michelet longed for.

He blamed himself for not being "in love enough" with his subject, not throwing himself into his book; or he attacked French as being dry, slack, abstract, and artificial. He was not yet willing to admit that he might be demanding of language something it could never deliver, that he was asking of it the virtues of silence, or at least the voice of something that does not speak. Gaëtan Picon in his introduction to *L'Etudiant* points to the impossible logic of such a typical romantic enterprise, for Michelet wanted to replace the historical agent and the historian with abstract humanity, with Prometheus: "One might even say: God. But God and history do not speak with words,"[8] so that at the very moment of this union of historian and agent no one can possibly talk about it.

In the early years of his career, especially at the time of the publication of the *Origines du droit français* (1837, subtitled "as found in the symbols and formulas of universal law"),

several texts, including the *Journal* (1820–1823), the *Mémorial* (childhood reminiscences), and the *Journal des idées;* future references will include the page number, not the individual titles. Michelet makes a case for the essential "French" quality of the *Imitation:* "Whether the *Imitation* was French or not, it had its greatest effect [*action*] in France" (*Histoire de France*, V, 10).

[8] Gaëtan Picon, "Michelet et la parole historienne," Introduction to *L'Etudiant* (Paris: Seuil, 1970), p. 49.

Michelet meditated upon the problems of linguistic representation; his lifelong visits to museums often transposed the same broodings to the plastic arts. Michelet was familiarly known in university circles as Monsieur Symbol. Yet he was slow from the beginning to admit that any rhetoric might be capable of the resurrection he desired. Perhaps twentieth-century writers and critics are overly self-conscious about how the formulas of language perform, but Michelet pursued many of the same quandaries in a less systematic fashion. "But language," writes Benveniste, describing a universal experience, "is what is most paradoxical in the world and unhappy are those who do not see this."[9] On the one hand, Michelet imagined a language or primitive expression, inspired by Vico and probably Creutzer, composed totally of symbols, still innocent in its natural poetry.[10] On the other hand, he saw that modern society, born of feudalism's verbal trickery, had broken the symbol into an equivocal sign whose blurred meanings covered betrayal. Michelet traced the first dispossessions, the first falsified contracts, to the ambiguity of *vassus* (*vaillant* or *esclave*) and *servus* (*votre serviteur*, as used by a prince or nobleman, or *serf*) (*La Sorcière*, pp. 58–59). The Jesuits, descendants of the feudal heresy, discovered in the duplicity of figurative speech a way to move in and claim the body: they pretended

[9] Emile Benveniste, *Problèmes de linguistique générale* (Paris: 1966), p. 42.

[10] Michelet began his translation of Vico in 1825, the same year he read Creutzer's *Religions de l'antiquité*, translated by Guigniaut. Creutzer's "symbolique" evoked the infinite network of universal analogy in nature; *symbol* itself referred to "the primitive form of human intelligence" characteristic, for instance, of the Egyptians, later to evolve into its narrative counterpart, myth. See Pierre Albouy, *Mythes et mythologies dans la littérature française* (Paris: Armand Colin, 1969), pp. 75–76; also Paul Viallaneix, *La Voie royale: Essai sur l'idée du peuple dans l'oeuvre de Michelet* (Paris: Flammarion, 1971), "L'Héroïsme de l'esprit." Michelet describes Vico's three stages of linguistic civilization in his *Oeuvres choisies de Vico* (Paris: Flammarion, n.d.), pp. 557–59: "divine mental language, language of heroic signs, articulated language."

that "in all the business about the Heart" it was a question of a *symbolic* object, but actually "there was no metaphor, they meant the flesh itself" (*Histoire de France*, XIV, 112). The word "symbol" could have a positive or negative nuance in Michelet's text. It could be the "living sign" by which heroes unite the country, or it could be artificial indistinctness. "*We wanted a symbol*, we got an encyclopedia. *We wanted a simple, applicable type* we could imitate" (*Histoire de France*, VII, 77–78). Michelet was horrified at the result of scholastic linguistic theory, "*that all ideas* (the most fantastic, the most arbitrary) *necessarily have a* corresponding *object* in nature" (*Histoire de France*, VII, 28); man, then, was irrevocably separated from nature. But ultimately, Michelet was reluctant to examine the very terrain of language, its autonomy: what Kenneth Burke has called the " 'we' that is separated from the nonverbal by the verbal" and that "would not even exist were it not for the verbal."[11]

Michelet would not have been so intent upon re-establishing unity between man and his words had he not felt their disparity, even though he did not develop a theory to clarify his intuitions. He knew, nevertheless, like Rimbaud (who learned much from him), that his only hope lay in the complete revitalization and actual re-creation of language. An impossible undertaking? At least one that would teeter at the edge of possibility, pushing expressiveness to limits previously undiscovered—though never beyond these limits. Somewhere between the oversophisticated "sustained style" (*style soutenu*) of Ronsard and the charming, dynamic naïveté of Rabelais, between unself-conscious innocence and wit, between a stately, aristocratic parlance and village conversation, Michelet would found a new language; no longer modeling himself upon Danton, he would be a *sober* Rabelais: "To dare a new language; not that of barbaric innocence, speaking without a

[11] Kenneth Burke, *Language as Symbolic Action: Essays on Life, Language, and Method* (Berkeley, 1966), pp. 3 and 5.

blush, without feeling the depths of things, not that of brother Antiquity, who used, abused, and despised humanity,—but that of modern tenderness . . . the language of a serious, loving Rabelais" (*Journal*, II, 334).

The new language would not be abased to the "frivolous" level of genres like poetry and the novel, but the *Histoire de France* did not seem the proper place for its flowering either, though history was Michelet's calling and he believed in it. Another history was coming into prominence, however, a history with traditions Michelet was schooled in and with advantages he was seeking—natural history.

Return to Nature

After finishing his *Histoire de la Révolution française*, Michelet returned to where he had left off in his *Histoire de France*—the Renaissance—and read this message: "Younger and older than them all, mother and nurse of the gods, as of men, she [Nature] cradled them in the old days and will smile again on their tombs. . . . 'Return to Nature' is the greeting [*salut:* salvation] the Renaissance extends to us, her first words" (*Histoire de France*, VII, 342).

In 1853, fatigue, despair, and ill-health forced Michelet from his dusty documents to the Mediterranean sun. With his young second wife, Athénaïs, an amateur naturalist, he moved to Nervi, near Genoa. It was logical that nature, Michelet's blind spot in both his intellectual and his personal development, began to take on a new interest for him; natural history in the backstage of human history appeared now to be asking the same questions that had always prodded him, so he began to look to nature for the new lease of hope, health, and professional inspiration needed after 1848.

The *Word-Deed* marriage exemplifies a fundamental ideological and stylistic strain in Michelet—union through dialectics. Innumerable groupings underlie Michelet's vision: life/death, subject/object, individual/humanity, past/present, reality/illusion, inside/ outside, up/down, fate/freedom, unity/ multiplicity, grace/justice, nature/man. They cannot, however, be reduced to the yoking of manichean opposites they sometimes seem, but rather must be seen as organizations of movement and change, ambiguous poles of value in the context of mutually dependent couples.[12]

The modification of nature's position in his ideological construct is central to an understanding of Michelet's four naturalist books. Before the 1840s, Michelet often associated nature with the supposed "bad guys" (led by "Fatality"), while Christianity (Joan of Arc and Saint Louis among its adherents) he largely admired and, therefore, admitted on the side of human freedom. In 1831, as proclaimed in the much-quoted passage from the *Introduction à l'histoire universelle*, nature was pitted against man and liberty: "With the world began a war to finish only with the world, and not before; that of man against nature, spirit against matter, liberty against fate" (the new edition of the *Oeuvres complètes*, 1971, II, 229). But sometime before 1848, Christianity, represented as Grace, gradually assumed for him its ignominious role against Liberty and was only much later reassimilated into the all-embracing republic of the future.[13] With the publication of

[12] See Lionel Gossman's "The Go-Between: Jules Michelet, 1798–1874," *Modern Language Notes*, 89 (May 1974), 503–41.

[13] During the 1840s, Michelet began to see nature from two new perspectives: nature composed of a *peuple* of defenseless and delicate *petits*, as is humanity; nature more consoling, especially in the face of death, than Christianity, whose injustices outraged Michelet. In 1842, even before Michelet's avowed support for nature's inhabitants in *Le Peuple* (1846), grief at the death of his friend Madame Dumesnil led him to find consolation in the natural world, and the first inklings of *La Mer* appear in his *Journal:* "I was digging into the source of all life, nature; I read the articles *Animal, Cetaceans*. The latter was most moving. There is a poem to write on these poor creatures, kind and intelligent for the most part, judging from their brain and family habits, but condemned by the contradictions of their organism" (*Journal*, I, 405). In 1846, Michelet became indignant that the Church refused to bury his father, a nonsectarian supporter of the Revolution.

the first naturalist book, *L'Oiseau*, in 1856, nature had clearly emerged as the new savior: "Time weighs heavy, life, work, the violent crises of our age, the breakdown of the world of intelligence we used to live in that nothing has replaced. The rude labors of history once had teaching for relief, as well as friendship. Their interruption brings only silence. Whom can we ask for rest, for moral replenishment, if not nature?" (*L'Oiseau*, p. 4). Primarily an abstract theoretical concern, nature had appeared only sparsely in Michelet's letters and in the *Histoire de France*, where images were typically ambiguous, and though he insisted retrospectively on nature's constant influence on his career, it was not until the 1850s that he considered nature a fertile field of investigation and formulated the dialectic between nature and history as the foundation of his method and the source of his undying energy. "When in my human endeavors, my breath was about to give out, I touched *Terra Mater* and took flight again" (*La Montagne*, p. 235).

L'Oiseau shocked the unprepared French public; on its heels came *L'Insecte* (1857), *La Mer* (1861), and *La Montagne* (1868). Superficial, sensational hypotheses about the genesis of a "new" Michelet spread, and Athénaïs Michelet's role in her husband's "retreat to nature" was exaggerated.[14] Although as

At this time, Michelet broke with Christianity and reconsidered his view of nature: "[The world] believes in justice, equal justice, without special privilege; no more elite. . . . This is human justice, which is to say, always balancing the weakness of humanity, the fatality of nature (extenuating circumstances)" (*Journal*, I, 659).

[14] One cartoonist depicted Michelet with a pair of love birds settled on his head, carrying the arms of Cupid, and driving a chariot drawn by a butterfly, a grasshopper, a beetle, and a bee. See *Michelet: Sa vie, son oeuvre 1789–1874* (Paris: Archives de France, 1961), p. 140. Athénaïs' influence on the nature books can be summarized in the following manner: direct: she collected notes; she wrote passages that were placed in quotes by Michelet; indirect: as physical inspiration through sex; as spiritual inspiration. "My life is a part of my work. Therefore, my closeness to her is useful and inspiring. Each time, it is something new. The last time was spontaneous, totally naïve and

an urban child he had very little contact with nature, as a young intellectual in Paris around 1830, he caught the fervor for natural history in contemporary debates and discoveries (for example, the Cuvier/Geoffroy Saint-Hilaire controversy). After those days, he never discontinued his avid, wide reading in several scientific fields. This consistency of interests was vivid to him when, late in life, he looked back over the long years of his career: "*Man makes himself, he is his Prometheus.* How? By means of two forces: one taken from himself, makes him liable to another, taken from nature. I perceived this in 1830, in a little book I wrote. Even at that date, my friendships —with the elder Edwards, a famous physiologist, then with Geoffroy Saint-Hilaire, and with Serres whose courses I took in 1840—gave me a foretaste, since I seemed to turn then, as for a charming diversion, to the natural sciences."[15] More than a simple stimulus, this "charming diversion" became an integral part of the greater structure of Michelet's ongoing lifework: "My secondary books, believed to be simple excursions, were studies, preliminary constructions, sometimes, in fact the essential blocks of the larger edifice" (*Histoire de France*, XVII, i–ii). Natural history provided the perfect arena for considering afresh those problems that were retarding his *Histoire de France:* the nature of time, the function of continuity and discontinuity in change, and the limits of history itself.

Revolution, Evolution, and the Masters of Metamorphosis

Around the turn of the nineteenth century, simultaneous with the French Revolution, another revolution was slowly

---

natural, the happiness of a delayed togetherness, the happiness of her attentions and her visible desire to bring joy and make one happy (a most complete communion). . . . I come from her made better, full of emotions and good thoughts. It is emerging from her that I have perhaps had my best ideas: *Love* on the 16th of March, 1856, *The Sea* on the 15th of September, 1857" (*Journal*, II, 524–25).

[15] The unpublished note (written by Michelet in 1872) is quoted in Viallaneix, *La Voie royale*, p. 434.

building—a radical remolding of consciousness.[16] Old modes of considering time and change no longer corresponded to recent scientific discoveries and intellectual perceptions. The Chain of Being (*Scala Naturae*, *échelle des êtres*, Ladder of Perfection) had dominated man's configuration of the world for centuries: all creatures stood in a hierarchy on the way toward Providence. Although individuals could aspire to promotion, they could not work a miracle of physical change in order to ascend the rungs. Not, that is, until the concept of evolution. Then time became a crucial factor in the development of life, and continuity was redefined in a paradoxical complexity. The word "revolution" began to fade beside the plethora of other terms and schools of change: uniformitarianism, catastrophism, progressionism, metamorphosis, and evolution. The bickering has persisted in historical and scientific literature, intent upon determining which camps were "closest" to being "right," that is, to being "evolutionist," before Darwin. It seems, however, that each great scientific thinker—all of whom were familiar to Michelet—contributed to the eventual discovery of evolution and that even Darwin had to bow to later advancements in his theory vaguely but imaginatively conceived perhaps by some of his predecessors.

Michelet understood the dispute between the two broad camps that were abstractly generalized under the terms discontinuity and continuity. And, though he sometimes seemed partial to one side, he always marveled at the well-matched titans. The French Revolution, which had monopo-

[16] "It is ironic and intriguing that the fixed hierarchical order in biology began to pass almost contemporaneously with the disappearance of the feudal social scale in the storms of the French Revolution" (Loren Eiseley, *Darwin's Century: Evolution and the Men Who Discovered It*, New York, 1958, pp. 9–10). "On the archaeological level, we see that the system of positivities was transformed with a wholesale fashion at the end of the eighteenth and beginning of the nineteenth century" (Michel Foucault, *The Order of Things: An Archaeology of the Human Sciences*, New York, 1970, p. xxii).

lized his perspective for so long, and everything it implied about time and change, had to be reinterpreted in the light of two cosmic revolutions looming in the background: "In a rather short period of about a half-century, we have witnessed two great revolutions. 'Which ones? 1815? July? February?'— No. I am speaking of vaster and more important revolutions, those that spread around the globe, over the earth" (*La Montagne*, p. 81). The first revolution pitted the "vulcanists" (Leopold de Buch and Elie de Beaumont) against the "neptunists," or "catastrophists" (Abraham Werner and, by association, Georges Cuvier). Michelet suggested an analogy between Napoleon's volcanic rise and fall and Buch's theory of geological change by heat and pressure. Werner "the neptunist" believed, on the other hand, that rock layers which were precipitated in separate stages from an advancing and retreating primal sea indicated completely different creations of life. It was easily inferred from this theory that a logical platonic morphology appeared automatically with each era, leading up to man's eventual rule. Cuvier added to the validity of these conclusions by dramatizing Buffon's "epochs of nature" into total and radical re-creations. The intellectual insurgents (Buch and Elie de Beaumont) gradually replaced the awesome Establishment (Werner, Cuvier, and supporters of the Biblical deluge theory).[17] "We should not forget that this daring revolution

[17] Epochs created by catastrophic change left the biblical Creation intact. Each epoch would show a new "creation" of new flora and fauna (except some possible rare holdovers from an older age), and the Deluge could have heralded the "last" Creation. Also, the change precipitating each epoch could be attributed to "supernatural" forces. Cuvier's semantic ploy was clever. Although Buffon used the word "revolution" to indicate the passage from one epoch to the next, he clearly meant simple "change." Buffon did not know what revolution was to come to mean after 1789 (see Eiseley, *Darwin's Century*, pp. 68–69). For a description of the difference between neptunists and vulcanists, see Charles Coulston Gillispie, *Genesis and Geology: A Study in the Relations of Scientific Thought, Natural Theology, and Social Opinion in Great Britain, 1790–1850* (New York, 1959), pp. 46–49.

of upheavals took place not only against the Bible, the Flood, and so on, but against the popes of that time, by Buch against his mentor Werner, by Elie de Beaumont against his, Cuvier. Not the least were the high authorities who accepted it: the Aragos, the Ritters, the Alexander von Humboldts" (*La Montagne*, p. 82). Buch's conception of change–rocks swelling and buckling under the earth's surface–with its violence toned down approached the famous uniformitarian theory proposed by James Hutton. "Uniformitarianism" formed the cornerstone of Lyell's later thinking. Hutton, whose language would be adopted by Lyell and, at last, by Michelet, claimed that the earth's surface was alternately raised and eroded, worn and rejuvenated: "Or may it [this world] be also considered as an organized body? Such as has a constitution in which the necessary decay of the machine is naturally repaired, in the exertion of those productive powers by which it had been formed."[18]

This "second revolution" led by Lyell (in Michelet's own history of science) corresponded to the peaceful English industrial revolution. Buch's "first revolution" stood, therefore, as the historical transition from catastrophic change to internal, almost imperceptible reproduction: "At the height of the upheavals, about 1830, when Buch and Elie de Beaumont seemed to rule, there arose a great voice, Lyell's geology. A forceful, ingenious book where for the first time the earth appears as a worker manufacturing herself, through constant and patient toil without any violent jolts" (*La Montagne*, p. 83). When Michelet discovered Lyell (a second Vico in his life), he knew that he had encountered a sympathetic mind.[19] The very image (reminiscent of Vico) Michelet had used to represent history—

[18] *Theory of the Earth* (Edinburgh, 1795; rpt. New York, 1959), p. 16.

[19] Charles Lyell's major work, *The Principles of Geology* (1830–1833), was translated into French twenty years after its appearance. An abridged version, *Elements of Geology*, published in England in 1838, was available in French in 1839.

"humanity creating itself"—reappeared in Lyell's geological vision: the earth, like humanity, struggled for her own development. Finally, Michelet seemed secretly content to recognize the edge that the "school of peace" gained over the "school of war" and, for him, Darwin was the opposite of anything sinister or violent: "This is the school of war and this, the school of peace. —The latter is gaining ground. A spirit of peace at all costs . . . seems to drive Lyell, Darwin. They suppress conflict in nature, want the earth to carry on without shock, want her to transform and change herself imperceptibly throughout millions of centuries" (*La Montagne*, pp. 83–84).

Joining forces with Lyell and Darwin meant becoming part of an international movement. Michelet dreamed again, as in his youth, of a "total science" enlisting brotherly luminaries of diverse backgrounds, all "masters of metamorphosis": "What strengthens this geology of peaceful transformations is the fraternal support it has among naturalists, among the great masters of metamorphosis, our Geoffroy Saint-Hilaire, Goethe, Oken, Owen, Darwin, who reveal how an animal, under the varied influences of its environment, and through the instinctive impulse leading it to choose what is best for it, how, I repeat, it has made and modified itself" [*Comment, dis-je, l'animal s'est fait et modifié*] (*La Montagne*, p. 84).

With the word metamorphosis, Michelet added his voice to the significant discussions of his day. Under the umbrella of this word, he united the faithful in their support for continuity. And yet this word in its many nineteenth-century contexts complicates the notion of change beyond the rather optimistic apocalyptic pattern suggested by "revolution" in Michelet's history. Metamorphosis evokes the continuous intermingling and ambiguity of empirical and transcendental realms. Before his commitment to the debates of natural history, he could order time with some confidence by dating progressive "incarnations" of the eternally latent principle, Revolution. Those days were over.

In the fields of geology, zoology, and botany, "metamorphosis" was used to describe the total transformation of an organism in its life processes, its coherences and disruptions. Lyell applied the term to the last stage of rock formation, to those rocks worked over for the longest time and modified most deeply. Swammerdam, a Dutch naturalist (1637–1680) whom Michelet paraphrases in *L'Insecte*, issued his astounding observations of insect stages under the name of metamorphosis: "The most general fact about insect life, the first law of their existence, is *metamorphosis*. . . . How would academic Europe receive this new science of metamorphoses?" (pp. 99–100). One of the greatest original propagators of this new vision in both botany and zoology was Goethe. In 1790, Goethe published the *Metamorphose der Pflanzen*, proposing that all parts of a plant represent modifications of a type-leaf and that all plants are the morphological developments of one type-plant. Thus, plant taxonomy gave way to the notion of a recurrent organic structure amassing all species into a living unity. Michelet was, of course, immediately fascinated by this overarching pattern: "It [the nineteenth century] created plants (not the simple varieties, but lasting species). It created different habitats for them with growth cycles that would remake and renew them" (*La Montagne*, p. 237). Goethe's poem "Metamorphose der Tiere" extends the same hint of a "unity of type" to the animal kingdom: "Every organism shapes itself after eternal laws. And the rarest form mysteriously preserves the primordial structure" (" . . . bewahrt im geheimen das Urbild"). Actually, Goethe outlined in his unsystematic work many of the premises to be formulated only a few years later by Geoffroy Saint-Hilaire (*Philosophie anatomique*, 1818). In order to support his philosophic premonition that all life forms derive from one ideal animal (not necessarily man), Geoffroy devised two principal theories: one of analogies, or unity of composition, and one of unity of structure, or principle of relations. These two theories state that the same organic materials or units of construction make up every vertebrate and that these units are always in the same relative position to one another. By concocting outlandish anatomical analogies supported by these two theories, Geoffroy was determined to link the Vertebrata to the Articulata, and, carried away with enthusiasm, he defended two of his followers who, by stretching imaginations and theories, extended the unity of life down to the mollusks. About the time the cephalopod became a vertebrate bent back at the umbilicus, Cuvier balked, and the great debate between Geoffroy and himself began.[20] Cuvier was said to have "won" then, for whatever it is worth now.

Michelet defined his own position, metamorphosis, through a motley crew of masters. The visionaries—Goethe and Geoffroy—rub elbows with the English empiricists—Lyell and Darwin. Whether he felt evolution in the air or not is ques-

[20] The flush of the debates has evidently faded with history. "In our time, a greater spectacle has attracted here the excited attention of all the world's nations, when two giants (more than men, methods), Cuvier, Geoffroy, rose in combat against each other" (*L'Oiseau*, p. 98). Geoffroy was traditionally held to be the champion of evolution against Cuvier's "fixism." Yet Cuvier, at least since the beginning of the twentieth century, has been judged the more serious and influential scientist. Cuvier did deliver the crucial blow to the Scale of Being by splitting it into four divisions (Vertebrata, Articulata, Mollusca, Radiata) and thus allowing species to branch into an infinite diversity. Eiseley sees Geoffroy, finally, as a hindrance to the acceptance of evolution: "The attempts to fill in all the gaps represented in the old Scale of Being were bound to fail and to stand as an impediment to evolutionary thinking" (p. 118). Edward Stuart Russell (*Form and Function: A Contribution to the History of Animal Morphology*, London, 1916) at least gives Geoffroy some credit for later "Darwinian" speculation: "Theories such as Darwin's, which assume a random variation which is not primarily in response to environmental changes, answer the problem in Geoffroy's sense. Theories such as Lamarck's, which postulate an active responsive self-adaptation of the organism, are essentially a continuation and completing of Cuvier's thought" (p. 78). For a complete and favorable view of Geoffroy, see Théophile Cahn, *La Vie et l'oeuvre d'Etienne Geoffroy Saint-Hilaire* (Paris, 1962).

tionable.[21] He sympathized with Geoffroy's obsession for unity but had second thoughts about the absolute truth of the "peace school" as opposed to the "school of war." There was something other than confusion perhaps to be learned from both:

The tide is turning in favor of this new school, justly so, I think, but not without injustice for the old school. Is it easy to suppress the crises and upheavals everyone recognized only yesterday with Ritter and Humboldt? So many mountains give evidence of violent commotion, but this is only the result of a first look. To change one's mind and believe in slow and peaceful action takes thought.

Even the best functioning and most regulated animal life can have crises; sometimes they are morbid, sometimes natural. Should we believe the *animal-Earth* has experienced nothing of the kind, that there has been no rough or violent passage in its long life? [*La Montagne*, pp. 84–85]

Harmonious life has its moments of crisis, and within apparent continuity there are examples of severe discontinuity: Are these paradoxical conclusions to be denied or synthesized? Michelet hoped that time and man's growing knowledge would heal the rifts and explain the mysteries of nature: "As our museums become richer and grow more complete, as they reveal fewer lacunae, one would assume nature does nothing

[21] Roland Barthes in his *Michelet par lui-même* (Paris: Seuil, 1954) puts Michelet in the camp of Lamarck and the "*transformistes.*" Geoffroy and Michelet are discredited too for admiring the German transcendentalists (Kielmeyer, Oken), but Cuvier was also a disciple of Kielmeyer's. No one in France was an "evolutionist" before Darwin—and perhaps Michelet really never read *On the Origin of Species* in the original (translated into French in 1872). He reported, however, in his unpublished diary (available in typescript at the Centre de Recherches Révolutionnaires et Romantiques, Clermont Ferrand) on 26 July 1862: "Baudry brought Claparède on Darwin." On 13 August 1862, he noted: "I read Darwin and Mlle. Royer." In 1863 he loaned "Darwin" to a friend in Montauban and in 1865 discussed the English naturalist with Quinet. It is at least safe to say that Darwinian theories and research were in the air.

brutally, but, rather, gently through imperceptible transitions. Where we think we see something skipped, a void, a harsh and clashing point of passage in her work, we should accuse ourselves; this lacuna is our ignorance" (*L'Oiseau*, pp. 98–99). The labels taken from Linnaeus and Lamarck for the museum exhibitions, which Michelet contemplated, satisfied some need for order, and yet the terms of catastrophism rooted themselves in his imagination. He worried as the graceful line of creation took on zigzags: "Let's stop a few minutes at the solemn passages where uncertain life seems still to linger, where nature questions herself, testing her will. *Shall I be fish or mammal? . . . Shall I be bird or quadruped?* Important question, troubled hesitation, long and varied combat" (*L'Oiseau*, p. 99). Michelet juggled in his mind the numerous alternatives. Time was easier to follow in history: France's events occurred one after another, with only intermittent and temporary hints of revolution, until the Revolution itself actually came, and, appearing from within and without as *both* rift and continuity, reconciled the distinction between the two.

Natural history offers no single reconciliation and, indeed, has always functioned well without it. In a sense, Michel Foucault is right to trace the rearranging of modern man's "positivities" (his epistemological "space," his mode of becoming) to Georges Cuvier. The comparative anatomy practiced by Cuvier uncovered similar functions in all creatures (respiration, digestion, reproduction, circulation, movement) and similar organic development. Geoffroy's comparative studies of skeletal structures, despite extravagances, led in the same direction. Foucault signals the important development when a "double" was created in existence itself, without recourse to being: "From Cuvier onward, the living being wraps itself in its own existence, breaks off its taxonomic links of adjacency, tears itself free from the vast, tyrannical plan of continuities and constitutes itself as a new space: a double space, in fact—since it is both the interior one of anatomical coherence and physiological compatibilities, and the exterior one of the elements in which it resides and of which it forms its own body" (p. 274). Life was no longer the working out of a preconceived goal but a constant juggling of infinite, temporary reconciliations and coherences. Animal and human forms could be diverse and bizarre on the surface while perfectly understandable from a perspective of development and depth. The earth's surface exploded and sputtered while its interior churned quietly all the while. Or the reverse was true: unsuspected underground cataclysms might take place on a calm day. Time was long and cyclical (Hutton, Darwin), linear and fragmented (Cuvier), neither or both. Change proceeded with mechanistic precision, in natural harmony, or out of sheer chance.

Yet Michelet still surrounded the endeavor, as serious as his questions were, with the usual trappings of the romantic poet. "This [book]—*The Bird*—looks for the bird in the bird, avoids human analogy as much as possible" (p. 8). Any text, evolving toward its ideal goal, was still supposed to disappear in its object: "Above death and its false separation, beyond life and its mask disguising unity, [*The Bird*] soars, making love on the wing, from nest to nest, from egg to egg, from its own love to God's" (p. 57). The ideology of unity penetrates the nature books even though, like the histories, they abound in prolific detail, so that, as Edmund Wilson commented, the reader seems not to know "precisely what is coming."[22] The reader does know who will triumph in the end, but this "suspense in full knowledge" (like that found in Hugo or Hitchcock) adds to the pleasure of reading a truly curious style.

After 1848, the divine *fiat* operated, however, with less assurance, for the hidden consciousness of Michelet as a writer was telling him that he was profiting from the devious powers of language. Therefore, two currents echo in the nature books (both may have been present, yet not so urgent, in the his-

[22] Edmund Wilson, *To the Finland Station: A Study in the Writing and Acting of History* (Garden City, N.Y.: Doubleday, 1955), p. 20.

tories). In the first, the ideology of unity in multiplicity is reaffirmed and Michelet's authority left unchallenged. In the other, Michelet is less intent on animating and dramatizing figures and events and guiding us discreetly through ordered time than he is intent on finding his own way. The two narrative points of view—one active and one more passive—correspond, in turn, to two different concepts of language. The first maintains Michelet's former insistence on language as a self-effacing force that fuses hearts and produces love and action. The second gives language its independence, and actually considers it in part difficult, if not antagonistic, to work with. Awarding language this space and identity of its own is, in the end, the secret of how Michelet reinvestigates his professional and personal concerns. It will lead him to understand differently the old assumptions or to experience other illuminations. The timely (and timeless) questions of nineteenth-century science, history, literature, and philosophy grow more compelling in each naturalist book. On the one hand, Michelet marvels in a firm voice before the Harmony of Nature, the Infinity or God, in every creature's soul. On the other, he feels the unknown closing in around him at his every move, as he attempts to use metamorphosis to thread a passage through a world of complex change: "So I could ascend in this book to a higher life, I took as my thread the hypothesis of metamorphosis and did not seriously consider constructing a *chain of being*" (*La Mer*, p. 423). Metamorphosis is a slippery, yet effective, muse. And Michelet wonders if, by abandoning himself to her, he will some day rejoin his original principles: "Today the same force leads me to embark with you under the earth on the vast living sea of metamorphoses. World of mystery and shadow. It is here, though, that one finds the light penetrating most deeply into the soul's two precious treasures: Immortality and Love" (*L'Insecte*, p. xxxix). The rhetorical machinery stands ready, and the eternal principles are there when they are needed.

2 Descent into the Dark

It was not until he wrote his fourth and last naturalist book, *La Montagne*, that Michelet could perceive, retrospectively, the grand design of the series. He realized from the beginning both a selfish and an altruistic goal: he would be revitalized and he would simultaneously familiarize his readers with the world of nature, to make them more observant, tolerant, and even sympathetic. He had not, however, foreseen the increasing difficulty of his mysterious subject: "The bird is a person. We accept that freely. But the insect! The problem here seemed more difficult. As for the children of the sea, their fleeting personalities could be grasped even less. It was rash to define such a project; to re-establish these hidden and confused souls disdained until then, denied; to return dignity to them in the fraternal rights of the great City. Today we continue this work in *The Mountain* and its forests" (*La Montagne*, pp. 4–5). As obscurity settled around an adventure that had once promised to be heartening, he remembered the fundamental sacredness of his task and the possible rewards of unusual knowledge and power, rewards more valuable than mere physical rejuvenation. At every turn he asked what the secret, what the source of life, was, what was behind immortality: "Old priests, almighty doctors, tell me, I beg you, the mystery of immortality. You have within you, within the forests of mountains, the power of initiation. We climb, and with each step, we leave behind a part of our miseries from below" (*La

Montagne, p. 133). Though he described in *L'Oiseau* his determination to unite man and nature and to exercise the "art of education and initiation," he accepts in *La Montagne* the basic experience of his books as his own initiation. The narrative structure of initiation, dim and disguised at times, emerges at the end to provide a revealing direction in the development of Michelet's ideology; he does not relinquish his joy of flight to descend into the swarming insect and polyp cities and climb back through eroding forests without undergoing change himself. And the narrator as initiate, as well as initiator, can best convey the inside story.

Although he succumbs for a moment or two in *L'Oiseau* to the Icarian temptation—"Winged dreams, the delight of our nights we so regret in the morning, if only you existed"—his muse, metamorphosis, will redirect him to the dark, misty form of the earth where man belongs: "The ability to drag himself from one place to another on the earth, the ingenious instruments recently invented to enhance this ability, all this does not lessen his adherence to the earth" (*L'Oiseau*, p. 84). For the first time, Michelet looks and does not recognize anything; it is like peering down the long sights of the *Histoire de France:* "After only two volumes, I perceived in these immense perspectives the *terra incognita*" ("Préface de 1869," xxxvii). Yet this descent will be even more disorienting: "This investigation requires what we have the least of today: the ability to escape time and space." His eyes are not accustomed to the "vast night of the sea, an infinite dark! nothing and nothing" (*La Mer*, p. 171). And even in the half-light of the forest something is sinister: "The night dimmed, sounds seemed to hush; even life appeared absent" (*L'Insecte*, p. xvi). Michelet has indeed caught the correct tone, for he is transgressing on territory usually invisible to man, where he must tread softly and with respect: "Man comes by grace alone to these dangerous sites, to this somber laboratory of Nature's enormous force" (*La Montagne*, p. 65). There is a vague churning and seething in the dark, an odd whirring in the silence, and slowly, as his eyes begin to discern obscure forms, a prodigious world rises before him.

The eyes don't believe what can be embraced only by the imagination–multifarious life extending from the infinitely small to the infinitely large, from a timeless past to the present. Gaston Bachelard, who was one of the first prominent modern critics to give Michelet his due, appreciates the imaginative power necessary to render such a slippery vitality. Although his own reactions to images are fundamentally subjective, Bachelard could not have found a better example of his material and dynamic imagination than Michelet. Change, for Bachelard, can never be comprehended from its capricious surface: "The most unstable reverie, the one most given to metamorphosis and completely open to all forms, still keeps a kind of ballast, a density and slow vegetation."[1] To contemplate a subject in its entirety means an appreciation of both its movement and its depth. When the material and dynamic aspects of imagination work cooperatively, an intimacy results, in which knowledge is a literal "being reborn with" (Claudel's *con-naissance*). As early as 1842, Michelet knew that the chemical oneness he established with things differed markedly from the external point of view practiced by contemporaries in philosophy and history: "Between the method that formulates (Hegel) and the plastic method that surrounds (like

[1] Gaston Bachelard, *L'Eau et les rêves: Essai sur l'imagination de la matière* (Paris: Corti, 1942), p. 2. Suzanne Hélein-Koss, in "Gaston Bachelard: Vers une nouvelle méthodologie de l'image littéraire?" *French Review,* 45 (December 1971), 353–64, distinguishes deftly between the material and the dynamic imaginations: "*the material imagination* that unites with the substance of an element and looks for contemplative rest there; the *dynamic imagination* that neglects the substance of the element to see in particular a force or principle of transformation—." In Bachelard, they are often inseparable: "The imagination of movement needs the imagination of matter" (*L'Air et les songes: Essai sur l'imagination du mouvement,* Paris: Corti, 1943, p. 300).

Quinet, who takes great strides around each object and embraces it with force), there is perhaps another one, an interior chemistry that remakes things, taking off again where they first began" (*Journal*, I, 382). An investigation comes about only after the observer enters into an existential participation with the observed, experiencing all its particular perspectives: inside, outside, still, in motion, developed, and in growth. Called "creative" observation, this is the method that led the great scientists of the nineteenth century to their discoveries and syntheses: "The sciences of observation actually only began in 1600 with Galileo. The sciences of creation began, slightly before 1800, with Lavoisier. The latter are the most original sign of our century" (*La Montagne*, p. 237). In the midst of modern diversity and flux, the "masters of metamorphosis" attempted to express an adequate projection of the living whole. Alexander von Humboldt, the century's archetypal naturalist, read by devotees as far away as Thoreau at Walden Pond, spoke for the generation that guided Michelet: "In the midst of this immense variety, and this periodic transformation of animal and vegetable productions, we see incessantly revealed the primordial mystery of all *metamorphosis* which Goethe has treated with more than common sagacity, and to the solution of which man is urged by his desire of reductive vital forms to the smallest number of fundamental types."[2] Yet the dynamic imagination must not be reductive in its synthesis, but through its images must approach only an "obscure unity," the unity suggested by the streaking symmetry of birds' wings caught in a sunset or by the strange appearance of underground springs that have traveled up through the depths from a hidden center.

Against the density of the night, the few flashes of synthesis are barely perceptible, and the mind reels in confusion before the countless indistinguishable populations. Rubbing his eyes

[2] *Cosmos: A Sketch of a Physical Description of the Universe*, trans. E. C. Otte (London, 1849), p. 21.

in the forest, Michelet sees, at last, the capitals of "the great populations of the shadows" that rival the ancient wonders of the world: "Thebes and Nineveh were nothing. Babylon and Babel, because of their astounding structures, are the only ones to sustain a comparison with these tenebrous Babels rising steadily in the abyss" (*L'Insecte*, p. xx).[3] Beyond these subterranean kingdoms lies still another "hinterland, hidden beneath the upper, real world, in the depths of life and darkness of time" (*L'Insecte*, p. 32). After the well-charted Revolution and Middle Ages, the monarchical period of the *Histoire de France* resembled a dark forest, and the historian could barely discern the minute in their great numbers, all the minor courtiers: "You hear no more noise; it is as if there was no one. Tiny men fill the scene, come and go, parade their ridiculous importance" (*Histoire de France* X, 42–43). But still history offers a poor comparison to the infinite legions the new sciences uncovered; the one huge burst of life in Michelet's prerevolutionary history is provided by the eighteenth-century *credo*: "Vertigo overtakes me, watching the prodigious scene of so many beings, yesterday dead, today so alive, creative" (*Histoire de France*, XVI, 321). This is still nothing in relation to the numbers that lie waiting, locked under layers of rock and time: "Who does not know that man has scarcely seen the entrance to the prodigious world of the dead! He has hardly scratched the surface of the globe. . . . If we imagine that the dead (already going back many thousands of years, with the earth) are considerably more numerous than the living, it is outrageous to draw conclusions from a few specimens" (*L'Oiseau*, p. 356). Michelet, the professional resuscitator of the dead, imagines being overwhelmed by clients. And if he could penetrate as far back as the primordial trilobites, he still would not have reached the end–in fact, he might have

[3] Michelet shares the impression with Victor Hugo, who also, in *Dieu*, encounters beneath the surface a swarming insect city: "Anthills are Babels [*Les fourmilières sont des Babels*]."

only touched upon a transitional species of vast generations disappearing in a lost past: "It is infinitely probable that far simpler beings preceded them [the trilobites], prepared for them, but their soft composition left no trace" (*La Mer*, p. 118). The future may be as hopelessly meshed in darkness as is origin, for the historian must capture, in his re-creation of millions of lives and lands, surface/depth, ephemerality/eternity, and metamorphosis/structure.

Sparks of light and stars are not much help in the confusion of this absolute night. An insect here and there, a firefly, will offer its services. "But one would not dare plunge into the peopled darkness of thick forests if luminous insects did not reassure the traveler" (*L'Insecte*, p. 163). Men would tie these tiny natural lanterns onto their sandals and scare away the snakes. But traveling the impenetrable black sea was worse; men finally had to resort to their own initiative. So the people of France created their own coastal constellations; for calm nights a steady beacon was appropriate, but for less dependable weather, moving, revolving lights were needed: "These, like the mysterious animals lighting up the sea, pulsate in the manner of a living flame that flares and pales, shoots up and dies down. On dark stormy nights, they go wild, seem to take part in the Ocean's convulsions, and, unabashed, they fire back with each flash in the sky" (*La Mer*, p. 93). Unlike Victor Hugo's astral savior Stella, who travels from some heavenly sphere to human shores, Michelet's man-made fraternal stars originate on earth. While a glow emerging from darkness in Hugo's poetry reveals an everlasting struggle for immortality and transcendence,[4] Michelet seems concerned foremost with

[4] Lines from Hugo's "Stella" (*Les Châtiments*) depict her as a divine apparition:

> She shone from the depths of a distant sky
> Formless and white with infinite charm.
>
> (Elle resplendissait du fond du ciel lointain
> Dans une blancheur molle, infinie et charmante.)

the possibilities of human community and the organic network binding everything together.

Water is more appropriate than fire, than the stars, electricity, or insects, as man's guide through nature. Water is the very essence of metamorphosis since it participates in almost every form of movement: "Strange and miraculous fairy! With very little she can build up anything; with as little she tears it down; basalt, granite, and porphyry. She is the great force, as well as the most elastic, which gives with the changes of universal metamorphosis. She encloses nature, goes deep inside, translates it, transforms it" (*La Mer*, p. 349). Water is more useful than fire in metamorphosis because of its ability to reveal indirectly. A universe in constant flux is best conveyed by what and where it is not—by its shifting boundaries, its wavy outlines, its relations, its reflections. The first metamorphosis of water, the mountain—a potential vast continent—was known by the way the ocean cradled it: "The sea, as boundary, is in fact what traces continental forms" (*La Mer*, p. 32). The geography of land masses seems disconnected without considering the missing links hidden by intervening water basins.[5] As elusive as air, yet more substantial because it is visible, water demonstrates how opposing shores are related: "The principle of geographical unity, the element of classification, will, more and more, be located in the *ocean basin*, where wind and water—faithful messengers—establish a relationship,

---

"Cadaver" celebrates immortality emerging from the dead mortal body:

> For the secret opens and being escapes.
> The beginnings of a star light up in the eye.
>
> (C'est que le secret s'ouvre et que l'être est dehors.
> Un commencement d'astre éclôt dans la prunelle.)

[5] Michelet's reversal of perspective is analogous to the perception of form as described in Gestalt psychology. A geographer might say, I see two opposing land masses; Michelet would reply, No, there is one sea basin.

assimilate opposite shores" (*La Mer*, pp. 33–34). No true shape appears without the help of mediation: a landscape without lakes is blind and cannot acknowledge its beauty, or divulge itself to others. A landscape with lakes operates like the lighthouse, as a common axis of earth and sky: "Lakes are the eyes of Switzerland whose sky is doubled in blue" (*La Montagne*, p. 39). Alpine lakes have the power to coax the invisible into view, to bring the rough, brown bulk of the glacier into the open: "These lakes, the mute confidants of the glacier that comes out of its night and stands revealed in them, were the terrifying object of a cult for our ancestors, the Celts" (*La Mer*, p. 39). The small bodies of water act as ambassadors and reinterpret the glacier in a slightly less terrible form, a form man could at least take courage in worshiping.

Reflection often anticipates reality before it is completely unveiled, and Michelet seems more interested in this vague revelation than the later brute straightforward appearance. The colors of sunrise explode on the snow-capped peaks before the early-morning riser even glimpses the sun. During this mysterious moment, the natural world shimmers between night and day, between formlessness and form. This ritual awakening of the world is more eloquent when apprehended indirectly: "It is not the sky that they look at upon awakening —the poor Savoyard farmer, the feverish Genoese sailor, the worker from the black streets of Lyon. They all look first to the Alps, consoling peaks releasing them, long before day, from bad dreams, and repeating to the prisoner: 'You will see the sun again' " (*La Montagne*, pp. 47–48). By fixing upon the reflection of an object, rather than upon the object itself, Michelet does not pretend to lose the reality of that experience but recognizes that the meaning of the reality is in its hesitation, in its growth into form. The polar world, *monde des glaces* (*glace* refers to both ice and mirror), is composed entirely of endless reflections whose instability gives the effect of an illusory landscape where dream is also reality: "If you like to dream, if you like to daydream watching the improvised changes and the play of clouds, go up north; all this is made real, though no less fleeting, in the flotilla of moving ice" (*La Mer*, p. 307). As ice thickens and grows opaque, it assumes the ambiguous state of a moving mountain.

This change of the primal "mediator"–water–back into the "mediated"–mountain–alerts one to the consequence implicit in a universe dominated by metamorphosis: everything, including symbols of greatest stability, functions as a link in a succession of transitions. Thus, the mountain can serve the same purpose as the insect, in that it skirts the border between man's world and the invisible unknown, inviting by an ambiguity of situation the exercise of the imagination: "For hours on end, we would be lost in a dreamlike contemplation, never indifferent, always amazed. How many dreams, whether from the past or imagined, pure chimera, we would hang on this uncertain cloud, though very real, reappearing for a time at the edge of the world, of the unknown beyond" (*La Montagne*, p. 58). Huge peaks fade into the clouds as snows and streams evaporate from its surface. The mountain's role as central conductor in the metamorphosis of water means that it is more accurately identified as a go-between in some ongoing process, as a mediator of mediators: "It is the theater of exchange, the theater of the high correspondence between weather currents and wind, vapor and clouds. Water is life that has already begun. The circulation of life, in the form of air or liquid, comes about here on these mountains. They are the mediators, the arbitrators of dispersed and opposing elements" (*La Montagne*, p. 58). The summit's edges are assimilated into an optical illusion of mist and rain; dissolving into thin air, the mountain has a deceptive levity that regularly disarms and charms man's imagination. The romantic commonplace–Sénancour, for instance, spoke of the sunset on the Savoyard Alps and the effect of vapors "lifting the mountains and separating them from the earth so that both top and bottom were indiscernible"[6]—was explicitly interpreted by Humboldt, for whom the archetypal experience becomes a symbol of man's consciousness oscillating between reality and subjectivity: "That which, in the vagueness of our impression, loses all distinctness of form, like some distant mountain shrouded from view by a veil of mist, is clearly revealed by the light of the mind" (*Cosmos*, p. 13). For Michelet and Bachelard the distinction between reality and the mind's eye, imagination, is not so clear. In fact, Bachelard, speaking perhaps for Michelet, would have us live out both sides of the dialectic—"a view or a vision, a pictured reality or a moment in dream" (*L'Air et les songes*, p. 21). In one last image, a mediator, the cypress tree, is infused with energy, movement, and light, with the flickering quality of passing between two worlds, earth and air, reality and dream: "The Persian idea, true as well as sublime, is that the cypress, a pyramidal tree whose tip imitates a flame, is a mediator of land and sky" (*La Montagne*, p. 129). An imaginable model for Van Gogh's hallucination, Michelet's arboreal burst of flame aims again at the precarious universal relationship; this ambiguity and volatility represent the tree's very identity.

The change from bird and insect to flame is conceivable, and the imagination can become accustomed to the idea of mountain and tree as elements of passage. But when other members of the vegetable and animal worlds, or finally even men, begin to slip in and out of stages and to assume different forms, the effect of instability is disquieting. A living form could not only vary from a liquid, solid, or gaseous equivalent of itself, it could also blur with anything vaguely related to it. Since the division of the "three kingdoms" no longer held sway in nineteenth-century science—"One had to leap over the sacred moat of the three Kingdoms, the old scholastic

[6] Etienne de Sénancour, *Obermann, texte original de 1804, précédé du Journal Intime d'Obermann*, ed. André Monglond (Paris, 1947), p. 13.

categories"–vegetables could look and act like animals and vice versa. The mistaken identity was more serious than the protective illusion of butterfly and flower, tree and toad; any organism might get caught in the constant process of change and development *between* two different forms or might seem a *blending* of these forms. Either produces a strange occurrence called the monster.

3 The Age of the Monster

In the nineteenth century, monsters were in fact not so strange; there were too many of them. "It ["our century"] produced races of animals—useful and admirable monsters" (*La Montagne*, p. 237). Scientific tradition, represented by Aristotle, Pliny, and Leibnitz, had isolated the monster, outside the general laws of nature, but Michelet agreed with Geoffroy Saint-Hilaire's hypothesis that the monster was "a most instructive spectacle" in nature's evolution, a necessary experimental step, if impotent and hesitant, toward adaptation. Cuvier presented, in his annual report to the Académie des Sciences in 1826, this résumé of Geoffroy's views: "He does not, as does Aristotle, regard these monsters as exceptions to the general laws; —but considers them rough beginnings, which will never be finished, representing the different degrees of organization" (quoted in Cahn, p. 180). Ideologically, Michelet was delighted to see the mysterious gaps between species beginning to be filled with logical links. Imagistically, however, the curious combinations, resulting from processes of blending and oscillation, provoked a strong ambivalence on his part; he was sometimes sympathetic to, or amused by, nature's futile efforts, but at other times he reacted with disgust and even repulsion. Perhaps simply the equivocal quality of the creatures themselves disturbed Michelet, or he fell prey, as most men do, to imagining animals in human poses and thus transferring immediately to them his own social prejudices.

A monster is anything that cannot be clearly labeled. Often a morphological deviation (and/or a change in the environment) creates the monster, but an animal or plant may be confusing simply because it looks or behaves like something else. Especially disconcerting is the case of an animal or plant that looks or acts like a man. The *Histoire de France* is populated with a menagerie of figures half man and half animal or half enigma. It is usually this unidentifiable zone that characterizes the true monster: Condé would not fit anywhere, "nothing of a man, something more or less, and from some different species" (*Histoire de France*, XII, 179).

Two ambiguous female figures of the natural histories bothered Michelet because they are neither pure vegetable nor pure animal—the orchid and the medusa jellyfish. "Fantastic orchids, the favorite daughters of fever, children of a putrid air" might as well be "strange vegetable butterflies" (*L'Oiseau*, pp. 142–43). The medusa, "an emancipated polyp" (*La Mer*, p. 167), appears part vegetable (the polyp's zoological identity was still in question) and part marine-animal. Michelet observed the medusa firsthand, stopping to pick up the melting gelatinous body washed in from the sea: "I must confess that touching it was disgusting" (p. 164). Although the magical quality of the viscous sea water and of the flexible fish passing through his hands evoked a feeling of excited amazement, the medusa produced a more negative response.

In the surge of life from sea to land and later into the air, several creatures were left in a middle zone: the whale, penguin, seal, walrus, dugong, and manatee. The first effort to emerge from an absolute aqueous existence is the whale's. Though equipped with lungs, the whale is unfit for life where air is available because its monstrous body cannot be lugged across the land. Forced to retreat into the sea, there it risks suffocation. Nature's living example of sublime failure, the whale, monstrous in its impossible makeup, manages at least to survive: "Let us be honest. From the grandiose conception of a giant mammal, there came an impossible creature, the first poetic upsurge of a creative force that shot for the sublime, then gradually returned to what was possible, and would last" (*La Mer*, p. 243). One step removed from whales and other cetaceans are what Michelet erroneously calls "amphibians." The loss of body mass and weight brings progress, and the whale's successors—called sea elephants—head toward land. After the difficult first attempts of the sea elephant, which resembles a huge, unwieldy "slug," the walrus and sea cow succeed in crawling up on shore. It is not until the development of the seal ("lighter, a good swimmer, a good fisherman, living in the sea, but coming on shore to make love"—p. 251) that a truly amphibious organism is created. "With big feet, hooked tight against its body, with a stubby neck balanced on a fat cylindrical trunk, with a flat head" (*L'Oiseau*, p. 77), the penguin, first cousin to the seal, makes the mistake of trying to walk and becomes the clown of monsters. These awkward races, "the first emancipated sons, ambitious creatures," gain Michelet's sympathy, for they are striving toward the realization of nature's highest stage—the bird. The promise of flight is inherent in the futile gestures of the flipper-wing. During his voyage aboard the *Beagle*, Darwin too was intrigued by the penguin's amorphous appendages: "In diving, its little plumeless wings are used as fins; but on the land, as front legs."[1] Penguins, though amusing, represent a privileged step in nature's metamorphosis; they partake effectively of two worlds, land and sea, and are "masters" of both. The highest known form of amphibian was a kind of "siren," which had some human traits, giving it the right to be called *demi-homme* or *homme de mer*. According to folklore, these unfortunate in-between creatures died out some time following the sixteenth century, after having been mistreated by

[1] Charles Darwin, *Journal of Researches into the Geology and Natural History of the Various Countries Visited by H.M.S. Beagle* (London, 1839), p. 256.

man, who could not tolerate recognizing himself in the eerie halfbreed. Man ruled nature with a double standard; if an animal resembled man, or man an animal, the misfit was obliterated: "Everything that did not conform to animality and everything that also came close to man, passed for a *monster*, and they did away with it. The mother who had the misfortune of giving birth to a malformed son could not defend it; they smothered it between mattresses. They thought it belonged to the Devil" (*La Mer*, p. 256). When, on the other hand, an animal tries to imitate man's social actions, not his physiological form, the result can be charming, like a pet we have trained. Michelet was moved by the madonna manatee and child; *la mère Lamantine* looked to him as if she were straining with a crude "hand" to hoist her infant up to her breast.

In addition to the creature of mixed or half kingdoms, an oscillation may occur between sexes, creating a strangely ambiguous body. Some mollusks (*l'haliotide, la veuve, la bouche d'or*) that demonstrate male and female traits are called biological hermaphrodites: "Inside their retreat, they also hide a solitary love. Each is double; in one is both lovers" (p. 193). Singled out as a particularly beautiful mollusk, the haliotis is later compared, and with a highly suggestive significance, to the earth. The earth rises toward the distant sun from whom she is permanently separated. The superficial contact of the sun's rays is dispensable, for she herself is endowed with astounding generative powers. The earth, the sea, and the haliotis are not necessarily bisexual, but can be females, sometimes even virginal, capable of parthenogenesis. This biological phenomenon sometimes horrified Michelet,[2] but he

[2] Often Michelet pretended to be horrified by the possibility of reproduction by one sex alone: "Judea by prophetic creation, Greece by dialectic creation, reproduce without women, are sterile. The Middle Ages dream of conception without sperm, do without God the Father" (*Journal*, II, 308). The human analogy to the hermaphrodite or parthenogenetic virgin troubled him: in *La Femme*, he always

implied in *La Mer* that autonomous sexuality might offer a superior form of pleasure: "She makes love her own way, and even more fully than many others. When her day comes, tiny spheres escape from the mother sponge, armed with weak fins that give them a few moments of movement and liberty. But reattached soon after, they take on the form of delicate spongillae that will in turn begin to grow" (p. 136).

The antithetical image to that of the "double sex," that is, the neuter, or sexless animal, falls as easily under the category of monster. Explicable in a completely different way, this malformation opens new possibilities for the understanding of teratology. Insect asexuality is caused by very early manipulation of environmental conditions. If, during the female bee's nymph stage, it is fed an inferior mixture of honey and flower dust, the young virgin will not develop sexual parts like those of the queen, who is nourished on a finer formula. The undersexed nature of the male bee is also determined in the first hours of life. His grotesque physical plumpness depends solely upon the geometrical design of the beehive's alveoli: fed the proper mixture and left to grow in an oblong cell, a pupa will automatically become a drone: "This form is obtained by a small round section that is the back [of the cell] and makes him almost circular, I was going to say potbellied. As is the house, so grows the inhabitant. The male will be born squat, with a big stomach; he was predestined to have this shape because of his cradle" (*L'Insecte*, p. 335).[3] These examples sug-

---

opted for the maternal or wifely woman who showed no resemblance whatsoever to the "odious Hermaphrodite." A woman with male social interests or habits was to be discouraged or condemned. Contradictory as usual, the historian was fascinated by the idea of artificial fertilization and by the possibility that all a woman's children would resemble the first love partner (*Journal*, II, 441).

[3] Maurice Maeterlinck, a poet-naturalist following in the tradition of Michelet, also portrays drones comically as paunchy (*ventru*): "They lead . . . the leisurely existence of honorary lovers, big and delicate: content, potbellied, taking up the passageways, blocking

gest that an organism's early life, even its prenatal existence, could be crucial in the difference between abnormal and normal development.

Embryology, given impetus by Geoffroy Saint-Hilaire, intrigued and troubled Michelet since it recognized the possibility of abrupt, far-reaching change in animal and human growth. The conclusions of Geoffroy's studies, with which Michelet was familiar, diverged from those of Bonnet and other natural scientists. Charles Bonnet, in his consoling theory of "préformation," also called "embedding of germs" (*emboîtement des germes*) in Malebranche and Réaumur, held that the germ of the adult is found in the earliest stages of animal development and simply realizes itself in growth. This belief coincides easily with the view of the species as fixed and opposes any radical possibilities of metamorphosis and evolution: the monster is a smooth realization of predictable forces. Geoffroy, however, observed that environmental circumstances could be crucial to the future development of an organism.[4] The embryo is particularly sensitive to changes in its environment, and, at times, only a minor alteration may eventually produce a monster. Geoffroy found, for example, that partially covering a bird egg with wax would permanently impair the future adult bird's respiration.[5]

---

traffic, disturbing work, pushing, pushed around, bewildered, self-important, totally swollen" (*Insectes et fleurs*, Paris, 1954, p. 159).

[4] Instead of using the word "evolution," Geoffroy understood this process in terms of "metamorphosis": "The body exists with certain traits, which, forcing it to relate to many things in the exterior world, encourage it to undergo diverse metamorphoses" (quoted in Cahn, *La Vie et l'oeuvre*, p. 173).

[5] From Cuvier's report to the Académie des Sciences (1833): "Mr. Geoffroy continues to think that the adhesion of the fetus on the egg is the unique cause, or, using his expression, the ordinate of monstrosity" (quoted in Cahn, p. 178). Geoffroy's experiments on the bird egg were reinterpreted by Michelet in a curiously significant way: a bird can actually lose a limb, an insect's insides become deadened and paralyzed, if the egg is not kept warm and if even one edge of it is exposed to the cold (see *L'Oiseau*, p. 64).

In Michelet's natural universe, filled with numerous fetuses and metaphoric premature creatures, *avortons* (walrus, sea cow, medusa, mollusk, slug, octopus, and insect), the chances for the proliferation of monsters are multiplied. Before reaching adulthood as a monster, the fetus itself, "torn by a cruel fate from its mother" (*La Mer*, p. 176), already presents both a horrifying and pitiful sight. The caterpillar charges out of its egg as a nude embryo armed for battle. A veritable monster, an egg covered with a fine fur and that moves, it is also thickly folded in layers of skin and has a large stomach. The octopus is another in the ridiculous and frightful guise of the warrior: "a cruel, furious fetus, soft and transparent, but stretching out and breathing forth a murderous breath" (p. 201).

When the nineteenth century began to study the fetus and to recognize the infinite combinations possible through evolution and through environmental adaptation, an orderly ladder of defined species became an amalgam of monsters. In the new organic flow of development gaps were not systematically filled. The opposite happened. The more monsters that appeared, the more gaps opened. The zoological space seemed infinite, like some sucking void. Michelet watched as each monster tried to bridge the gulf on either side; like Zeno's paradox, there was always room for another half monster, and another, and another, which were in themselves beings that demanded full rights and recognition. Still, however, a portion of dark always remained, a parcel of emptiness. In the end, the monsters were anything but consoling.

Undesired consequences might result from an irreparable break in the tenuous fabric of life forms, caused either by a natural aberration or by environmental destruction. It is bad enough that certain species or classes of species should disappear entirely from the scene—the word extinction is not pronounced, but the concept is there. But to compensate for the glaring hole a greater evil is performed. And all this happens "naturally." For some reason, an African red ant species lacked the important worker class; they could not survive without it, so they forced a smaller class of black ants into their service: "One is less shocked by the depraved means the red ants use to survive than by the *monstrous lacuna* that forces them to resort to this" (*L'Insecte*, p. 271, my italics). Whether from negligence or necessity nature had committed an unpardonable sin by leaving an unbridgeable hole that led to slavery in the ant society. Michelet discovered that sometimes transitions are completely missing and that for these gaps his own ignorance could not be blamed.

4 The Lacuna

A vision of harmony has often been ascribed to Michelet, and it is true that to guard against the disturbance of any great discontinuity, he insisted on discovering the links between life forms. He forced himself to find explanations for any deviation: if not through science, then through the imagination. Certain discoveries in *L'Insecte*, however, gravely challenged the certainty of a homogeneous, or *lisse*,[1] view of organic development. The shocking practice of slavery in the ant republic might have been an isolated incident in nature's harmonious processes, leaving intact the deeper, more pacific cycles. Michelet still wanted, therefore, to get to the bottom of the metamorphic system. As he closed in on its different phases and examined the personality of each class type, he finally conceived of the inner metamorphosis of a single individual. In both history and nature, he always thought that a long preparation preceded any change in an individual, whether plant, animal, or nation, but rarely was he given the opportunity to see the intermediary steps unfold before his eyes. Usually any new existence emerged out of ignorance into surprise; such

[1] "This is to state Michelet's great thematics, that of a world without a seam." "To pass from vague water, viscous, neither fluid nor form, to the transparent fish that seems to grow out of water is to open one's hand to the absence of seam and to spread oneself out over this ideal slickness [*lisse*]" (Barthes, *Michelet par lui-même*, pp. 27–31).

a model, most frequently associated with Michelet, is epitomized by the agave, point of comparison for the *sorcière*. For ten years this African cactus sleeps with hardly a sign of life until, one morning, it breaks out like gunshot. So the witch appears one late spring day "all the more violent" (*La Sorcière*, p. 102) and explodes into power. Michelet criticized historians who focused only on "victories, holidays, official events" and rarely on "the mute circulation of life, a certain latent work that bursts forth one morning with the sovereign force of revolutions and changes the world" (*Histoire de France*, XIII, iii). This very unseen development defined for him the real material of history, so that *L'Insecte* reversed the conventional pattern and the history that often escaped archives and documents was disclosed: "Here the revolution other creatures hide so well is bared" (p. 71).

The basic questions, asked over and over again by Michelet in terms of the larger cyclical systems of history, are applied to the insect as individual: Does the continuity break down at any point? Is the hidden revolution of a certain subject predictable, effortless evolution or constant crisis? Are the different metamorphoses of the self actually different "selves" with an entirely new identity? While observing a caterpillar molt, Michelet was astounded to see that its whole body is wrenched apart: "How this nymph, short, weak, soft, and gelatinous, manages, without using her arms or legs, only by skillfully dilating and contracting her rings, to free herself from the heavy and awkward machine she was, how she finally throws off her legs, pulls free of her head, and, I can hardly say it, tears several of her major internal organs away and casts them aside!" (p. 71). The new second self, which emerges, has apparently no connection with the original one: "There she will establish herself in her new self as a nymph, while the old *self*, that beats about on the wind, soon flies away no one knows where. Everything is and must be changed" (p. 71). The possibility of beginning again from zero, of getting another, new self, is exhilarating, for it represents complete freedom from the past: "that life can change to such an extent, dominate its organs, that it sails off victorious, so free of its former *self* [*tellement libre de son ancien moi*]!" (p. 72). Michelet was not so sure, however, of life's victory over loss; as he reflected on that crucial moment of transition between an old body and a still unseen new form, he found no guarantee of safe crossing, no place where something was not hidden. This moment may last an eternity. At the most important passage for any individual, one may meet—instead of continuity—the "terrifying lacuna." "There is (for many species) a moment when nothing old is left, nothing new begins to appear. When Aeson was cut up into pieces and put into Medea's caldron to become young again, you would have found, by searching there, his limbs. But here, no such thing" (p. 73). In the volume of the *Histoire de France* preceding the Revolution, Michelet admits that his history had accumulated lacunae. Louis XVI and his void become the attention of history, and the historian painfully leaves aside all the martyrs and heroes he would rather describe: "Because of this, numerous lacunae" (XVII, xiii). From the point of view of a nation slumbering, of a history of omissions, nothing was less certain—or more—than the Revolution.

Face to face at last with the awful alternative, Michelet maintained a blind hope in the triumph of life and justice over lacuna: "Still confident, the mummy wraps herself in little bands, docilely accepting the darkness, the inertia, the captivity of the tomb" (*L'Insecte*, p. 73). In general, the law of metamorphosis as it applies to the natural environment is a reason for optimism: there is an underlying unity to it. The tree grows new leaves with difficulty, but they are "thousands of nurses, building up its sap and life" (*La Montagne*, p. 215). The "death" of the Alps provides fertile land for Holland so that "dissolution is nothing but creation" (p. 231). In the same way, the annihilation of France's most industrious population fed into an eventual rebirth of freedom: "Because Protestant France, out of her fertile wound, engenders the France of Holland" (*Histoire de France*, IX, vi).

Yet a closer look at metamorphosis on the scale of the individual reveals danger. An insect or animal, first thrust into the world of weather and confronted by enemies, must cover itself with an encumbering outer protection. While it grows, it has to endure periodic molting. It trades one type of suffering for another and does not necessarily gain in the exchange. Certain mollusks, for example, spend their entire lives refortifying their defenses, never achieving greater freedom: "Every step is taken at infinite cost, the cost of a complete house. Something that ruins itself in this way just to go on living can only vegetate, poor and unable to make progress" (*La Mer*, p. 178). If a slightly more desirable life is enjoyed by the insect larva—a fetuslike orphan—the cost is no less than an almost fatal illness, but it is by this "malady," like that of menstruation, that it is supposed to grow. Each state, however, seems only to represent a provisional approach to some very distant integration of personality. The sickness of self is not resolved in a supreme effort to change once and for all; the process is endless, with no specific goal in sight. Unrealistically, the larva hopes it can rest at its present stage of development: "If struggle or pain gives it the glimmer of intelligence, it probably would say after each molting: 'It's over at last! I have finished and will be at peace, this is my last change.' To which Nature replies: 'Not yet! No, not yet! You have not yet given birth to yourself.... What are you? only a *larva*, a mask soon to fall' " (*L'Insecte*, p. 62). Even more troubling is the possibility that each stage of change may not even provide a reality in itself, not even offer a viable existence. It may only "prepare" some vague future being; it may, in essence, be only the mask of a lost or unattainable self—so much suffering for an existence that is not only ephemeral but, perhaps, after all nothing but an illusion.

Where there is the image of molting, one finds almost inevitably the image of the mask; but of the various masks one wears, which is the actual self? "It truly is her intimate self she courageously leaves out to dry, be smashed apart, but to become what?" (*L'Insecte*, p. 73). The lost self, which withers and floats away in the wind, relinquishes its "soul" to an "other." Michelet's voice anticipates Rimbaud's; each "I" is a metamorphosis of many others: "You might say another *she* moves, stirs inside her, follows traces already laid and wants to become... what? does she know?" (pp. 62–63). In the *Histoire de France*, "mask" sometimes connotes a monster, the evil of a double personality: "Coligny had precisely the reality of the virtues whose mask the other (Montmorency) wore" (IX, 24). But, as in the natural histories, the meditation on masks, proliferating like insects, soon becomes complicated: the facial mobility of Henri IV gives way to the multiple masks of the seventeenth century: "We speak of the *double*, but this one was *multiple!*" (XIV, 190). Molière's Sosie testifies to the demise of the ego; the French people, serving as audience to the empty mask of the monarch, knew no identity but that fickle surface: "But under the mask, inside this royal actor who alone *was*, and the rest, nothing" (XIII, 98).

Michelet the ideologue preferred progress to the procession of equally deceptive masks; the insect should make us confident of the ultimate resurrection; the scarab is our Christ: "From the most offensive tomb it rises resplendent" (*L'Insecte*, p. 68). Even if as human beings we cannot see beyond our tedious early stages, perhaps our family or community, even humanity, will evolve like a scarab. Nevertheless, the preparatory stages continue to be prolonged: "I have gone through painful moltings, laborious transformations. . . . Over and over again I have gone from larva to chrysalis and on to a more complete state, which later, because incomplete in other ways, headed me off on a new circle of metamorphoses. All this, from me to me, but not less from me to whoever was still me, who loved me, wanted me, who made me, or rather whom I loved and made. They too were or will be my metamorphoses."[2] The concept "Jules Michelet" is, therefore, disseminated in different states of development everywhere, leading no telling where.

Although the abstract vision is minimally comforting, Michelet was still obsessed with the possibility that nothing is connected–no parts of the person, no family. A small child may resemble the grub whose development must remain a mystery as it sees no farther than from day to day. To calm these fears, Michelet actually picked apart a nymph to look for the vague beginnings of the butterfly. This "germ" of the insect's future would prove omniscient nature's ability to plan; all metamorphic stages would be comfortably interlocked. The most terrifying vision for Michelet returned consistently in cases of more radical metamorphoses, especially those suffered by lower marine animals, such as the mollusk and crustacean. At one point in the metamorphosis of the shrimp or crab, the animal is exhausted and weak, actually absent (*absent de lui-même*), a living void, vulnerable to every passing predator. The human being, along with the higher animal forms and fish, is spared this physical blotting out, this private lacuna of the body, by means of his very gradual but constant metamorphosis: "He is never broken down by it, only weakened, in a vague and dreamlike moment, when the flame of life pales in order that it may return sharper" (*La Mer*, pp. 213–14).

When Michelet fixes upon the gaps in animal and human

[2] "J'ai subi des mues pénibles, des transformations laborieuses. . . . J'ai passé mainte et mainte fois de la larve à la chrysalide et à un état plus complet, lequel au bout de quelque temps, incomplet sous d'autres rapports, me mettait en voie d'accomplir un cercle nouveau de métamorphoses. Tout cela de moi à moi, mais non moins de moi à ceux qui furent encore moi, qui m'aimèrent, me voulurent, me firent, ou bien que j'aimai, que je fis. Eux aussi, ils ont été ou seront mes métamorphoses" (*L'Insecte*, p. 74).

existence, his fantasies take on such urgency as to fill the initial nothingness with their own world and time. The lacuna becomes a universe. If one believes blindly that the passage through symbolic death back to life again will be accomplished, any suspended time "in-between" can be optimistically called the *prenatal* period: "The insect, in its chrysalis, seems to forget and ignore itself, to remain apart from its suffering, one might even say it relishes this relative death, like a baby in a warm cradle" (*La Mer*, p. 214). Prenatal life, associated with the deepest pleasures and pains, is hardly uneventful; rather than being an inferior existence, it offers refinements of sensitivity and consciousness. The prenatal inhabitant, the fetus, is able to profit from its unprotected delicate body, a privilege rendered almost impossible once out of the womb. Whereas all attempts at union with another body are frustrated outside of the womb-world, the isolation imposed by the necessary protective covering (like fatty skin or shell) makes prenatal sex ideal. The expression of this almost unbelievable possibility existed in Egyptian mythology: Isis and Osiris, growing inside Isis-Athor's womb, make love, resulting in the birth of a son, Horus. The three are then born together at the same time.[3] In the zoological realm, Michelet understood the reproduction of the bisexual sponge in the same way; not yet a fully developed organism, "she" gives birth without having to be born: "As in the story of the Egyptian gods, Isis and Osiris, who gave birth before themselves being born, Love arises before being" (*La Mer*, p. 136). In fact, bodies still close to a pure embryonic form permit a special contact, for they have the best of both worlds: the nervous system—developed early (*ébauché d'abord*)—stimulates feeling but not to the

[3] "For they were already so much in love inside the womb that Isis conceived. Even before being, she was a mother. She had a son named Horus, who is none other than her father, another Osiris gifted with goodness, beauty, and light. So they are born together, the three of them, mother, father, and son, all the same age, the same heart" (*La Bible de l'humanité*, p. 289).

point of fear. One of the few unions in all four nature books considered successful is the coupling of slugs, "ceux qu'on croirait les plus froids," as Michelet calls them, using understatement, for they are repulsive as well as "cold." Yet they are transformed into an image of almost prenatal eroticism. "Happiness has, for instance, been noted in the snail that finds a mate after a painful search for love. Both of them, with a grace full of emotion, undulating their swan necks, share eager caresses" (p. 176).

A second microcosmic life cycle can occur *inside* the womb, mummy case, or cocoon—a place where the unborn live, love, and die, where a privileged time and space function both within and beyond the greater metamorphic process. Michelet is fascinated by an idea related to his own, which he pretends to borrow from an unidentified American. His unnamed source reminds us curiously of Edgar Allan Poe, whose "Colloquy of Monos and Una" relates the levels of semiconsciousness after death. Poe's "deceased" protagonist retains, all the while, degrees of sensitivity to time and place.[4] Michelet's vision of life-in-death does not permit the usual activities of a "normal existence," but his figure of the tree as a captured soul, like the fetus–nymph–mummy, illustrates a kind of subliminal intelligence: "An American imagines, with much truth in it, that between life and death, there are many intermediary states, that these two worlds are entirely relative. A dead life and an alive life, vague and unconscious thought, impotent dreaming that cannot act or understand and analyze itself, these are aspects one must find in the long existence of those trees, embalmed, so to speak, just like the mummies of Egypt, yet still

[4] "My condition did not deprive me of sentience. It appeared to me not greatly dissimilar to the extreme quiescence of him, who, having slumbered long and profoundly, lying motionless and fully prostrate in a midsummer noon, begins to steal slowly back into consciousness, through the mere sufficiency of his sleep, and without being awakened by external disturbances" (*Great Short Works of Edgar Allan Poe*, rpt. New York, 1970, p. 338).

living under their mute mask."[5] This conception of "another world" is more fertile for Michelet than the traditional notion expressed in *L'Oiseau* of the mortal's dream for some immortal, timeless, heavenly paradise.[6] Instead of the latter, Michelet has created a mysterious shadow zone between, not beyond or above, life and death;[7] an existence where no irreparable act can be committed, but where future action and thought are incubating: a world of the unconscious, an *earthy* paradise, a *relative* eternity.

Finally, in order to obliterate the ambiguous lacuna, both the entrance into and the exit from this perfect transitional world must be rendered practically imperceptible. Death, a well-modulated passage, can no longer be associated with the sting of pain, violence, and sorrow. This is conceivable under one condition—that life become almost interchangeable with a secure, warm, and generous "prelife." Then death would be a simple transfer from one live maternal universe to the other, like sliding from the sea into the cavern of the whale: "In this marine world of rapid ingestion, most creatures are absorbed

[5] "Un Américain imagine avec beaucoup de vraisemblance qu'entre la vie et la mort, il y a nombre d'états intermédiaires, que ces mots sont tout relatifs. La vie morte, et la vie vivante, la pensée vague, inconsciente, le rêve impuissant pour agir, et même pour se comprendre bien, s'analyser, ce sont des choses qui doivent se trouver dans la longue existence de ces arbres embaumés pour ainsi dire, autant que les momies d'Egypte, mais qui vivent pourtant sous leur masque muet" (*La Montagne*, p. 218).

[6] The verses Michelet quotes from the German poet Rückert, "Wings above life! Wings beyond death," would suggest that man desires escape from the life/death cycle (*L'Oiseau*, p. 83).

[7] Whereas Michelet synthesizes the aspects of continuity and severe discontinuity, which he sees in both "insect" and "human" deaths, Maeterlinck contrasts insect "eternal life" with man's definite "death": "When an insect dies, it is only one cell transformed into a larger organism, whereas each one of us thinks he is a larger organism in itself. The insect dies much less than we do, perhaps it does not die at all. For us death, except for fairly uncertain religious beliefs, is an absolute end; for him it is a metamorphosis like any other, back to the beginning of the eternal return" (*Insectes et fleurs*, pp. 461–62).

live" (*La Mer*, p. 114). Life would pour smoothly into new life without rupture, without the blackout of death: "Happy and blessed three times over, this world where life is mended, without costing death, this world generally free from grief" (*L'Oiseau*, p. 75).

The only possible way this imperceptible passage could be realized is to strip the subjects in question of nervous systems, deny them their "means of suffering." But that removes all possibilities of enjoying pleasure, which is so rarely encountered. Thus, only the amorphous, primitive, microscopic plants or animals can avoid pain and death. Michelet's imagination, searching for the perfect condition, runs headlong into the truism that to bypass death, one must miss life: "Innocent and peaceful, they [whales] swallow a world scarcely organized, which dies before having lived and passes asleep into the crucible of universal change" (*La Mer*, p. 238). Michelet is ambivalent about how he wants to conceive of prenatal or primordial time; he has arrived at such an extreme point in his thinking that he has only minimal help and almost an open field for contemplation.

5 The "Organizable"

The muted death of microscopic plant and animal life whets Michelet's curiosity again, and he plunges into the sea of metamorphosis, determined to ascertain once and for all if there is a break or smooth transition between end and re-beginning, between deaths and renewals. At least the once grossly general questions—"Which is death? Which life? What is awake or asleep?" (*L'Insecte*, p. 68)—have changed focus to the biological beginnings of life: "Where did the first animal beginnings come about? What would have been the primitive theater of its organization?" (*La Mer*, p. 120). What seems to be a flight from the last lacuna turns out to be a relentless pursuit, a challenge Michelet throws into the face of nature that he will find her center yet.

Now the quester is invited into a completely unknown and nightmarish realm, a Dantesque Hell of infinitely descending or ascending circles: "It was not the case here of a decreasing scale of abstract sizes or of inorganic atoms, but of a successive enveloping, the prodigious movement of one thing inside another. For the short distance we can see, each animal is a small planet, a world inhabited by still smaller animals, lived in by others smaller still" (*L'Insecte*, p. 106). Michelet is no longer carefully stepping down the rungs of a ladder; rather, he is growing or shrinking according to the dictates of the sphere he awakens in. He is no longer on a leisurely walk through the museum but caught in a series of unexpected displacements like Alice in Wonderland.

Michelet can only hope that if he abandons himself to the river of metamorphosis he eventually will come out at the sea or at the court of the queen, a Sibyl who will tell him the truth. He compares the exploits of a naturalist to those of a daredevil in a barrel or boat upstream from Niagara Falls, floating in a deceptive calm and trying not to think about what lies ahead, because his imagination runs frighteningly and insightfully rampant. Like Rimbaud in "Le Bateau ivre," Michelet may regret the structures of his past, his constrained puddle. Like Baudelaire's paralyzed ship ("un navire pris dans le pôle"), his boat may be wedged into its inescapable prison—or like Dante, the voyager may discover at the center a triumphant way out.

Michelet always had some intuition that the secret he was after lay in the sea. As early as *L'Oiseau,* he questioned the notion that stagnant or thick waters were places of poison and death and wondered if they weren't instead "a first living fermentation." No one had absolute proof that seawater might hold the basic element of life, but naturalists, including Humboldt, Bory de Saint-Vincent, and Geoffroy, were tempted to believe it. Michelet has Bory de Saint-Vincent articulate some of his own speculation: "What is sea *mucus?* The sea's general viscousness? Is it not the universal element of life?" (*La Mer,* p. 113). Geoffroy Saint-Hilaire called this mediating ingredient between the inorganic and organic worlds the "animalizable": "the first degree of organic bodies" (p. 115). Michelet seems to prefer a general word that does not refer to a specific kingdom but to a functional moment in an ongoing process, the "organizable."[1]

A prime example of the "organizable" is a drop of seawater, or mucus, since it embodies in its small space the entire cosmos

[1] Charles Bonnet in his *Contemplation de la nature* separates all life forms into beings that are primitive and unorganized; organized and inanimate (vegetable); organized and animate (animal); organized, animate, and reasoning (man). For a discussion of Bonnet's "evolutionism," see Foucault, *The Order of Things,* pp. 147–52.

and initiates a microscopic construction that would "through its transformations, recount the universe" (p. 116). Michelet has extended his imagination far into the visible realms of time and space since his first steps in *L'Oiseau* and *L'Insecte*. The insect, whose tiny multitudes once dazed him, seems young and oversized when compared with protozoans. But has he at last gotten back to the beginning? Is his drop of water the lacuna? When seen under a microscope, that original drop of water is composed of millions of universes. To arrive at the real beginning he will have to make himself smaller still. Like the frustration of monsters subdividing into other monsters with room for more, the various planets of life regress infinitely: it looks, for a minute, as if there is nothing in sight and yet some vague form always begins to emerge.

If the "organizable" is the source so sought after, Michelet meets still another obstacle: how does one observe the "organizable"? Its unstable composition means that it changes immediately either into a liquid or a solid; like the fetus, it cannot maintain its totally open and natural state for long but must seek shelter or start an instantaneous reaction of closure. Resin and blood have the same capacity of renewal as seawater, but lava is the closest relative to the miraculous mucus, for it too participated in the first days of creation when the earth itself was an "organizable"—a *pâte molle* (soft dough or paste). Not even this supposedly perfect state of sensitivity could the earth prolong; the tragedy of the earth was the cooling of its crust or veil.

The Fall for Michelet is not sin, but the hardening of one's malleable nature outside the womb—the point at which the organizable becomes organized and openness is no longer feasible. If we could exist forever as a slightly thickened bloodstream or as a soft fetus, we would never experience alienation from others or from the environment. Relationships would be a simple matter of osmosis. Although he realizes that animals must allow their exterior surface to toughen for their own protection, he prefers that they be content with a minimal covering—a kind of porous, transparent skin that would reveal, rather than hide, the inner self, and that would leave the body vulnerable. The whale's blubber wavers in this privileged area between resistance and hypersensitivity: "Fat protecting it from the cold does not, in the least, fend off shock. Its skin, intricately composed of six different tissues, quivers and shakes for any reason" (*La Mer*, p. 239). The fish, whose flexible scaled sides offer both movement and durability, takes on the slippery characteristics of the sea, appears "identical to the element it swims in" (p. 112). It is one of the rare creatures to have avoided the need for a hard outer envelope, perhaps because it still inhabits a womblike element. Man, animals, and the tree, forced to live in a more destructive, changeable universe of weather, cannot be sufficiently sheltered by a thin coating of scales. Man must build a house; the bird, insect, and spider must build their nests; and the tree must cover its precious sap with rings of wood and a layer of bark. Given these harsh realities, Michelet still yearns for the undersea, underground world. In *La Mer,* he spends a chapter constructing his "dream house." The house overlooks the sea while sheltering in back a garden of calm; Eden is partly restored: "The concave side of this half circle, its interior, would be protected by the crescent's horns, so they embrace the mistress's pretty little garden" (pp. 377–78). The houses he found in the Engadine region of the Alps inspired his enraptured description. The "pleasures of the North" are heightened by the house's secret "paradise," its cozy room hidden just above the stove. Not only does this inner sanctum protect the couple from the inclement exterior; being completely closed off, its inhabitants cannot have any contact with the outside world. The male, especially, appreciates such absolute security: "A quick observation gave me the favorable impression of a woman totally devoted to her house, with little curiosity for what was happening outside; this is because the windowpanes, often convex, scratched and quite thick, let in daylight but not the image of passers-by" (*La Montagne*, p. 205). The secret erotic chamber par excellence, which is for Michelet the polished alcove, has its counterpart in animal and plant life. The awkward woodpecker, who is endowed through love with the gift of sculpture, builds a nest that is transformed into a luxurious marble and ivory bedroom. The sheen does not come from the material itself but from love, glowing, like a hearth, against the walls. The thrush, building its nest with the usual materials, rubs its breast around and around,[2] molding a circular room and polishing the walls until they shine: "Its nest, openly exposed under the damp shelter of vines, is made with moss outside and remains invisible, entwined with vegetation; but look inside: there is a marvelously clear cup, polished and shining, that would not dull next to glass. You can see yourself in it" (*L'Oiseau*, p. 272). When the flower's room hardens into

[2] Bachelard is inspired by Michelet's description of the way a female thrush shapes and is shaped by her nest: "What an unbelievable inversion of images! Here, is not the womb created by the embryo? Everything is internal pressure, its physically dominating intimacy. The nest is a swelling fruit pushing at its limits" (*La Poétique de l'espace*, Paris: Presses Universitaires de France, 1957, p. 101). It is interesting to note, however, that Bachelard and Michelet often infuse the same themes with a very different tonality: Bachelard's cosmic confidence radiates from an image that produces anxiety in Michelet: "Thus, by contemplating the nest, we are at the origin of a confidence in the world, we respond to the beginnings of confidence, to a call for cosmic confidence" (*La Poétique de l'espace*, p. 102). For Michelet, the nest can mean pain: "The house then is the person himself . . . I will say, his suffering" (*L'Oiseau*, p. 269). While polishing with its own body the inside of its nest, the thrush actually sacrifices itself for its family (like Musset's pelican). Bachelard's chrysalis harmonizes man's two most fundamental desires—flight and repose. Michelet's chrysalis is, on the other hand, locked in an uneasy sleep with no knowledge of what is in store for the future. The shell is associated in Bachelard with rest: "Man, animals, the almond, all find maximum repose in a shell" (p. 121). Whereas the man who lives inside Bachelard's "shell grotto" loves solitude and has no fear, Michelet's shell becomes a prison.

jewels, the atmosphere is still a strange welcoming combination of softness and mirroring: "The bee lies back in an alcove worthy of a fairy, on the softest carpets; under fantastic pavilions; and walls of topaz and sapphire ceilings" (*L'Insecte*, p. 321).

As with any of Michelet's images, paradise can eventually slip into nightmare. The perfect house that fits snugly onto the body, that comes out of the body's own fluids, can slowly metamorphose from comfortable protection into a prison. The sea urchin, other mollucks, and crustaceans, admirably armed in their brittle houses, can find themselves trapped in what is intended to save them. The sea urchin's perfect circular form turns against it: "This defensive miracle made a prisoner; not only did it close itself in, but entombed, it dug its own grave" (*La Mer*, p. 186). This natural phenomenon, recurring in history, condemned both the Spanish and French dynasties. Philip II built the "pleasure dome" of the Escurial that also worked against him: "palace, monastery, and tomb" (*Histoire de France*, IX, 244). The successive Louis' of France, retreating into larger and larger palaces until Versailles, paradoxically remained in smaller and smaller bedchambers, and France itself, drawing in with its kings, became a *cachot*, a prison cell.

Each creature, shut inside itself, reaches out for light, for air, for something or someone else. The mollusk, whose very identity is its shell, takes special pains to breathe: "It is not surprising if these poor creatures, shut inside and suffocating under their houses, found a thousand apparatuses, thousands of kinds of valves, to ease things a little" (*La Mer*, p. 191). Stomata, antennae, tentacles, hands, branches, and pine needles develop out of a need for the enclosed, animal, insect, or tree to maintain contact with the outside world. But as long as there is any small opening in the house, the enemy can slip in. The ear-shell, or haliotis, extends one foot outside, and this foot, which must fulfill the function of all the senses, is already too much: "I'm afraid... the crab is watching; if I crack the door, he'll be in my house" (p. 192). Certain birds, the wasp, the bee, the termite, and, especially, the spider build impregnable houses because of their need for security, often at the cost of their freedom. The life force, the only hope of continuity through offspring, the force preserved in the female, must be religiously cared for. Neither house nor "home" will suffice for the wasp, but rather a "home within a home." Almost imperceptively, the labyrinth begins to close in.

No fortress is buttressed enough; no city adequately guarded. The jittery spider locks itself behind sixty doors and then, without peace of mind, secures the last door with its own body, a "living lock" (*un verrou vivant*) (*L'Insecte*, p. 8). Despite all precautions, the enemy cannot be stopped. The hawkmoth (*Sphinx*), quiet and velvety, slips at night through the narrowest chink in the hive to plunder, pillage, and kill. The Sphinx of history is Richelieu who "walks without walking, who advances without seeming to and without making noise as if sliding along a thick carpet..., then, arrives, overturning everything" (*Histoire de France*, XI, 244). Though noisier than the Sphinx, the hurricane, described in *La Montagne*, gives Michelet the same feeling of insecurity behind his own tight shutters. He tries all day to write despite the unrelenting wind, but he finally cannot stand the pressure of the storm, which he imagines as a pack of dogs, a mob of black faces, the sinister monotony of madness: "In the overall uniformity (true though contradictory) there was a diabolical swarming" (*La Mer*, p. 85). Michelet begins to understand that wherever he looks, he can find the opposite of what he expected. A kind of black magic is being worked on him. As he draws closer to the basic element of pure potential, the "organizable," he sees it transform before his eyes into forts and prisons. Unity could be a nightmare. Nor are the circles, enclosed one within another, turning on some recognizable axis. In fact, the fundamental principle of all being is reduced perhaps, like that of a monster, to formlessness and blurring.

Michelet had not bargained for this. Nature was supposed to uplift his spirits, not challenge his consciousness, not double his questions while everything dissolved around him. It is all very fine for the mountain to quiver in a morning mist or evening sun, but when the bottom started to crumble under his own feet and still the flowers bloomed, he no longer could trust any reality—in nature or in history: "From four to five thousand feet, this danger underfoot is masked by rhododendron, by wild juniper. . . . Under these flowers even more erosion continues in silence, only to appear one morning stripping everything to a hideous nudity, which nothing will ever return to cover. How like man nature is! As I was writing this, a horror of the moral lapies [*lapiaz*] I witness these days came over me" (*La Montagne*, pp. 178–79). Nor did "moral erosion" take place on some abstract level; chaos was close to home. During the hurricane of 1859, a shutter banged loose, and Michelet looked out to see the *fourmillement* he had already sensed behind the droning wind and rain. His intuitions and fears became hallucination: "Monsters, what more do you want? Are you not drunk with shipwrecks I hear about from all sides; what are you asking?—'Your death and universal death, the suppression of the earth, and the return to chaos' " (*La Mer*, p. 86). The roles are reversed. Before the spirits of nature will answer any questions, before they will tell any secrets or perform any feats, they will place the burden on the questioner. Michelet will have to undergo precisely the insect or mollusk metamorphosis that so troubled him. Nature was giving the old reply of the mirror.

6 Metamorphosis of the Personality

In the naturalist books Michelet reorders and defines his protagonists as they suit his need to work out, on an imaginative scale, the ideological impasse of history and personality. Certainly his *Histoire de France* is a symptom of the same crises, but natural history provides a different field where interpretation does not have to pass through the problematics of the individual, the controversies surrounding a Robespierre or a Richelieu. The basic issues and structures of Michelet's work have different disguises in natural history, where they are perhaps easier to read. As early as 1830, Michelet reduced his historical dialectics to intersubjectivity:[1] "The *self* [*moi*] is placed on one side with human liberty; on the other is the *not-self* [*non-moi*], or physical fatality.... Our victory can be explained by a single consideration. That is: nature does not change and human nature changes and profits" (my italics).[2]

[1] In a reading of English romanticism, Harold Bloom signals the central importance of the internalized quest-romance pattern: "The internalization of quest-romance made of the poet-hero a seeker not after nature but after his own mature powers, and so the Romantic poet turned away, not from society to nature, but from nature to what was more integral than nature, within himself. The widened consciousness of the poet did not give him intimations of a former union with nature or the Divine, but rather of his former selfless self" ("The Internalization of Quest Romance," in *Romanticism and Consciousness*, ed. Harold Bloom, New York, 1970, pp. 15–16).

[2] From Michelet's course notes, 1829–1830, at the Ecole Normale, quoted in Viallaneix, *La Voie royale*, p. 444.

This overly categoric distinction was not to be examined until later, when the intertextuality of the *Journal* and naturalist books provided the occasion for a dialogue that could protect, while ultimately undermining, the uninterrupted project of France's history. Whereas the *Journal* is obsessively devoted to its subject, the self, constantly chiding or justifying it, the naturalist books, while seeming to relieve these tensions are only the excuse for further exploration.

Nature was not just a not-self to be discarded as irrelevant, because within it the same dialectics of *moi* and *non-moi*, the dialectics of identity, were still operative and still naggingly difficult to resolve. Natural history provided a testing ground for the study of relationships between the individual and any counterforce: a loved one, society, even time and evolution. Whether an antagonist or faithful shadow and guide, nature generated for Michelet the dynamics of a complete, though complex, personal mythology.

In the beginning was community (sometimes male, sometimes female, sometimes bisexual); the community was one being—like a cosmic primitive god—or it was many. Again, no distinction was made, no other alternatives considered: "The first state, a patriarch, is, then, like the budding of related existences, the closed world of a family foreign to the world. . . . There has been no individual yet like the human community, the human polyp, an original union, so close there is not even the feeling of union" (*Journal*, II, 308).[3] Society was a coral reef swaying in time to universal currents. At some critical moment, an individual appeared and, by definition, had to abandon the original community. But "he" was never happy, and he ironically spent his entire existence working his

[3] Darwin was also intrigued by the confusion of individual and community in polyp colonies: "Of these polypi, in a large specimen, there must be many thousands; yet we see that they act by one movement; that they have one central axis connected with a system of obscure circulation; . . . Well may one be allowed to ask, what is an individual?" (*Journal of Researches*, p. 117).

way slowly back to the first formless unity in which consciousness and anxiety were unheard of: "Upon contact with the general atmosphere of the globe, the boiling matter begins to ferment, to rise. It yearns for more being. Life catches fire.... This enviable increase is achieved with the budding of related animals. Then the individual appears and with him the desire not to be alone but to return to the state of sweet society."[4] Yet Michelet was not satisfied with this cyclical vision; nature faithfully mirrored his ambivalence. When the medusa became a kind of case study, he praised her feeble but courageous attempts at autonomy—"trying to be herself, to act and suffer on her own" (*La Mer*, p. 167). Predictably, the medusa can never rest at ease in her state of independence, so nature allows her a lifestyle fixed forever in flux. She can alternate between free-floating and stationary forms. Michelet, who, as usual, personifies the medusa, gives her uniquely human motivations: "The polyp cluster makes the medusa; the medusa makes the polyp. She enters into association with it. But this vegetable life is so boring that by the next generation she frees herself from it and launches out again into the hazards of pointless navigation. A strange alternative, where she floats on eternally. Active, she dreams of rest. Inert, she dreams of moving again" (p. 169).

Such is the dilemma Michelet lived with, always caught between *alternatives bizarres*. He thought existence should be strictly regulated in dialectical terms: *individual*/historian of the *people*: "Is individuality not the symbol of a collective? Then, self of a multiple not-self that will appear at my death. Breaking up the individual disperses life so it will flourish, multiple and more beautiful. Therefore, an alternative mirror

[4] "Au contact de l'atmosphère générale du globe, la matière bouillonnante commence à fermenter, à se gonfler. Elle tend à être davantage. La vie s'allume.... Cette augmentation désirée s'accomplit par bourgeonnement d'animaux associés. Puis l'individu apparaît et, dans l'individu, le désir de ne pas rester solitaire, de retourner à cet état de douce société" (*Journal*, II, 307).

of concentrated life. . . . I go from my individual self to my literary self, concentrating the world as beauty, and then to my moral self, absorbing the world as good."[5] But again the problem, uncovered by the example of the insect, reappears: is there a *moi,* or simply an assemblage of numerous *non-moi,* a series of alternating negatives that give the illusion of something positive?

Although Michelet yearned to promote total unity and, like his sea urchin, to be at one within himself as well ("to be one, . . . to be gathered up, strong in myself, round"), he conceded that two complementary forms might be a solution to the problem of unity: "The beauty of the world to come will be the harmony of double forms, their balance, the grace of their oscillation. From mollusk to man, every creature in between is made of two related halves. In each animal (better than unity) there is union" (*La Mer,* p. 186). He was willing to see the couple as a sacred configuration, and, in order not to abandon his original ideal of oneness too abruptly, he would prefer that couple to be twins. He called the fission of polyps a splitting of twin life (*vie géminée*); he marveled at the concept of male and female in nature. He even patterned his own life after this image—or vice versa—and sought out his "double." His second marriage was to exemplify the advantages of dual harmony: "Communicating everything is so sweet with this other self, so different from me. It is me and is not me. I am glad for the likeness, glad for the difference" (*Journal,* II, 115). Successful oscillation between two "halves" demands some distinction between them. They may be twins, but not identical, or they must at least sustain different interests and

[5] "L'individualité ne serait-elle pas symbole de collection? Ainsi moi d'un non-moi multiple, qui apparaîtra par ma mort. La dissolution de l'individu éparpille la vie, pour la faire fleurir plus multiple et plus belle. Ainsi, miroir alternatif de la vie concentrée. . . . Je vais du moi-individu au moi littéraire, qui concentre le monde comme beauté, puis, au moi moral, qui absorbe le monde comme bonté" (*Journal,* I, 219).

exhibit different personalities. Because of his partiality to the image of twins, it would seem that Michelet adopted the myth of the androgyne as the model of a perfect couple. The platonic concept is as close to a oneness-in-two as any that has been imagined.[6] Here again, however, a juxtaposition of Michelet's texts reveals ambiguity. He hates to compromise absolute unity—"any division is against nature"—but also insists that a couple be a true *double* unit.

The condition of the double prepares the only possibility for a developed personality. The self is formed in a continuous dialectical exchange with its other self or another person. Self-love represents the necessary transition between an absolute confusion of mother and offspring to the birth of an individual. The very first stirrings of primitive identity depend upon a baby's sensation of self when the infant—or possibly the fetus—vaguely takes its own body as an object of love (Freud discusses this early narcissism in "Anxiety," Stand. Ed., XX, 135). Michelet actually attributes the process of self-development and definition to an intuitive narcissism; he combines this concept, strangely enough, with Darwin's theories of natural selection and survival of the fittest: "So they create themselves, the tiny lives have an obscure instinct, like an attraction, like the internal gravitation that is love. First, love of the self for the self (as Geoffroy Saint-Hilaire would say). They love themselves and want only good for themselves. And that is behind all the detail of each developing individual: its tastes and choices, how it prefers (Darwin) what is best in itself for it, what will save its life, enhance it,—make its small fortune,

[6] Plato's myth is so attractive to Michelet that he reads it into the story of Isis and Osiris: "In the universal mother [Isis-Athor, or night], a daughter, a son, Isis-Osiris, were conceived, who, being two, were only one" (*Bible de l'humanité*, p. 289). "This is the mystery of life: twins [Isis-Osiris], indistinct from each other until the third month, were separated, and will soon be dispersed throughout the vast world to spend their life trying to remake their unity" (*Journal*, II, 302).

transform it perhaps and send it higher."[7] The critical moment when the infant seizes the concept of identity, of his wholeness (or Gestalt) depends upon the conceptualization of the other. Jacques Lacan has called this experience the *stade du miroir*, for he represents it as the subject's perception of himself as different from his mother's reflection in the mirror.[8] The response to this discovery is usually contradictory. On the one hand, the child feels the excitement of recognition and has some vision of stability. On the other, he experiences anxiety. The mirrored self exists, after all, in the tenuous realm of the image and is nothing more than a mental construct (an ideal ego). It is easy to imagine a counterproposal of destruction. The infant projects onto the "other" in the mirror his own insecure reactions; he feels he must act against a threatening enemy before he is acted upon, and thus initiates with himself the first "drama of jealousy."[9] In the inevitable dialectics of

[7] "Les petites vies, pour se faire, ont dans l'instinct obscur, comme une attraction, une gravitation intérieure qui est *l'amour*. D'abord l'amour de soi pour soi (pour dire comme Geoffroy Saint-Hilaire). Ils s'aiment et se veulent du bien. Et cela fait tout le détail du développement de chaque être, le goût, le choix, la préférence (Darwin) pour ce qu'il a en lui de bon pour lui, pour ce qui doit le sauver, l'augmenter,—lui faire sa petite fortune, le transformer peut-étre et le porter plus haut" (*La Montagne*, p. 240).

[8] LaPlanche and Pontalis have traced the logical development from Freud's theories of narcissism to Lacan's *stade du miroir:* "One can, in a genetic perspective, conceive of how the ego is constituted as a psychic entity, correlative to the constituting of the body as specific outline. One can also think that such a unity is precipitated by a certain image the subject receives of himself, based on the model of the other, and which is precisely the ego. . . . J. Lacan connected this first instant of self-formulation with the basic narcissistic experience he calls the 'stage of the mirror' " (Jean LaPlanche and J. B. Pontalis, *Vocabulaire de la psychanalyse*, Paris, 1967, p. 262).

[9] "The moment that brings the stage of the mirror to an end inaugurates, through the identification with the *imago* of one's likeness and the drama of primordial jealousy . . . , the dialectic that from then on links the *I* with socially elaborated situations" (Jacques Lacan, *Ecrits*, Paris, 1966, p. 98).

narcissism, the self becomes its principal rival, and aggression is the logical conclusion. "Aggressiveness is the correlative tendency of a mode of identification we call narcissistic."[10]

Michelet never really resolved his ambivalence toward the whole (community, mother-infant) and the couple (mother/son, brother/brother, husband/wife). To grow and develop, the individual must subject himself to a fall, which makes him susceptible to pain, constant insecurity, and a consciousness of lonely death. Again, the fall is a hardening of undifferentiated matter into barriers or into definitions of selves; a cyclical return to the amorphous mother would naturally alleviate any sense of personal struggle and annihilation. Michelet perhaps spoke more profoundly than he knew when he made his easy remarks in 1830 about nature as *non-moi* against the *moi*. He prefaced this statement with a nervous retraction of his previous declaration of war, realizing, nonetheless, that the combat was not yet over: "I am not willing to declare myself the enemy of *this nature* man was made for. It is more like a harmonious antagonism, if I can say it that way, that brings about *human nature's* glory and necessity" (quoted in *La Voie royale*, p. 444). In his public stances and *Journal*, Michelet wanted the harmonious aspects of the inevitable duel to override threats of aggression. In the nature books, it is as if Michelet's imagination were seeking vindication for the suppression of omnipresent violence.

The alternative to wholeness is, therefore, not loving twins but two opponents who, knowing they cannot be equal, struggle not to be defeated. Images of the whole disintegrate into images of split, torn, mutilated bodies. Lacan calls the representation of this aggressive correlative to narcissism "*imagos du corps morcelé*": "These are images of castration, emasculation, mutilation, dismemberment, dislocation, of disemboweling and devouring a body, of ripping it open, in short, the *images* that I

[10] Lacan, p. 110. See "L'Agressivité en psychanalyse" in *Ecrits*, pp. 101–24.

personally have grouped under the heading, which is, in my opinion, structural: images of the body-in-pieces" (*Ecrits*, p. 104). The *Histoire de France* provided some notably gory examples of mutilation—Coligny, Ravaillac, Damiens, a poor woman caught in the frenetic crowd of a financial depression—but in the panorama of nature's incessant battles for survival, the maimed bodies are everywhere. Insects, equipped with every imaginable instrument of torture, go to work on the human body, dead or alive, and tear it to bits. The alligator can not avoid having its tail severed by the snapping jaws of the piranha, "razor fish," and would never survive had it not evolved a thick body armor. In addition, it is not uncommon to come upon these disembodied parts, still twitching on the ground: "The bee stabbed to death, the wasp saws it up with three slices of the teeth, leaving its head and corselet there to keep fighting alone for a while" (*L'Insecte*, p. 301).[11] Ravaillac's quartered limbs danced with the sinister life of the not-quite-dead insect; though the crowd carried what was left of his body, it seemed to move on its own: "From then on, the trunk that was pulled around, paraded everywhere, began to beat about from pole to pole. Except it was still living!" (*Histoire de France*, XI, 141).

Certain species, deformed out of proportion, have become nothing but living weapons of destruction. The cachalot or sperm whale, which is almost all head, has forty-eight teeth. The piecemeal world of Michelet's nature recalls the hallucinatory images of Hieronymous Bosch, whose creations exemplify for Lacan "the atlas of all the aggressive images that torment men" (p. 105): "Stingers, terebrae, suckers, razor-thin teeth, pointed claws, an arsenal of unknown arms with

[11] Cf. Victor Hugo's *image du corps morcelé* as revealed in the violence of insects: "The ferocious scarab opens up the maybug, forces his head inside and then his copper corselet, digs around and empties its stomach, disappears up to his middle in the other's miserable body, and devours it on the spot, live" (*Promontorium Somnii*, Paris, 1961, II, pp. 458–561).

no names as yet, were born and grew and sharpened so they could go to work on living tissue" (*L'Insecte*, p. 132).[12] These are like the bodiless, nameless monsters Michelet conjured up during the hurricane.

It is not hard to see in the *Journal* the psychic violence Michelet directs against himself. His earliest diary was intended to provide a forum for self-judgment and castigation. "Let's get on with our censuring." His theoretical uneasiness about the individual—as if the individual were in some way sinful and had to be purged by history—may reflect his own feelings toward himself: "I needed distance from myself; I am much the better for it. What would it be like if you only had before your eyes thoughts transporting you as far away as possible from this vile self you always fall back into?" (*Ecrits de jeunesse*, p. 117). Not wholly explicable as a Christian sentiment of sin, this feeling of worthlessness probably dates back to Michelet's childhood. The year of his birth seemed to him to mark the decline of his family and the symbolic death of both his mother and his father. That was the year when poverty started to besiege them, causing both the bad humor and, later, the prolonged sickness of his mother: "Ninety-eight, the year of my birth, saw the beginning of the decline and death of the press, the ruin of printing, destroyed under Napoleon. I can say that before 1800, my father began to die inside, to live through me, with faith in my future."[13] Michelet believed somehow that he spread death and ruin in his wake,

[12] Although Maeterlinck's most violent and melodramatic passage depicting insect life—the slaughter of the drones by the worker bees—is vivid, he tends to humanize where Michelet dehumanizes: "The wings of the unfortunate creature are lacerated, their tarsi torn out, their antennae chewed; and their magnificent black eyes, mirrors of exuberant flowers, echo of the blue and innocent pride of summer, now softened by suffering, only reflect the distress and anguish of the end" (*Insectes et fleurs*, pp. 161–62).

[13] "A mon père," quoted in Gabriel Monod, *Jules Michelet: Études sur sa vie et ses oeuvres* (Paris: Hachette, 1905), p. 234, and also in *Journal*, I, 657.

that his inner evil was contagious, and, finally, that he was a kind of sorcerer who had actually corrupted his first wife. His narcissism includes the usual dialectic, self-love and self-hate: "I loved in her the evil [*le mal*] I put there" (quoted in Monod, p. 77). Nor did his insecurity abate with his romantic second marriage. Perhaps Narcissus never loved more than half himself; Michelet's rendition of the myth, addressed to Athénaïs, might be closer to the psychic truth: "Lovable and deep source I am so changed by, where I take such pleasure in mirroring my heart, God help me from mixing you, without knowing, in the troubled and bitter waves of the ocean I have in me" (*Journal*, II, 17). Sometimes Narcissus sees a pure garden fountain and, other times, an opaque sea.

Related to what Lacan calls the process of identification on the "imaginary level" is R. D. Laing's "ontological insecurity." Laing suggests that the alternative avenues of behavior open to such a person are radical: isolation and/or engulfment.[14] A person will try to survive alone; when he cannot, he either capitulates his entire self to the other, or he reverses the process out of self-defense and forces himself to be the tyrannical partner. At the age of twenty-two, Michelet had already formulated a plan of emotional invulnerability: "We should close up tight; it is perhaps, for someone who is too accessible, the secret to happiness. We should build walls around inside, where we will let in those we love but according to each one's feelings and understanding; as for other men, plenty of good will, little confidence" (*Ecrits de jeunesse*, p. 77). Michelet complained bitterly and eloquently about the "harsh and unjust barrier" that grew up between himself and Athénaïs—"between those who should be but one together!"—although he realized he contributed to it: "I see myself too clearly, I judge myself" (*Journal*, II, 620–21). True to his youthful design, once Michelet let Athénaïs into the stronghold, he became her jealous jailer. It is hard to imagine that

[14] See R. D. Laing, *The Divided Self* (Baltimore, 1960), pp. 39–61.

Athénaïs, more moral than Michelet, could have given him any cause for worry; nevertheless, she wrote in her diary on 7 April 1849: "I come home after making my marriage social calls. I feel sick at heart. Perhaps my husband does too, yet he is wrong to. Never did I love him more. This jealousy that he shows after a few days of marriage and that I did not mean to cause makes me worry for the future" (quoted in Monod, p. 243). One can understand why Michelet, Molière's Arnolphe incarnated, sang the praises of the cozy Engadine house where the woman could not see outside: "For the most part, these houses are true fortresses" (*La Montagne*, p. 201).

Michelet was not content with possession. Arnolphe wanted to be Pygmalion. Athénaïs was less Michelet's double, his twin, than his own creation. He explains in a letter to his aunt, written 26 March 1849, that his fiancée derived her ideas and character from his own writings: "I had, as I already told you, this rare advantage of finding someone formed solely by my ideas, books, and teaching, and who, having in me all her intellectual life, is the most useful assistant I could ever have" (quoted in Monod, p. 239). In the nature books, his Galatea fantasy can bloom uninhibited. After metaphorical journeys to the tropics and poles, he turns his attention to the temperate zones. He personifies the geography of his home as his wife, and his masculine ego soars: "This one was made for me, she is my legitimate wife, I know her as such. And all this time she has resembled me; like me, she is serious, hard-working; she has an instinct for work and patience. . . . With what delight I find here today my image, the trace of my will, the creation of my effort and intelligence! Thoroughly molded by me, she reveals my work to me, reproduces me to myself" (*L'Oiseau*, p. 222). Michelet's literary figures, as well as his human relationships, never remain in a state of precarious paradise but always flip over, always show the dark of their dialectic. He himself knows how easy it is to slip into the opposite temptation; Athénaïs has within herself the power to engulf him:

"I sense that I am becoming more and more avid for her and all she is. I tried for several days to write, to pull out of this absorption. For her and in her interest, I must not lose myself in her and must keep somewhere outside of her where I am strong and she can find strength and support" (*Journal*, II, 126–27). This insidious reversal of control where the woman, in her position of supposed dependence, subtly dominates her mate, sets in motion the mutual needs of a sadomasochistic relationship. For the French, the praying mantis is nature's archetypal warning of what a woman can do. Perhaps for an English public, the analogous metaphor would be the black widow spider.

7 A Strange Sexuality

The young Michelet was ambivalent about sex and women. Whereas Gabriel Monod recognized a contradiction in Michelet's temperament and morals—"the conflict between his passionate and sensual nature and the moral ideals that defined his life" (*Jules Michelet*, p. 250)—the conflict seems internal. Intermittently attracted to women, Michelet gives, nevertheless, the impression of being fundamentally shy or afraid of them sometimes, even repulsed by them and suspecting that they are repulsed by him: "Monday, I went to Poret's house, and not too far from his door I saw his sister, who crossed to the other side of the street, undoubtedly because she caught sight of me. Was it timidity or aversion?" (*Ecrits de jeunesse*, p. 111). Naturally, he seemed more at ease with his friend Poinsot, to whom he writes: "Disengaged from the love of women and afraid of it as well, too weak to rise to the love of God, this friendship is at the moment . . . my only concern" (p. 254). The best way to deal with women socially, Michelet reasoned, was to keep them at a distance; otherwise, "the society of women is unbearable" (p. 77). Was Michelet's interest in Marcus Aurelius at this time purely philosophic? He began a "soliloquy," inspired by the Roman Stoic, with another admission of inadequacy, saying he was "used to being avoided by women who considered him some kind of savage"; the tone of the discussion turns Baudelairean: "What then are these objects that charm us? What are they physically? It is the same matter as this horrible insect you are afraid to touch. . . . This perfect being, divine, you say, is subject to the nastiest needs, the most disgusting affections. . . . Pleasure will fool you; you will never be able to achieve this union that is the chimera of lovers. In despair you will tear with your teeth at the adored body in which you cannot lose yourself" (p. 102). Mixed with sadness and despair, this analysis uncovers an uncomfortable reality that Michelet dealt with only vaguely.

His fascination with the body was fed as much by disgust and fear as by sensuality. The worker bees seem to spare him from the ambivalent encounter: "She is born very pure, to the point of not even having an organ of inferior needs [*l'organe des nécessités inférieures*]" (*L'Insecte*, p. 343). Athénaïs, too, offered an apparently welcome reprieve from his heavily sexualized universe: "You can hardly say she was the work of nature. She ate less than a sparrow. She slept little, toward morning. She did not perspire, always had cool skin. Her clothes, even the cashmere sweater she sometimes put over her skin, never got dirty. She took it off, I think, cleaner than when she put it on. She did not have a handkerchief and had no need of one; if she happened to catch a little cold, it was mine she was giving back to me. She was not, moreover, in the least repugnant to me" (*Journal*, II, 587). If Athénaïs made love with indifference or difficulty, Michelet believed in willfully abstaining from sex: "You can arrive at a fullness of heart only with a little solitude and, especially, infrequent physical pleasure" (*Ecrits de jeunesse*, p. 89). What was the use if the result was only disappointment, "in this world that knows no fixed union" (*La Mer*, p. 103)? Whales—the symbol of the most valiant attempt at harmonious love in all Michelet's natural world—try to overcome the prison of their skin, but their supreme effort, while they roll and heave like oceanic cathedrals, appears cosmically clumsy and would look like an epic sea battle, if one did not know better: "Their slippery sheaths separate them, keep them apart. They fall back, in spite of themselves, missing each other because of this frustrating [*désespérant*] obstacle. In the midst of total agreement, you would say it was mortal combat" (*La Mer*, p. 242).

Michelet's propaganda for marital bliss is deceptive. He celebrates very few happy unions in the nature books. His world is dominated, rather, by horrifying virgins, monster amazon-mothers, emasculated males, and grotesque pairs. Occasionally there is a sadistic scene of symbolic male retribution. A city of large carpenter ants is ripped apart by a pack of smaller, but ferocious, mason ants. Pale, defenseless, nude embryos, sleeping in gauzelike wombs, are jerked mercilessly from their prenatal paradise, raped, and buried alive. Here, the "*corps morcelé*" is definitely female, and the tableau has the combined effect of Bosch and Delacroix. "A cruel and tragic change for these daughters of love, excessively pampered until now and treated with much more care than princesses, brutually torn at by claws, teeth, and pincers, stripped naked by the executioner. Immediately thrown into the burning sun, dragged, shoved, rolled over all the sharp points of coarse sand, sensitive in their new nakedness, infinitely sensitive to the shocks, jolts and quick jerks their violent enemies rarely refrained from inflicting on them"[1]

If a dominant male meets an equally strong female, the result is still not a successful marriage: the dialectic of mutual aggression transforms love into a butchery. The embrace of two sharks is like medieval torture: "The female fearlessly lets herself be grabbed, mastered by the terrible hooks he throws out. . . . Entwined, the furious monsters roll like this for

[1] "Cruel et tragique changement pour ces filles de l'amour, traitées jusque-là avec une gâterie excessive, et ménagées beaucoup plus que des princesses, d'être brusquement mises nues, dépouillées à coups de pinces, de dents, de tenailles, déshabillées par le bourreau. Jetées tout à coup au soleil brûlant, trainées, poussées, roulées par toutes les aspérités d'un sable grossier, sensibles, infiniment sensibles, dans leur nudité nouvelle, aux chocs, aux heurts, aux sauts brusques que leurs violents ennemis ne leur épargnaient guère" (*L'Insecte*, p. 286).

whole weeks, unable, though starving, to bring themselves to separate or pull apart and, even at the storm's height, invincible in their unchanging, ferocious embrace" (*La Mer*, p. 321). The sexual violence of Maldoror and his shark in Lautréamont's love poem is perhaps cruder, but no less fantastic.[2] Still, the most ghastly of Michelet's couples—a suspension of two voids—pits two historical figures, Fénelon and Madame de Monbéron, against each other, but they seem dwarfed by, almost incidental to, the extreme paradigm they represent: "Arid and desperate spectacle of two souls worn out to the point of exhaustion by the friction of their emptiness, beyond the death of their hearts, still trying, never satisfied, who cannot stop, nor live nor die entirely" (*Histoire de France*, XIV, 270).

Brutal males are generally in the minority. The masculine element hovers often around "greenish" virgins, who look down on them from a majestic but severe throne of purity. The bright blue gentian flower, pumping her green sap, lies beyond the reach of her pale golden lovers groveling at the base of her stem. She is as distant to them as the immaculate virgin peak Bernina is to a mountain climber. But most formidable of all is the virgin of the Alps: "At the chateau of frozen summits sits enthroned a merciless virgin who, with her forehead wreathed in diamonds, teases all heroes, and laughs at them with a laugh crueler than the sharp face of winter. They climb, foolhardy, and arrive at the fatal bed, where they lie enchained, married forever to a crystal bride" (*La Montagne*, pp. 19–20).

[2] "Two sinewy thighs clasp tightly about the viscous skin of the monster like two leeches; and arms and fins interlace about the body of the adored object which they surround with love, while their throats and breasts soon fuse into one glaucous mass exhaling the odors of seawrack. In the midst of the tempest that continues to rage, . . . rolling upon one another towards the depths of the ocean's abyss, they join together in a long, chaste and hideous coupling!" (Lautréamont, *Les Chants de Maldoror*, tr. Guy Wernham, New York, 1965, pp. 112–13).

The females in the natural world begin to grow as the males shrink. Swammerdam's brilliant discovery showed that the king bee or ant was in reality a queen; nature was run by mothers: "Crucial discovery revealing the true mystery of the superior insect, initiating us into the real nature of these societies, not all monarchies, but maternal republics and huge public cradles where each one breeds a people" (*L'Insecte*, p. 99). Subordinate to these mighty females stand useless, inactive males who are only tolerated in the republic for reasons of reproduction. From this vacuum of laziness the "women" usurp more and more masculine roles, easily compatible with their maternal capacities, and from them, build a powerful species. They organize a military force of Amazon warriors: "For us, feminine means feeble; for them, it is the synonym of force and energy. . . . For this reason in particular the insect is a creature of war, furnished with frightening weapons" (p. 180). A race of terrifying Joan of Arcs, the virgin wasps, despite (or rather because of) their maternity, takes the responsibility of massacring their entire city as an act of euthanasia and suicide before the arrival of winter. Eventually, these "women who wear the sword" will exert a castrating influence. Growing more self-sufficient, the females develop, as would be expected, less need for their weaker counterparts. Even in the area of reproduction the males are dispensable. The love of the bee, like that of the spider, wreaks disaster upon the poor male, exhausted after one afternoon and discarded as "multilated," but she is fertilized for life. In the *Histoire de France*, drones were allowed to be kings: "[Henri IV] was worn out at twenty-five years of age. After two minutes of lovemaking, he was in bed for three days" (IX, 216).

The next step is inevitable. If the bee is impregnated only once, she will soon find a way of dispensing with that one inconvenience. The savage virgin workers, as in a religious order, totally replace their need for males: "They will have no husband other than the city" (*L'Insecte*, p. 296). Finally, certain species actually achieve self-fertilization. Earlier scientists would not entertain the outrageous possibility—Réaumur, Michelet reports, "denied it, saying 'Nothing comes from nothing' "—but parthenogenesis was at last firmly entrenched as fact, at least for silkworms, certain butterflies, and bees. The queen bee and queen termite (whose bodies are prodigiously larger than those of the drones) or even the Virgin-Alps are nothing compared with the monster mother who conceives death over and over, *Mère Typhon:* "Seeing her gorge herself like that and swell, absorbing waves and ships, the Chinese thought of her as a horrible woman, mother Typhoon, who, while soaring in the sky and selecting her victims, conceives, begins to fill, becomes pregnant with the children of death: *waterspouts of iron* [*tourbillons de fer*]" (*La Mer*, pp. 299–300). Michelet's most fearful fantasy of engulfment found its appropriate expression. These funnels of tremendous centripetal force appear in the *Histoire de France* in the guise of a powerful enemy, a conquering empire, or elusively as an insidious form of friendship. Madame de Maintenon's young woman friend, *la Maisonfort*, backs instinctively away from "this very demanding friendship always swallowing her up" (XIV, 37). Catherine the Great of Russia incarnates the *Mère Typhon* of history, its myth of malevolence: "Then purged, fertile with dying and dead children, she herself ages, grows fat, gay and merry, during our frightful miseries" (IX, 38). Finally, as the insect's instruments became autonomous, the sucking void from a Jules Verne world of marine nightmare represents all destroyers of the French people: "But what is the vulture, a beast with only a beak and claws, compared with the power of these horrible sea spiders, these formidable suckers breathing in to make a void, attaching itself everywhere, extracting the very marrow out of bones, and smart enough to salvage prey from a crumbling skeleton?" (XV, 178).

A slight tip in the balance of a relationship has the potential of horrible consequences; the transitions, imperceptible as usual, progress with the speed of fatality. Yet these very monsters of absorption could be transformed into symbols of the deepest voluptuous pleasure.[3] Only such magnitude achieves the illusion of the womb. A prodigious parade of generous nurses exploits Michelet's dream in its every detail. The female whale's anatomy allows her young to feed from the breast while remaining close to the womb; the infant feels doubly protected and cared for. Superior to the passive human mother, the active whale carries an endless supply of sweeter, richer milk, for which the young whale does not have to work because its mother discharges generous spurts of it like an engine: "By a powerful piston, she sends out a ton of milk" (*La Mer*, p. 274). Yet the whale is no comparison with her cosmic and miraculous model, the sea. Michelet expands the conventional word play *mer / mère*[4] to its logical extremes: in the sea, the distinction between breast and womb dissolves, and every plant and animal is a fetus afloat in the world of milk, a *mer de lait*, which sounds more conducive to reverie than what it is: a term for a winter sea covered with millions

[3] One of R. D. Laing's case studies (James) resembles Michelet in his ambivalence toward absorption, especially as manifest through his relationship to nature. "He knew of no half-way stage between radical isolation in self-absorption or complete absorption into all there was. He was afraid of being absorbed into Nature, engulfed by her, with irrevocable loss of his self; yet what he most dreaded, that also he most longed for" (*The Divided Self*, p. 91).

[4] Kenneth Burke extended the pun on *mer* to include an assortment of meanings: *merde, mère, Mère* (mother of Jesus), *Mère* (mother earth), *mère* (pure). See William H. Rueckert's development of the various meanings in his *Kenneth Burke and the Drama of Human Relations* (Minneapolis, 1963), p. 91. Bachelard would, of course, hear the same reverberations, though, as usual, he tends toward the optimistic interpretation, omitting, for the moment, possibilities of ambivalence: "Michelet's poetry of the sea is a reverie surviving from the deepest zones. The sea is maternal, water is a prodigious milk; the earth prepares in its wombs a warm, nourishing food; on shore, breasts are swelling, giving to all creatures *atoms of rich grease.* Optimism is abundance" (*L'Eau et les rêves*, p. 161).

of microscopic organisms. Michelet imposes his own image: thousands of little beings, rocking in liquid arms, suck peacefully on the infinite nipples, the "volcanoes of milk."

The French word for breast, *sein,* facilitates Michelet's imaginative blending, since the word for female organs can also refer to womb, and to the English "lap." The sea, where the arts of maternity were first practiced, washes the shore into her own shape: "She gives it maternal contours, and I was going to say, the visible gentleness of a woman's womb [*sein:* breast?], that which the infant finds so sweet, shelter, moist warmth, and peace" (*La Mer,* p. 124). *Seins* begin to haunt Michelet's landscape; everywhere he looks, the mystic female presence literally rises before him. Mother Nature is more than an abstract figure for him who is involved with her as if she was his own mother. Michelet makes no distinction between his reaction to the majesty of Asia and his respect for the once flesh-and-blood figure of his childhood: "The feeling I would have seeing my mother herself I have contemplating the one whose large, rich breast, both to East and West, has poured out to the nations" (*La Montagne,* p. 91). A poetry of the mother surfaces on every level of the natural histories; from microcosmos to macrocosmos she is at work, creating the privileged atmosphere for her children. Inside the hummingbird's eggshell, Michelet imagines the suave existence of a sheltered sea: "Understand that this dot [a hummingbird egg], though it seems imperceptible, is an entire ocean, is the sea of milk in which the germ of the sky's favorite child floats. It floats there without fear of shipwreck; the most delicate ligaments hold it suspended in place; it is spared jolts and knocks. It swims ever so slightly in this warm water as it will in the air. Absolute security, the perfect state in the heart [*sein*] of a nourishing home! and how much better than feeding on the breast!" (*L'Oiseau,* p. 68). Michelet's books bathe in the radiance of immeasurable maternal love. There is no end to his dream, nor perhaps to his imaginative needs: "Loved? All mothers love, from the Ocean to the stars. But I mean cared for, surrounded by infinite love, enveloped in the warmth of maternal magnetism" (*L'Oiseau*, p. 64). Like Baudelaire's, Michelet's muse inebriates and engulfs him in sweet perfumes where he languishes,[5] a "*faible enfant.*"

The erotic force of Michelet's hymn to maternity invades the images of the women in his own life. Confused in the contagious myth, they are resurrected with all the ambivalent power of their sister races. When Michelet speaks of his life with Athénaïs, one would think he was the nymph in its cocoon, the embryo in its eggshell, the primitive protozoan in the sea: "I felt how many delicate and charming threads close in around the heart in this life so thoroughly and minutely entwined. . . . I found in her [Athénaïs], in her varied gifts, the complete keyboard of human life. Not a note missing, except physical love perhaps. For the rest, so positive and right in every way. And yet, basically a poetic nature with bursts of energy and aspiration sometimes. All this, deeply felt, savored during the storm, snug here as in a sea."[6] Much has been

[5] Compare Baudelaire's "Parfum exotique," in *Les Fleurs du mal:*

(When, with my eyes closed, on a mild fall evening,
I breathe the odor of your warm breast,
I see happy shores unfold
brightened by the fires of a constant sun;

A lazy island where nature gives
rare trees and savory fruits.)

(Quand, les deux yeux fermés, en un soir chaud d'automne,
Je respire l'odeur de ton sein chaleureux,
Je vois se dérouler des rivages heureux
Qu'éblouissent les feux d'un soleil monotone;

Une île paresseuse où la nature donne
Des arbres singuliers et des fruits savoureux.)

[6] "J'ai senti combien de fils délicats, charmants enserrent le coeur dans cette vie si profondément, si minutieusement entrelacée. . . . J'ai trouvé en elle [Athénaïs], en ses dons si variés, le clavier complet de la vie humaine. Pas une note qui y manque, sauf l'amour physique peut-être. Du reste, si positive et tellement propre à tout! Et pourtant

written about Michelet's strange relationship with Athénaïs. Certainly, she did not represent the abundant, maternal, and sensual woman of his literary fantasies. But she held for him some undeniable attraction.

The most obvious answer is repressed incest. Michelet is the first to admit that marriage, "the most permissible of incests," is often built upon the mother/son and father/daughter paradigms. He acknowledges that his first wife, older than he was and with whom he shared little of his intellectual life, served as a mother substitute. Athénaïs, he also admits, would not have married him had society ruled otherwise on the incest taboo: "She would have married her father and most willingly. And that is what happened. I am as much her father as he" (*Journal*, II, pp. 323–24). Gabriel Monod and Paul Viallaneix have hinted that Michelet played the father role as a means of coaxing Athénaïs into at least some minimal physical contact. It is true that Michelet encouraged the direct association of himself with her real father; if the husband called up the beloved memory, it allowed feelings to replace more readily the wife's habitual reserve: "I caressed and consoled her with all my tenderness; she was looking at her father's portrait and wept while embracing me" (*Journal*, II, 92). Michelet becomes many things to Athénaïs—father and child—while restricted to a sparse sex life, but he seems to derive pleasure from the relationship. Viallaneix suggests that as a true libertine Michelet

---

pleine de sens poétique, d'élans parfois et d'aspirations. Tout cela senti, goûté bien profondément en pleine tempête, enfermés ici comme en mer!" (*Journal* II, 214). The same image is adapted to a more hostile tone in Victor Hugo's "Tristesse d'Olympio" (*Les Rayons et les ombres*):

> Nature, I know your calm brow and how you forget,
> And how your metamorphoses tear at the threads,
> The mysterious threads, binding our hearts together.
>
> Nature au front serein, comme vous oubliez!
> Et comme vous brisez dans vos métamorphoses
> Les fils mystérieux où nos coeurs sont liés!

learns the joy of prolonging a rare culmination of his desires; in *Michelet par lui-même*, Barthes weaves a piquant portrait of the historian as *femme de chambre*. The beginning and end of Athénaïs' menstrual periods are faithfully marked in her husband's diary as he dotes over her delicate body. But his obsession is more than a passport to her room or closet; it comes as close to an imaginative return to the womb as possible: "I had the good fortune of following, day by day, her intestinal life—and, even better than at Fontainebleau, was able to observe at all hours, finally getting to know her *as if I had lived in her entrails*" (*Journal*, II, 393, my italics).

In the same way that women have converted an initial position of inferiority into subtle control, the "humiliated" male operates a clever reversal.[7] As an eternal man-child, he is once more on the verge of being swallowed up in the Common Mother when it becomes apparent that the mother-wife, while growing more important, is also depleting her strength. The child has sucked from her the precious liquid that she is not always able to replenish. Though earth and sea may seem completely regenerative, the twentieth century knows as well as did the nineteenth that this is not so. When Michelet moved to the warm Italian climate, he saw himself as a weak child asking for his nurse's last metaphoric milk, because the rocky Mediterranean soil was indeed barren: "Nurse? Yes, she still was, as much as she could be, given the poverty of her resources, the natural poverty my health reduced me to. Incapable of eating, I still received from her the only nourishment I could take, life-giving air and light" (*L'Oiseau*, p. 47). When both parties admit to being dependent, a moment of reprieve is gained in the mutual struggle for possession. No matter how overbearing the mythical woman becomes, for Michelet she is still essentially sickly (*malade*)—she is still in-

[7] This chapter discusses a few of the paradigms thoroughly presented in Jeanne Calo's *La Création de la femme chez Michelet* (Paris: Nizet, 1975). For a general analysis, see Jean Borie's *Le Tyran timide: Le Naturalisme de la femme au XIXe siècle* (Paris, 1973).

capacitated once every month. When Michelet himself was suffering once from a stomachache, he waxed sentimental over the scene in which one *malade* was soothing another: "She was already in bed, a word from her, a little friendly sign (a little tap) made me forget everything. The happiness of almost being called over restored me and one sick person tenderly kissed the other at the edge of her bed" (*Journal*, II, 339). During the darkest days in the *Histoire de France*, the archetypal relationship of *malade* to *malade*, even of dying to dying or living dead with living dead, recurs with a frequency that confirms the centrality of this paradigm. A sinister parallel of the Michelets' bed scene is the intimate confrontation between Richelieu and Louis XIII: "Sick, he [Richelieu] was put on a bed facing the patient, and, whatever care the cardinal took in reassuring him, in diverting him, neither one was ever deceived again. They were two enemies" (XII, 178).

If one person begins to recover, it is usually the male of the couple. Michelet's exaltation of the prodigiously fertile woman is joined to the demand that she be willing to sacrifice all, even her life, to keep her sustenance flowing. The woman, in this revolution of dialectical roles, must not only agree to be possessed by her Arnolphe, to be made over by her Pygmalion, but also to become, if need be, a sacrificial victim: Iphigenia-as-mother. The ultimate in motherhood, returning again to a sadomasochistic relationship, is a young woman in *La Femme* who is literally being killed by the hungry child she continues to feed merely to stop his crying. Her words return as a kind of refrain: "Drink, my child! drink, it is my life! . . . Enjoy, drink.... It is my pain. . . . Drink, it is my pleasure!" (p. 85).

The final paradigm of the couple whose dynamics are always fluctuating corresponds to the extreme Baudelairean duality of victim/executioner; except Michelet, as usual, must add a saving grace to this stark conclusion: the weak child grows up to become a resuscitator of sacrificial victims. He redeems the mother who gave her life so that he might live.

Perhaps this dialectic informs Michelet's attraction to

Athénaïs. Michelet was aware of Athénaïs' health problems and the frigidity that might result, but he was willing to take the risk;[8] there was something about a suffering, sickly woman he liked. Viallaneix also recognizes Michelet's fascination with a wan woman and draws an analogy to the historian's goal of resurrecting the dead. Athénaïs becomes the loving symbol of the nation, and her revitalization gives Michelet the impression of having reanimated all France. In an imaginary dialogue with the historian, whom he conjures up from the dead, Viallaneix recreates Michelet's first reaction to Athénaïs, who appears at his door, pale and dressed in black: "You are not disappointed, on the contrary, that Athénaïs seems drained, that her complexion lacks color. You love death. You love to revive the dead. Your history is a 'resurrection.' That is why, at the thought of giving warmth to the cold-blooded girl whom you help into her coat, a familiar joy shoots through you. Clio in person is standing before you. . . . You say to yourself, with a conviction only you could know: 'Oh! the lovely dead girl' [*oh! la jolie morte*]" (Introduction, *Journal*, II, xx). *La jolie morte*, the epithet originating in Athénaïs' serious illness in Vienna, returns as an endearing phrase in Michelet's prose. He imagines how she must have looked at the height of her illness: "Those who saw her pass in the carriage in which she rode with the good doctor found her pale, so pale they asked what this apparition was. 'The lovely dead girl!' they said. 'She has something so touching and pure about her! Did we not hear she

[8] Michelet wrote to the doctor in Vienna who had treated Athénaïs for a blocked urinary tract, which probably permanently damaged her kidneys, perhaps causing intercourse to be painful for her, although Dr. Bischoff later replied that, if willing, Athénaïs should enjoy normal sex. Michelet's letter to Athénaïs written 23 December 1848 shows his state of anxiety: "The answer, so late! from Vienna, I await it eagerly, anxiously" (*Journal*, II, 620). Michelet describes her malady in the following manner: "The absolute fullness of the entrails, hard as a rock, pushed the neighboring organ back, closed it off, hermetically, and she was in horrible pain, rare for a woman, and could not urinate" (*Journal*, II, 580).

was in the tomb yesterday?' " (II, 580–81). Were she to undergo childbirth Michelet would fear for her life. Their first child did die within the first year, and there was no question of trying to conceive again. Michelet's friends thought this marriage to a twenty-year-old woman was sheer lunacy on his part: she would lead him to the grave. "They said this charming young woman of death, this pale *Fiancée of Corinth* would be my tomb" (II, 595).[9] But Michelet himself had the opposite image in mind: "*Risuscitare le cose morte*" (II, 88) was like a sacred oath accompanying his marriage.

Athénaïs, however, was not the first "*jolie morte*"; she was preceded by Michelet's mother, his primary model, the shadow behind all the other metaphorical mothers. Though horrified by the "living death" of her sleep, young Michelet cannot overlook the sensual element of his mother's slightly morbid expression: "—a long illness so altered her features you might say she really died a long time ago. . . . Her lower lip protruded a little, almost as when she slept and you could hear her breathe" (*Ecrits de jeunesse*, p. 216). Again the element of ambivalence is strong, because Marie-Antoinette, another of the malevolent figures of history, reflected, for Michelet, the image of his mother: "Her lower lip pouted and appeared sensual" (*Histoire de France*, XVII, 154). The "pharmaceutical perfumes" of the sickroom (Montaigne's) repelled him, but the most taboo of all images, making love to someone dying, returns in disguised terms. Half-dead nuns and sorceresses were subjected to the visits of their jailors, and the sick did not necessarily content themselves with a friendly tap: "For twenty years, mistress of a sick man, and miserably sick herself, [Diane de Poitiers] undoubtedly had certain consolations" (IX, 14).

[9] The fable is recounted in the first chapter of *La Sorcière* and follows Goethe's poem "Die Braut von Korinth": the young pagan lover is drained of his life by trying to revive the cold Christian virgin promised him before her family converted.

His mother's death triggered complicated reactions in Michelet, who was sixteen years old at the time. Although he tried not to blame her for the difficult family situation of the previous years, the bitter arguments and the poverty—"You cannot say mother's illness brought about our ruin" (*Ecrits de jeunesse*, p. 212)—her death freed something inside him, and life seemed to take a turn for the better: "The change of life and locale following shortly thereafter stopped the blow from going too deep. A freedom not experienced before, a calmer and less fretful existence were great consolation for a sixteen-year-old. Sometimes I was surprised and blushed at my hard heart, I reproached myself for this cruel happiness, as if I had got it in return for her life" (p. 216). The guilt Michelet felt at the time of his mother's death may have stemmed from the unconscious but early belief that he caused her weakness, that his life sapped hers. A nervous outburst interrupts his sober thoughts on Oriental mythology: "At this point, I started thinking about the mystery of pity and grief. How they [women] suffer because of us, for us. How my mother suffered for me, physically and spiritually! A deep sense of Indian devotion for this first, this supreme religion overtook me" (*Journal*, II, 302–3).

Michelet's mother occupied the center of his life for many years; for most of his childhood and youth, she was his unique companion. Looking back on his childhood, he pretended to be alone, but he was instead "with mother": "Too clumsy to play with the other children, who would have laughed at me, and forced to live a sedentary life with Mother, I read, I learned little, but I learned on my own" (*Ecrits de jeunesse*, p. 183). Michelet was not sent to a *pension* until the age of twelve. Whenever the question of enrolling him in school arose, he immediately broke into tears; his mother could not stand the sight; and his inevitable break with home (with *maman*) was continually postponed: "Mother took pity on me and I got out of it for the time being" (p. 185). This image of the child, who stays as long as possible with the mother and begins his first learning experiences with her, permeates Michelet's work and is glorified by him. Instead of indicating immaturity, prolonged contact with the mother establishes the very foundations of the family and society. In *La Mer*, Michelet heralds the dawn of civilization as the moment when the baby sea cow, because of morphological evolution, climbs to its mother's breast: "Family stability, heartfelt tenderness growing every day (we could also say, Society), these important things begin once the child sleeps at the breast" (p. 248). The father recognizes the social benefits to be gained from a long association of child with mother and converts any feelings of hostility into benevolent surveillance: "The child resting on the mother's heart, and slowly drinking her life, staying near for a long time and at an age when he can learn, all this depends upon the indulgence of the father watching over his innocent rival. And this is what makes progress possible" (*La Mer*, p. 255). But rarely is the paternal force so tolerant, and if not present, it is at least internalized as unconscious retribution whenever the temptation of incest, no matter how innocent, beckons. The all-embracing mother-sea is not even exempt from the stern law: transgressing men and animals that throw themselves into the sea, confident, like oysters, that their shells are protection enough, "only emerge mutilated" (p. 210). Regret over some act that appears to be insignificant haunts Michelet as a boy as much as it did his model Rousseau. He confides to his diary: "I upset my poor mother to the point of tears and she was already so weighted down by our other misfortunes; I was sorry soon after but too proud to go back on it. I'll end here and tell later the things I did to her that still leave me feeling a terrible remorse" (*Ecrits de jeunesse*, pp. 184–85). Some innate wickedness controlled his tongue, he argues, and would not loosen it for a moment's surrender to humility until it was too late: "Such, however, was the deplorable violence of my personality that harsh words sometimes slipped out, words I would now like to expiate with all my blood, one in particular that I said just after giving the school fifty francs we badly needed at home; I had barely said this cruel word when I felt torn apart by it, but I don't know what terrible shame kept me from asking forgiveness while there was still time" (p. 215). Thus, Athénaïs can be understood not only in the immediate terms of incest, but as an opportunity for relieving this long-standing guilt toward his mother. The scenario of remorse-reconciliation is played out by the couple with the regularity of ritual. After Michelet believes that he has wounded Athénaïs, a short period of alienation spurs his desire, and reconciliation is all the more delicious. The complete scenario of exacerbated and relieved guilt is spelled out in the *Histoire de France* when the historian elaborates the relationship of Louis XIII to his *favori*, Cinq-Mars: " 'Chastisement' [*le castoiement*] (as the Middle Ages called it), the pleasure, not of chastising by blows, but by scolding, correcting, humiliating, making the other cry, quarreling always in order to be making up all the time, that is the entire pastime of these kings" (XII, 162–63).

Michelet may have tried to right the wrongs of the years spent with his mother by reliving them through the two people he loved as much–Poinsot and Athénaïs. It is as if he wanted to share his mother's fate. He provoked as many chances to forgive and be forgiven as possible, but he wanted even more to "save" his metaphorical children, weak and sick ones at that, by giving all he had, his life if necessary. To escape into eternal childhood, to penetrate the mysteries of womanhood, these were nothing. But to be the sacrificial mother, this was Michelet's underlying desire.

Michelet claimed that Athénaïs had been deprived of the total loving care a mother should provide. She had been a lonely child, studious and contemplative, and had been sent away from home at an early age. So Michelet filled the void: "She married her real mother" (*Journal*, II, 104). A real mother is the only chambermaid and confessor to be trusted.

Again, she does more than observe, she molds subtly, but for life: "You needed a mother who without dominating you would envelop you, even without your knowing, who would be allowed to give the care, the attention a young girl scorns, though her life depends upon it—a mother who would overcome by an excess of tenderness any repugnance, who would cry when necessary and throw her arms around you to get you to decide what is right" (II, 631). It is this kind of mother who understands the true means to power. Michelet-mother insisted that Athénaïs needed special care to compensate for her past deprivation; she was—he kept her so—frail and dependent. His ultimate wish was expressed as a mutual transfusion: "So I imagine . . . that the immense vitality in me always overflowing in what I produce should be most beneficial for you in this intimate relationship; that you should gain in me life and health; that by holding you tight, my child, as the prophet who gave life back to the child, I could add (from my life, from my breath) hours, days, years to yours. Mine! Ah, if only I could bring about the exchange. And if I could die so you would live from me!" (II, 620). The image is still fundamentally sinister, instead of sensual.

As Michelet re-created his own childhood by playing the mother, he caused sexual distinctions to blur. He had the metaphorical possibility of being both sexes, and his "child," as a younger version of himself, also combined male and female traits. Athénaïs—so unmatronly—redeemed herself by her spiritual bisexuality, the essential trait of heroines in the lineage of Joan of Arc and the insect workers: "Rare and singular enjoyment of this unique love, of this feminine and virile company, with the spirit of both sexes, even more fertile in that it is pure and conceives, begets always in the sphere of ideas. . . . In a person of so complete a spirit, combining sexes and ages, child, young man, and woman, all closeness is felt deeply, as if infinite."[10] What might have characterized the

[10] "Rare et singulière jouissance de cet amour unique, de cette société féminine et virile, avec un esprit des deux sexes, d'autant plus

odious virgin or hermaphrodite are turned back to a desirable advantage.

The tenor of Michelet's relationship to Poinsot is openly ambiguous: "My friendship with the friend from Bicêtre has the gentleness of a friendship with a woman (to be examined)" (*Ecrits de jeunesse*, pp. 89–90). Truly, theirs was an important friendship, comparable to that of Montaigne and La Boétie. Michelet, who repeated to Poinsot, "We alone are alike," seemed more emotionally involved with him than with his mistress, later to become his first wife, Pauline. Of her, he said "Someone not enough like me" (p. 259). More than a friend with whom he shared mutual interests, Poinsot was Michelet's only real candidate for a "double": "This relationship has a certain 'je-ne-sais-quoi' (would I say romantic?) ordinarily only found in love. I keep trying to explain this touching and singular harmony of soul. It is the mistake of the *demiourgos*, who twice executed the eternal copy of the same soul (to speak as would Plato)" (p. 98). Yet this one chance for an androgynous union–Plato's androgynes could be composed of two males, two females, or one of each–this chance for a balanced relationship he saw as a freak of nature, not as the original and ultimate state of society. After Poinsot's death when Michelet was twenty-three, that rare potential disappeared. A case could be made for latent homosexuality in the Poinsot-Michelet relationship, in which the latter played again the role of mother, choosing a younger replica of himself as a lover. After Poinsot's death, Michelet notes his reaction: "Dear child, dear child! This name was all I could call him" (p. 134).

The historian would have been too moral to follow up what was an "antisocial" instinct, yet the important thing is that he breaks down traditional sexual roles and thus is able to arrive at some more suitable and perhaps stronger identity. Called

---

fécond qu'il est pur, qu'il conçoit et enfante toujours dans la sphère des idées. . . . Dans une personne si complète d'esprit, mêlée de sexe et d'âge, enfant, jeune homme et femme, tout rapprochement est senti à fond, comme infini" (*Journal*, II, 297–98).

effeminate and immature after the publication of *L'Amour* and *La Femme*,[11] Michelet probably understood, as Bachelard later articulated, that "whoever speaks of androgyny, skirts with a double antenna the depths of his own unconscious."[12] Successful initiation requires that the initiate take on characteristics of the opposite sex. Michelet's descent into nature involved a discovery of what is generally referred to by him and by others as "female"—certain shapes and functions, visions of change and growth. Michelet had to undergo a metamorphosis into his opposite, into woman and mother, before becoming himself "organizable," a personality whose growth would be change, not repetition. But did Michelet overcome the dialectics of human relationships by merging all roles into one? It seems that any imaginative solution is fatally inflicted with an inevitable will to power, with some general terms of possession; when a wife is expecting a child, the husband must, according to Michelet, become the "largest" mother, the "third" womb: "She carries a child nine months, makes it with her flesh and she becomes his child, living innocently in his hand" (*Journal*, II, 330). In the guise of this symbolic supermother, Michelet takes on the stature of a primitive divinity. As Isis-Athor (also called Night), he/she incubates in his/her womb the parent(s) (Isis-Osiris) of a child who will also be incubating soon in its own smaller membranous pocket. But is this encirclement infinitely regressive? Each god can be surpassed by a god farther back (or forward), patriarchies giving way to matriarchies and perhaps to other unimaginable godheads beyond that. When the universe is an egg within an egg,[13] or rather a womb within a womb, a last circle always remains to be drawn.

[11] "His vigorous talent is becoming effeminate, dealing with these subjects; he is losing his masculinity and forgetting his age": the judgment of a contemporary journalist, Leon de Wailly, quoted in *Journal*, II, 817, note 2.

[12] *La Poétique de la rêverie* (Paris, 1960), p. 50.

[13] "The child insect, so to speak, at this stage when the caterpillar is only an egg that moves (Harvey), this child, this egg that moves, contains, in turn, children, eggs" (*L'Insecte*, p. 69).

8 Sorcerer and Serf: Myth and History

For Michelet history was not a compilation, but a cure. The resurrection of his subjects was not simply a matter of listening, but an attempt to articulate what remained hidden, in the heart, in the code of another language, unreadable, silent. Michelet interpreted his mission himself in terms of myth and prophecy: an Oedipus, he would explain mysteries; he would incarnate in himself the couple, patient and healer—the "unformulable," as Lévi-Strauss calls it, and man's symbol-making capacity—assuring thus "the coherence of the psychic universe, itself a projection of the social universe."[1] "The silences of history must speak . . . " (*Journal*, I, 378):[2] this sorcerer's formula has captured a particular tendency in Michelet that reveals him as a forerunner in certain methods of modern historiography. The medieval serf, the peasant under the ancien régime said nothing, left no records; the medieval witch, the Protestant martyr were misinterpreted in the lists and accounts of their enemies. Michelet proclaimed this the goal of his *Histoire de France:* the cure of all forgotten nations, the cure of his "dying wife." But the major subject of his history often appeared, frustrated, in a note or developed elsewhere, as in the experimental ethnography of *La Sorcière;* or it hardly appeared at all: "Only a few rare pages about a little

[1] Lévi-Strauss, *Anthropologie structurale* (Paris, 1958), p. 201.

[2] See Paul Viallaneix's "Les Silences de l'histoire," in *Michelet cent ans après* (Presses Universitaires de Grenoble, 1975), pp. 49–61.

peasant (Duval), and almost lost, tell the profound horror of herds of men pursued by hunger" (*Histoire de France*, XIV, 222). Whereas later, the talkative, overdocumented kings of France would not be quiet, silent subjects were more readily found in nature.

From a contemporary psychoanalytic view, Michelet's initiation looks like regression, the stage of male adolescent desire for the vagina,[3] but from the anthropological view, he is undergoing the strict training required to become a shaman. In addition to effecting psychic and social assimilation, shamanistic ritual collaborates with the cosmos: the temporary return to an embryonic state dramatizes rebirth and repeats the original "creation of the world."[4] If Michelet's desire for a truly prophetic speech was obstructed by a mass of material in the histories, he compensated in the nature books. He is like the ocean voicing all creation: "They defer to their sublime father, the Ocean, who speaks their discourse for them. They explain themselves through his powerful voice. Between the silent earth and the mute tribes of the sea he leads the dialogue, huge, strong and grave, generous,—the harmonious accord of the great Me with itself, this stirring debate which is in essence Love" (*La Mer*, pp. 28–29).

The nature books seem to fulfill two contradictory functions. They provided an obvious release, a freer genre of expression, but they also opened up to the same patterns that rendered history almost intolerable: they remade the same discoveries. Nature, in fact, becomes the combination utopia/

[3] Adolescent boys at the Orthogenic School in Chicago (a residential treatment institution for emotionally disturbed children) expressed the wish to possess female organs: breasts and vagina. Bruno Bettelheim believes that this wish is for bisexuality, not just femininity: "More persistent than the desire for female organs, however, was the obsessional wish to possess *both* male and female genitalia" (Bruno Bettelheim, *Symbolic Wounds*, New York, 1954, p. 30).

[4] See particularly Mircea Eliade, *Rites and Symbols of Initiation*, tr. Willard Trask (New York, 1958), p. 36.

torture that was history, with one major difference: the fullness of this complex vision is restored, its dynamics and gradations are clearer. History is nature, in which the smaller history of France operates.

The easy parallel between the two disciplines appears as a constant reminder to the reader. Nature is its own flowing underground stream in touch with the Revolution, both a part of it and autonomous: a feature not uncommon in Michelet's work, where microhistories (the woman, the witch, legal institutions, families) circulate in the larger *Histoire de France*, itself a microhistory. Paracelsus enacting a "marriage with Nature," Palissy puttering in the royal garden—the first natural history museum—within earshot of the Saint-Bartholomew massacre, both initiate a lineage continuing through Harvey, Galileo, Newton, Lavoisier to Larmarck and triumphing in Geoffroy Saint-Hilaire and Darwin. Michelet, coming full circle, rejoining Paracelsus by his own marriage to the earth in *La Montagne*, incarnates this micromovement just as he hopes to reanimate in himself the descent from Joan, through Luther, Coligny, Gustave-Adolphe, Diderot, and Danton. Nature has its own revolutions in concert with those of history. The schematic progression of Michelet's four nature books might even duplicate the lineaments of his history.

In 1856, when *L'Oiseau* was published along with volumes nine and ten (sixteenth century) of the *Histoire de France*, the bird was already making rarer appearances in history: a lark would act as an image of hope, often contrasting with the ominous state of the present closing in around it; this lark is reminiscent of *l'alouette*, Joan of Arc: "O! intrigue, force, and patience can not always do what they want. . . . At dawn perhaps a song will spring forth from a simple heart, and the lark will find it while flying off from its April furrow to the sun" (*Histoire de France*, X, 311). After Rabelais and Luther, Michelet had the impression of sinking into little history, "*la petite histoire*," the account of minute intrigue, a narrative of court gossip. "One must look for the mystery of action in the infinitely small, in the shadowy world of insects seething, stirring, working underneath" (X, 75). The seventeenth and eighteenth centuries encouraged the rule of the spider; in 1858, year of the publication of *L'Insecte*, Richelieu was weaving his diplomatic webs: "But events tore the tangled threads of this spider web" (XII, 68). Especially while the Jesuit spider spun, the waters of the sea, the Revolution, were rising; millions of mute Frenchmen (infusorian) came vaguely into the view of history. In 1861, *La Mer* appeared; in 1863, Michelet's volume on the eighteenth century began with a recognition of the popular swell: "Masses until now immobile, ignorant, who, like the bottom [*bas-fonds*] of the Ocean, had never been able to hear storms, classes neither the Fronde nor the Revocation had stirred, this time raised their heads, asked about the public affairs" (*Histoire de France*, XV, iii). *La Montagne* (1868), published after the completion of the *Histoire de France*, is literally a return to the Mountain of the Revolution, a re-strengthening, a necessary transition before going on to the *Histoire du XIXe siècle:* the "death of the Mountain" in history, the execution of Romme, Goujon, and the last jacobins, is both foreshadowed and positively overshadowed by the "death of the Mountain" in the nature book, for the erosion of the Engadine is balanced by the repair of the earth somewhere else.

After leaving the thread of the Revolution behind in 1853, the historian embarked on a long labor of tracing the transformation of feudalism into monarchy. When at last the *Histoire de France* linked up with the *Histoire de la Révolution,* it proceeded as far as the Terror; still to be written was the culmination of history's negativity, the story of Napoleon. The nature books were necessary as the larger setting for this long and painful history, which otherwise would have been as unbalancing as the heavy wig of Louis XIV itself. While nature and the Revolution made forays into the history of the monarchy, their real residence was in the nonhistorical texts. There, myth was allowed time and was not swallowed up by the exaggerated importance of miracle.

The mythical model in Michelet is fragmented throughout the *Histoire de France* but emerges as more autonomous in the *Journal* and in the nature books: one being, eternally giving birth, eternally young, one coherent person-people, exists in its own intimate cosmos. Related to the child-genius, the orphan that springs from no one (the Renaissance, eighteenth-century science and ideas, the Revolution), this more maternal being is, however, the force underlying the superficial occurrences that are actually different perspectival manifestations of the same thing. This personified force abides more likely in the hidden recesses of time, some distant past or future that is myth, ethnography, and unwritten history. The *Histoire de France* documented a time that was either too early or too late to embody fully the mythical concept. Before the fourteenth century, France was a conglomerate of wandering tribes, which evolved into mutually exclusive provinces, but with the rise of unification, so came the beginning of the Fall: feudalism, the church. Now and then, imagination revives this state that slipped away, as, for instance, when the earth's crust began to cool and animals took on too much house; a song survives, translating the feeling of what it was like, "These songs, already old [*déjà antiques*] under William the Conqueror in 1066, are not, as might be believed, the work of a lumbering feudal period, which only weakened them. Such things do not date from an age of servitude, but from a living age, still free, one of defense, one that resisted, built the refuge of resistance, and saved Europe from the Norman, Hungarian, and Saracen invasion" (*Histoire de France*, I, 15). The *first* Sorcerer, really a kind of Diana whose trace, like anything before trilobites, is lost, not even resurrected in *La Sorcière*, knew this ageless age, the *early* Protestants did too, but usually history was born *déjà antique.* The seventeenth century, for instance, was grotesque, old, disguised in the powder and frill of youth, *une époque coquettement vieille.* Of the volumes devoted to the *Histoire de la Révolution française*, very few events reveal the true nature of Revolution as Michelet defined it; very little remains to be remembered: "This utterly pacific, benevolent, loving character of the Revolution seems today a paradox:—so unknown is its origin, so misunderstood its nature, and so obscured its tradition, in so short a time!" (*History of the French Revolution*, ed. Gordon Wright, p. 5).

The *Histoire de France* was slowly invaded by everything that was not the true history of the French, yet Michelet, martyr and sorcerer, continued his mission. Anti-nature (anti-history), though reigning in its sterile matriarchy, crouched, always prematurely old, in the dark, damp cell of the *in pace;* this inverted giant was finally only visible from the perspective of the anus, through which it appeared as an overblown Nothing. Nature could reverse these historical proportions: an anti-nature is always present but never does the positive mythical element retreat into an apparently permanent silence. Whereas man's sights moved ever inward, magnifying a smaller and smaller history, nature was always expanding as well as shrinking; its infinite, spontaneous perspectives could spread out any of the choices one wanted to enjoy.

The same multiple ranges of time are apparent in the *Histoire de France* as in the nature books, but readers make the mistake of reducing them to a radical dialectical pair, a reduction which, in the end, denies Michelet's richest attribute as a historian, his acute sensitivity to time. Previous readings of his work have pointed out the obvious ambivalence between a maternal time of return and repetition and a paternal time of progress and praxis, of erection. Critics have chosen to emphasize one side or the other, or their opposition. Claude Mettra speaks of the "Stomach and its Realm": "A stomach being in perpetual birth is outside death, outside anguish. Here the word becomes silence."[5] Roland Barthes also elaborates Michelet's homogeneous time, more typical of Renaissance writers,[6] his *lisse*, seamless flow, faultless continuity. In the midst of this flow, this fabric, which is not progress, shoots up the broken piece of time, a messianic eruption. For Barthes, this "theophanic moment of history"[7]—prepared by Joan of Arc, the Sorceress, and realized in the Revolution—gives history its signification, represents its praxis. For Georges Poulet, the revolutionary moment is seen in erotic terms as the release of male energy out of a female dormancy; in these terms, the act is radically separated from its context: "Instantaneous time, time condensed into the very moment it seems to spring from and contrasted by this instantaneousness to preceding time. . . . It is this projection of the moment outside historical continuity that Michelet excels in depicting."[8] Juxtaposing these several models, one arrives at a history composed of dialectical timelessness. Eternity and immobility are interrupted by moments of divine apparition, of radical discontinuity. The distinction of these moments, supposedly the only "time" in which history means and moves, is too tenuous when the slightest notions of relativity come into play, when a broader consciousness of time sets to work.

Rather than an immanent/transcendent model putting emphasis on revelation or a pantheistic scheme of recurrence, Michelet's time(s) project a series of infinite variations from an almost-eternity to an almost-chaos: yet any of these projec-

[5] "Le Ventre et son royaume," *L'Arc*, no. 52, p. 39.

[6] Robert Glasser's *Time in French Life and Thought*, trans. C. G. Pearson (Manchester, 1972), traces its theme from medieval to modern periods through literary expressions and images; writers of the Renaissance conceived that "the moving and transient world was transformed to a calm, regular plain, the plain of time" (p. 176).

[7] Barthes, "La Sorcière," *Essais critiques* (Paris: Seuil, 1964), p. 116.

[8] Poulet, "Michelet et le moment d'Eros," *La Nouvelle Revue française*, 30 (October 1967), 622.

tions resemble or oppose one another solely on the basis of perspective.

In the vague area of disappearance into eternity, at the ultimate point of comparison for all temporal variation, is located Michelet's myth of approximation. He is unabashedly attracted to the secure stagnant womb, and pages of his *Journal* and his prefaces are written to chide himself out of such temptation. History, an "*oeuvre virile*," allows none of the somnolence of the womb; while enticing, a withdrawal into the womb naturally arouses shame: "The mother has to . . . push the child away from her breast. Seeing him return home, defeated, put to rout, the mother of Theodoric, King of the Goths, lifts her dress, shows her vulva, and says: *Is this where you want to return for refuge?* The child usually says *yes* and the mother agrees. But time says *no*. Progress says: Become a man. Do not stay inside the woman, if you want to fecundate the future's daughter or wife. To return is weak and cowardly."[9] Moments of fantasy or discouragement elicit the image of absolute repetition and return. But this is not the pattern of nature and history, it is the result of exhaustion. Aleksandr Hertzen, the Russian revolutionary who corresponded with Michelet and who, exiled in Paris and London, had become discouraged after 1848, felt history had slipped into the rhythms of frustration: "Here we are, after all our philosophizing, like a squirrel in a wheel, back at the *corsi e ricorsi* of old Vico."[10] Certainly from reading Michelet, one comes

[9] "Il faut que la mère . . . pousse l'enfant hors de son sein. La mère de Théodoric, roi des Goths, le voyant revenir battu, en déroute, lève sa robe, montre sa vulve et dit: *Est-ce là que vous voulez rentrer et vous réfugier?* L'enfant dirait généralement *oui*, et la mère de même. Mais le temps dit *non*. Le progrès dit: Deviens homme, ne reste pas dans la femme, si tu veux féconder la fille ou la femme d'avenir. Le retour serait faible et lâche" (*Journal*, II, 321, written in 1857).

[10] Hertzen, *From the Other Shore*, trans. Moura Budberg, and *The Russian People and Socialism: An Open Letter to Jules Michelet*, trans. Richard Wollheim (London: Weidenfeld and Nicolson, 1956), p. 34.

upon a convincing series of what was even worse than repetition: imitation. The change in political leaders after 1793 was still like going "from Robespierre to Robespierre"; the devils of Louviers could no longer improvise but regurgitated from their worn manuals; Napoleon, the usurper, pretended to belong in the lineage of incest that characterized kings and regents. Mitigating against these evidences of despair was another logic that did not admit to the possibility of imitation in time: "We cannot begin again. We can only create" (*Histoire de France*, IX, 64).

Geological time, a constant, imperceptible, minimal movement, defines the slowest, most distant boundary phasing history into eternity: "[The Earth] only changed with the passing of centuries. Why does it need to hurry? It seems to know it has time in its sway, all of eternity lying ahead" (*La Montagne*, p. 84). In this almost infinite context, "outcome" becomes a meaningless concept. The familiar figure of the primitive earth or cosmic goddess reigns over a rare combination of realms: "The divine idea implies gentle life processes, tender incubation, being enveloped by a maternal presence, but especially patient laws of succession, time's infinity" (p. 241).

Shading out from this almost timeless time, all the possibilities of change sift in and out of one another, as different forms of progress and of circle. Masculine time, a forward or backward "march," becomes the simultaneous ascensions and declines of history and nature that appear in Michelet's pages as crisscrossing, dovetailing. One direction's primacy over the other is only a matter of perspective. From the point of view of '89, pinnacle and watershed of all history, major milestones all point to eventual victory: "The Renaissance rallies under the memory of old Rome, the glimmers of the future Revolution of '89" (*Histoire de France*, X, p. 306). From the point of view of royal succession, each stage is an ever graver bottoming-out. Like the polyps' naive expectation that they, while only the merest middle in the long evolution from waterdrop to island, might gather all civilization into themselves and stop, the historian hopes each time that the nadir in kingship has been reached: "You would have thought that Charles's madness, stumbling one day to the right, the next to the left, was the worst form of government. You would have thought this, but mistakenly. There was still a little financial order, some obstacle to ridiculous expenditure. That barrier was torn down, toppled with the coming of Henry III. So this will mark the bottom of the bottom [*le fond du fond*]? . . . Oh no, we are not there yet" (X, 132). Nature's planet within a planet, parasite on parasite, become the successive engulfing of one age in the next, a Dantesque inferno, possibly emptying out, as far as Michelet knows, into the "desert" of the nineteenth century: "This was an immense Dantesque poem which, from circle to circle, lowered France into the inferno, still little known even to those who had just come through it" (*Histoire du XIXe siècle*, I, 70). The victorious dance of the Fêtes des fédérations, where all of France, from every province, rushed together into the circle, is inverted into the antirevolutionary tradition of time and the vacuum of Napoleon. The dialectic of the Revolution is better expressed by two spirals turning in and around each other: "Theology flinging aside the demure mask of grace, abdicating, denying herself, in order to annihilate Justice, striving to absorb—to destroy her within herself, to swallow her up. Behold them standing face to face; which of them, at the end of this mortal combat, is found to have absorbed, incorporated, assimilated the other?" (*History of the French Revolution*, ed. Wright, p. 32). One Mother Typhoon is pitted against the other: two massive egos. Linear time, especially given to dialectics, evolves quickly into the spiral, a compromise between progression and return, neither masculine nor feminine but androgyne.

The extreme of masculine time is the unraveling Michelet confronted more frequently from the eighteenth century on:

"a time that does not walk but jumps, with turns and reverses, a violent jerking pace constantly throwing one into confusion" (*Histoire de France*, XV, xi). The historian describes himself in his vocation at this point as the "serf of time": "I follow it by year, by month, even by week and day" (XV, xii). The monarchy too has its "diabolic," if not "theophanic," moments, as when Louis XIV retires to bed (with Madame de Maintenon) and decides whether to go to war or not: "Thirteen years of universal war, several billions toward bankruptcy, several million human lives that will perish from misery and hunger, all depended on this hour (11 November 1700), between ten and eleven at night" (XIV, 127). What was a "chronological thread" becomes chaos because of such myopic attention. The *Histoire du XIXe siècle*, murky hellish circles, something other than traditional historical analysis, stands as Michelet's ultimate testimony to time's disruption. Bergson's subjective time, Heidegger's *Sein und zeit*, the obsession of Flaubert, James, and Proust, all derived from similar sensations. The *Histoire du XIXe siècle*, related to Flaubert's enigmatic literature "*sur rien*," is time pushed to the purest and tortured of all its forms. How could Michelet go beyond the "*pur du pur*" (Robespierre) and the *fond du fond* already passed by over and over? After the Terror, any experience had to be dream, overwhelming the latest dream, if it would attract the least attention; it had to be a miracle.

At times, Michelet praises the "natural mobility" of his age as flexibility, at times he assails it as "sickness," madness. This curious century is treated by critics as a misfit in Michelet's historical pattern, or as the logical consequence of history's culmination with the Revolution. It has been implied that Michelet could not decide what to do with this extra century and therefore proclaimed it nonexistent: "Time is dead. It has perished!" (*Histoire du XIXe siècle*, I, 289). A sharp sense of temporal relativity gives rise to precocious nostalgia coupled with apocalypse: "Sweet memory of times so close and yet so far, this brilliant and airy dawn so joyously preceding, announcing the end of a world" (I, 31). And yet the distinction between the end of "a" world and the end of "the" world implies that something lies ahead: "I am not one of those complainers who think with each new century the end of the world is coming" (III, xviii).

Michelet never accepted either death or nothingness as the end, and despite his despair, the meaning of his descents into a darker and darker time is substantive, if clever, and not evasive. The *fond du fond*, passively going "*de la chute à la chute*" (from one fall to another), narrows history down to its primary theme, "Here are eighty pages to narrate three years. And what did I say? Not a thing. This nothing is something. For it is the depth of time [*le fond du temps*]" (*Histoire de France*, XII, 57). The double entendre suggests both the bottom of time and what time, in the last analysis, is. Foucault equates this growing consciousness with the birth of modern history itself: "a whole mass of time in depth given the rejuvenated name of history."[11]

There is, therefore, no death of time as there is no true recurrence; every age, masculine or feminine, mythical or historical is an *entr'acte*, an intermission, an act within itself only definable as in-between. In the *Histoire de France*, the nuance of *entr'acte* is often negative: "this miserable intermission when everything is suspended, and the sense of the age does not come" (XVI, 59–60). These lapses of time are associated with the immobile, useless ages of history, especially the seventeenth century. The nature books themselves have been considered the intermission of the *Histoire de France*, and again the word has had negative connotations, like "diversion." In *La Mer*, its use as historical concept does not change: "Between two eras of strength, the strength of the Renaissance, the strength of the Revolution, there was a slump [*un temps d'affaissement*] when grave signs pointed to a moral and

[11] *The Order of Things*, p. 138.

physical breakdown. The old departed world, the young one that had not yet come, left between them an intermission of a century or two. Conceived out of nothing [*conçues du vide*], generations were born feeble and sickly" (*La Mer*, pp. 346–47). But later in the same text the word fills out the other, more positive side of its meaning. An *entr'acte* is a period of silent restoration. A woman left her city residence and identity, her husband and his life, and went courageously (for the nineteenth century) to spend time alone by the sea: "What grace of solitude is in this short intermission from life" (*La Mer*, p. 380). The Regency of the duc d'Orléans, between Louis XIV and Louis XV, was a "happy intermission of kindness, humanity, and tolerance" (*Histoire de France*, XV, 150).

The intermissions, or passages from one age, one world into the next, are actually stages of the eternal metamorphosis. History is no longer divided into times of strength and weakness but into a series of transitions, without identifiable beginnings or end, without apocalypse or origin, ever rooted in time. Limited to the history of France, Michelet could have clung to his desire for a goal-oriented time, but immersed in the vastness of natural science, his models underwent revision. Frank Kermode's *The Sense of an Ending* relates a similar conceptual evolution: "Naively predictive apocalypses implied a strict concordance between beginning and end. . . . Such a concordance remains a deeply desired object, but it is hard to achieve when the beginning is lost in the dark backward and abysm of time, and the end is known to be unpredictable."[12] Kermode, however, assumes that such a vision of time results in an age of constant crisis: "In so far as we claim to live now in a period of perpetual transition we have elevated the interstitial period into an 'age' or *saeculum* in its own right, and the age of perpetual transition in technological and artistic matters is understandably an age of perpetual crisis in morals and politics" (p. 28).

[12] Kermode, *The Sense of an Ending* (New York, 1966), p. 30.

"Perpetual crisis" seen in terms of metamorphosis can vary from the painful molting of the mollusk to the regular sloughing off of cells in women and to the earth's barely perceptible shifts. Revolution remains violent but it is no longer an aberrant function out of time, or, if so, then everything is aberrant and monstrous. "At last '89. . . . We are saved for sure. On the contrary: France undergoes something unheard of. For two years, no culture at all. It is a terrible operation in natural history to have to go through metamorphosis, to change skin."[13]

The concept of the French Revolution that emerged after Michelet's refocusing on natural history may have looked different from that which is defined in his 1847 study; even twenty years of "servitude" to the "little history" made Michelet more aware of the different levels of permanent revolution. In the sixteenth century, barricades thrown up in Paris were part of a larger circle: "So that this long, vast, and terrible revolution in France was an episode in the gigantic poem of Philip II" (*Histoire de France*, X, 143). In the geological overview, in cosmic time, who is in whose poem?

Michelet must still not be reduced to relativity, but rather allowed, under a homogeneous exterior, a gamut of configurations. From the microbiological second to the geological eon, everything is a stage of passage. Neither the progressive myth of insect metamorphosis nor the perfect oneness of a God, Michelet's personal myth holds precariously between being and nonbeing; it is becoming at the breaking point, a symbol of restless generosity, of permanent pregnancy. Again, the *Histoire de France* is the record of successive gradations evolving from a personal myth more clearly elaborated in the nature books. Both series of history are heavily sexualized and both are dominated by pregnant females. As much as Michelet

[13] "Mais voilà 89.... Sans doute nous sommes sauvés. Au contraire: la France subit une chose inouïe. Pendant deux ans, point de culture. C'est une opération terrible en histoire naturelle de se métamorphoser, de changer de peau" (*Histoire du XIXe siècle*, I, 7).

speaks of the two sexes of the spirit, and of marriage, his history is primarily homosexual and structured by incest. After the sorceress joined with the jesuits and exorcists, history became effeminate;[14] and even in the age of the sublime witch, her fertility was marred by incest since she loved only her son. The monarchy hardly disguised its identity as matriarchy: Diane de Poitiers, Catherine and Marie de Medici, Anne of Austria, Marie-Antoinette were only the obvious witches behind whom stood rows of progressively insignificant mistresses before one reached the king. Another view is the king's domination by his "favorites," also an effeminate element. From Henri II on, the pattern was set: "The famous guarantee of order, the strong monarchic unity (which was always a republic of favorites), was going to give us another, a republic of nursemaids, mothers, and visitors of the sick" (*Histoire de France*, IX, 135). These queens were obliged, for their own survival, to be permanently pregnant, like the termite queen, and often their suspicious pregnancies gave rise to abortion or monsters. By the seventeenth century the historical *avortons* (runts, embryos too soon from the womb) are as abundant as those in *L'Insecte:* Marie Leczinska has two *avortons* with Louis XV; the English, surveying the underfed French, consider them *un ramas d'avortons.* Instead of springing full-born from God, Louis XVI will always be nodding his own monstrous embryo head, "*sa grosse tête d'embryon.*"

The dialectical double of the abortively pregnant queen is the "Mother" (whether male, female, or androgynous) who participates in a unique generative process. She incarnates the *entr'acte*, time's lacuna, in that she has lost contact with whatever abstract husband there was and will never see her children: "It is sad to think of the thousands and thousands of sea creatures who still experience only a vague love, ele-

[14] Alain Besançon's thorough psychoanalytic reading of the first half of *La Sorcière* invites a psychosexual reading for the entire *Histoire de France:* "Le Premier Livre de 'La Sorcière,'" *Annales ESC*, 26 (Jan.–Feb. 1971), 186–204.

mentary, impersonal. . . . They love, and they never know the loved one incarnating their dream, their desire. They beget, without ever having the happiness of rebirth found in posterity" (*La Mer*, p. 230).

The same pattern is slightly transposed when the begetting process is seen from inside, instead of from an overview; then the *entr'acte* is experienced as an *acte incessant*, one long unbroken state of striving. The two concepts might appear antithetical: one vision is lonely, fraught with separation, history as crisis and fragment; the other evokes the constantly growing, literal, and physical apparition of the banquet, of the mystical Revolution. Edward Kaplan's interpretation of Michelet emphasizes this powerful propulsion of evolution that is an inevitable part of physiological generation from small creatures to angels: "Knowledge grows from one generation to the next, like the body of one being."[15] Still the impression from the point of view of the subject, pregnant with the future, is the same as isolation, for nothing is proven, nothing apparently happening:

This invisible son, continually being born of you, existed even before your birth, in the germ of history. He has, like a fertile seed, prepared your birth that was to be a degree of his successive apparition. He is your son and father. He will engender himself so you in turn can engender him. . . .

Do not, therefore, go out in public places asking your neighbor for the future: Where is it? Have you seen it? Eh! How would they have seen it? How can you yourself see it since you carry it within you? It is not a matter of seeing but of doing and willing the deed. You carry it as seed and you carry it as will and desire, as your unceasing act.[16]

[15] Kaplan, "Michelet évolutionniste," in *Michelet cent ans après*, p. 125.

[16] "Cet invisible fils, qui va naissant de toi, a pourtant préexisté à ta naissance dans son germe historique. Il a, comme germe fécond, préparé ta naissance même, qui devait être un degré de son apparition successive. C'est ton fils, et c'est ton père. Il s'engendra pour que tu puisses l'engendrer lui-même.

Ne va donc pas sur les places, demandant l'avenir à ton voisin: *Où*

Instead of proceeding by traditional generation, from the parental couple to child, passage in time is operated by a string of single androgynous mediators; less "jet" or erection, not the full-blown orphan, but concealed energy and movement, felt and never seen.[17] Mediators of the "unceasing act," they are pure functions in a continuous transition or the transitions of transitions.

The family model or ego-structure emerging from the nature books dramatizes the element of desire, essential to the unceasing act since it forms the basis for propulsion, rather than goal or apocalypse. The earth, like the sea and all other smaller creatures under the mother's dominion, re-enacts on the cosmic scale fatherless love. Though she is an autonomous androgyne because of her regenerative capacities, a "male" principle, not only distant and impersonal, but hidden, orients her being: "Whether father or lover or both, it is certain that he is the one she watches and follows in her large movements, and no less in every act of circulation and fertility. In the dark times, when vapors covered her under a veil of opaque atmosphere, she still felt him there, sought him in the depths of her dream. This obscurity lingers, because of an enormous thickness" (*La Montagne*, p. 79). A vague sensation of presence-in-absence is all that remains of this mythical relationship; paradoxically both a center and something outside, the sun, by

---

est-il? L'avez-vous vu? Eh! Comment l'aurait-on vu, comment le verrais-tu toi-même, puisque tu le portes en toi? Il ne s'agit pas de voir, mais de faire et de vouloir faire. Tu le portes comme germe et tu le portes comme volonté et désir, comme ton acte incessant" (*Journal*, I, 590–91).

[17] Transition is not always effected as Poulet would suggest, by *jet*. The original *jet* has now been frustrated and replaced by a slow aspiration, for example, the image of the earth, *La Montagne*, p. 86: "Can she [the Earth] still recall times so far-off . . . ? It was a sweet pleasure to have so few obstacles, to send, in a free upsurge [*d'un jet libre*], her inner impulse [*élan intérieur*] so high. . . . Today her crust has veiled her."

causing a displacement of the greater ego, endows it with energy, with desire: "Without seeing him the way we might, they certainly perceive the warmth, the luminous glory coming to them from outside, from a great center, powerful and gentle. They love this other Me who caresses them, brightens them with joy, overflows with life for them" (*La Mer*, p. 194). Like Jacques Lacan's Name-of-the-Father (or Symbolic Level),[18] the signifier that posits an orientation for desire is itself pure desire, the desire of desire, the *fond du fond;* and structure depends upon its activated absence. The phallus is always missing, but creation, as in the myth of Osiris,[19] continues despite or because of the lack.

Virile love, therefore, the advent of fraternity, of the father-son, the victory of law over metamorphosis and history, the

[18] "This proves that attributing procreation to the father can be the effect only of a pure signifier, of a recognition not of the real father, but of what religion has taught us to invoke as the Name-of-the-Father" (Lacan, *Ecrits*, p. 556). The Father is represented by the Phallus, not as object, fantasy, or image, but as signifier, that is, signifier of desire. For Lacan, desire, based upon the desire of the Other, "what the mother desires," becomes, in that this desire is unconscious, "what the Other desires." Since the phallus enters the domain of the signifier in terms of castration (the realization that the organ is absent in women posits the menace of its being missed in the male subject), it is called, and operates as, a *manque à être*, a *lack of being*, or lack of object. This perpetual lack and endless signifier are symbolically illustrated by the Osiris myth that so haunted Michelet: "The object of desire assimilated by the imaginary function into what is felt as *original loss:* the phallus of embalmed Osiris that Isis is looking for" is among a list of "imaginary substitutes in which desire finds a way of prolonging itself" (Catherine Backès, "Lacan ou le 'Porte-Parole,'" *Critique*, 24, 1968, p. 150).

[19] Michelet describes the dismemberment in *La Bible de l'humanité*, faithful to Plutarch's narrative in *De Iside et Osiride*, although not quite as detailed: "He was sacrificed by his cruel brother Typhon who chopped him up with a sword, dismembered him, dispersed his body. The man's honor, his pride and force, his virility, were brutally cut off. Where are his poor remains? Everywhere on earth, in the waters. The outraged Sea carries them as far as Phoenicia" (p. 292). Isis and the emasculated Osiris make love, however, one last time before he descends into the underworld, and Horus is conceived.

unity of the People, all become essentially metaphorical projections, figures of constant displacement, permanent pregnancy. The Revolution signifies this desire.[20]

"Weak and unarmed, and ready for temptation, the nation had lost sight of the idea by which alone it had been sustained; like a wretched man deprived of sight, it groped its way in a miry road; it no longer saw its star. What! the star of victory? No, the sun of Justice and of the Revolution" (*History of the French Revolution*, ed. Wright, p. 6). The Nation, the People, heroes, sorcerers, and historians are swollen with the desire for Revolution, though they are like blind men, like globes frozen over, like prisoners of themselves. Out there is their displaced center, the sun, though they know it only intuitively and by the will and hope of carrying it inside them. How do they know for sure if one kind of pregnancy swirls in spirals out to the Father, is pulled to his absence, and the other churns with nothingness, sucks on its own turnings and storms? The Revolution pits its simultaneously centrifugal and centripetal force against the vacuum of tyranny; Grace and Justice both breathe deeply within and around each other; France will hopefully evolve beyond Catherine and Napoleon, the Sea beyond Mother Typhoon.

Only a slight imbalance assures a beginning. No timelessness, no perfect union, no absolute roundness. The "too-harmonious" harmony that might have been the earth's fate without the sun would have brought death, nothing:

If she [the earth] had consulted us about the shape she would take, would we have given good advice? Some, with their ideal of a too-harmonious harmony, would have imposed on her surface the perfection of the circle, monotonous uniformity, hardly able

[20] Desire as the fundamental function of the Revolution should not deny time: "According to Michelet's own realization, the Revolution has no future. It is, rather, immersed in the secret geology of the people, it is a burning fusion of subterranean forces in the species. It is pure passion" (Claude Mettra, "Le Ventre et son royaume," *L'Arc*, no. 52, p. 36).

to encourage life's diversity. Others, less mathematical, more artistic, would have preferred twins, like man, so she would have the human form, two halves appearing equal. Equality that looks exact in our statues, but much less so in nature. The real inequality of the two halves is precisely what allows for the action. If the two sides were of exactly the same force, each one pulling equally hard, in a perfect balance, being would remain immobile. Life would not take off. Nothing could begin.[21]

Every now and then one of the pulling, engulfing sides is absorbed by the other, or one splits off from its original body because of different tensions and attractions. This may indicate progress, at least it is movement. Michelet wants the surface clear and simple, he wants orderly successions, but moving way in or way out between geology and algae, between clusters of revolutions, he can have no definitive judgment whether the *bizarre alternatives* of multiple dialectics are a stepping-in place or a stepping-off place, whether climbing the ladder is indiscriminate swarming from another angle. "But to ascend, to pass to a higher level, [all things] must have exhausted everything the lower-level contains in the way of trials—more or less painful—or in the way of stimulants leading to invention and any instinctive art. They must even have exaggerated each stage, confronting its excesses so that, by contrast, they feel the need for an opposite kind. Thus, progress is made by a sort of oscillation between contrary qualities, which little by little

[21] "Si elle [la terre] nous eût consultés sur la forme qu'elle avait à prendre, l'aurions-nous bien conseillée? Les uns, dans leur idéal d'harmonie trop harmonique, eussent imprimé à sa surface la perfection circulaire, l'uniformité monotone, peu propre à favoriser la variété de la vie. D'autres, moins mathématiciens, plus artistes, auraient voulu que géminée, comme l'homme, elle eût les formes humaines, deux moitiés qui semblent égales. Egalité qui se voit exacte dans nos statues, mais bien moins dans la nature. L'inégalité réelle des deux moitiés est justement ce qui permet l'action. Si les deux côtés étaient tout à fait de même force, chacun tirant également, dans un balancement parfait, l'être resterait immobile. La vie ne prendrait pas l'essor. Rien ne pourrait commencer" (*La Montagne*, p. 90).

break apart and assume, each one, a form in life."[22] Once the motion has begun, which is inevitable it seems, time contorts and expands in all of its forms, and the primordial goddesses swell with their eternal young, or the abortion machine cranks and grinds for its puffs of nothing. In the end, the most impressive metamorphosis is not the progress, not the ladder from which the completed insect opens its colors for flight, but the strange reversals and mutual exchange of absence: "How far we are from our departure point where the insect seemed a purely voracious thing, a machine of absorption! Great, sublime metamorphosis, more marvelous than the molting and transformation that calls the egg, the caterpillar, and nymph to wings" (*L'Insecte*, p. 373). The real metamorphosis, though Michelet will not make it explicit, takes place in his book. Certainly his specimens have not changed. His own apparent blind spot, replete with its logical desire, is "ex-centered" on language; this is the vacuum confronting silence of which he as sorcerer has to become the serf.

[22] "Mais, pour monter, pour passer à un degré supérieur, il faut qu'ils [des êtres] aient épuisé tout ce que l'inférieur contient d'épreuves plus ou moins pénibles, de stimulants d'invention et d'art instinctif. Il faut même qu'ils aient exagéré leur genre, en aient rencontré l'excès, qui, par contraste, fait sentir le besoin d'un genre opposé. Le progrès se fait ainsi par une sorte d'oscillation entre les qualités contraires qui tour à tour se dégagent et s'incarnent dans la vie" (*La Mer*, p. 177).

Part II

THE POETICS OF METAMORPHOSIS

9 The Spider: A Chapter's Moving Texture

In *L'Oiseau*, the naturalist's plans for universal brotherhood were foiled by birds of prey. But they, like the wide variety of insatiable beetles, caterpillars, and bugs, "metamorphosed" through the text into beneficent agents of rapidly renewing life.[1] Most insects, however, seem hideous to man: feelers swaying, compound eyes open, upside-down bodies moving forward to the clack of mandibles and pincers. Michelet nevertheless found ways of redeeming them morally and metaphorically. Either as young nymphs they were to be pitied, or under the magical, instantly poetic eye of the microscope the most banal of them, like the maybug, were dressed up in gold-skeined wings. And the highly developed states of the bees and ants offered man a lesson in community.

In the middle of *L'Insecte*, Michelet stops to "rehabilitate" a creature that seems to have few recommendable traits and is not even a bonafide insect—the spider: "Before going on to the insect societies of the last [section of the] book, we should talk here about a recluse" (p. 201). One feels that Michelet goes out of his way to study the spider: this crucial diversion

[1] The pivotal point of *L'Oiseau* is the "revaluation" of vultures. In a chapter at the book's center, they are transformed from birds of prey with terrible, almost mythic appetites ("They will eat a hippopotamus and still be hungry," p. 153) to orderly bureaucrats in charge of public health, *la salubrité publique*, and finally into venerable birds of the Egyptian religion, in which dead souls depend on their wings to pass into immortality.

in the announced chronology of the book suggests the same kind of excitement that made Michelet interrupt his *Histoire de France* after the Middle Ages to take up the Revolution.

Although certain tropical species cooperate in large societies, the spider's basic tendency toward isolation has been misunderstood and used to perpetuate the traditional prejudice against a misfit of nature:

> Mais cette vie sociétaire est tout exceptionnelle, bornée à certaines espèces, aux climats les plus favorisés. Partout ailleurs l'araignée, par la fatalité de sa vie, de son organisme, a le caractère du chasseur, celui du sauvage qui, vivant de proie incertaine, reste envieux, défiant, exclusif et solitaire.
>
> Ajoutez qu'elle n'est pas comme le chasseur ordinaire, qui en est quitte pour ses courses, ses efforts, son activité. Sa chasse, à elle, est coûteuse, si j'ose dire, et exige une constante mise de fonds. Chaque jour, chaque heure, de sa substance elle doit tirer l'élément nécessaire de ce filet qui lui donnera la nourriture et renouvellera sa substance. Donc, elle s'affame pour se nourrir, elle s'épuise pour se refaire, elle se maigrit sur l'espoir incertain de s'engraisser. Sa vie est une loterie, remise à la chance de mille contingents imprévus. Cela ne peut manquer de faire un être inquiet, peu sympathique à ses semblables, où elle voit des concurrents; tranchons le mot, un animal fatalement égoïste. S'il ne l'était, il périrait. [*L'Insecte*, p. 202]

(But this life in society is most exceptional, limited to certain species, to suitable climates. Everywhere else the spider, by the fatal nature of her life, her organism, has the personality of a hunter, a savage, who, living on uncertain prey, remains envious, defiant, exclusive, and solitary.

In addition, she is not like the ordinary hunter who breaks even, after all his forays, efforts, and activity. Her hunting is costly, if I dare say, and requires constant reinvestment. Each day, each hour, she must extract from her own self and substance the element necessary for making the thread that will feed her and renew this same substance. So she goes hungry in order to eat, she is exhausted in order to be remade, she grows thin on the vague hope of fattening out again. Her life is a lottery, relying on the luck of a thousand unforeseen contingencies. This cannot help but make any living thing anxious, hardly likable to its own kind, which it considers rivals; let's be honest, an animal forcibly egotistical. If it was not, it would perish.)

A metaphor develops immediately out of the idea of the solitary animal: the primitive hunter who hides, waits, then dashes out for his prey. Associating the pejorative adjectives "envious" and "defiant" with "exclusive" and especially "solitary," which are not necessarily pejorative, forces a disagreeable nuance into the semantic field of solitude. But Michelet is immediately impatient with his simple metaphor of the hunter: "*Ajoutez*" he begins again, warning us of the linguistic play to come with the marker "if I dare say." At the word *coûteuse* (costly), Michelet plants the surprise of a new metaphor.[2] Imposed upon the description of a hunt is a modern economic vocabulary: *mise de fonds* (investment).[3] The life of the

[2] Michael Riffaterre's definition of a pertinent stylistic device hinges on the notion of the unexpected *contrast* within *context:* "We can therefore define the stylistic context as a *pattern* broken by an unforeseeable element. Style is not produced by a succession of figures, tropes, and processes; it is not continuous emphasis. What defines the stylistic structure of a text is a sequence of elements marked [*éléments marqués*] in contrast to unmarked elements [*éléments non marqués*], dyads, binary groups whose poles (context, contrast in relation to this context) are inseparable and connot exist independently one without the other (each fact of style [*fait de style*] comprises then a context and contrast)" (*Essais de stylistique structurale*, tr. Daniel Delas, Paris, 1971, pp. 65–66).

[3] I am treating metaphor not as a process of substitution, something figurative for something literal, one word for another (Proust), but as interaction. Metaphor by its very etymology suggests passage; it is a *transference*, or more precisely, *metamorphosis*. "Metaphor is not simply a change of meaning, it is the metamorphosis of meaning" (Jean Cohen, *La Structure du langage poétique*, Paris, 1966, p. 214). Metaphor, used in this active sense of a generalized figure that can change nuances and central meanings of words, becomes a dynamic, organic part of a text, itself a *forme signifiante* (Mikel Dufrenne, *Le Poétique*, Paris, 1963). Several theories of metaphor (which have

savage arthropod is subject to the capitalist cycle. Two sentences, one based on epanalepsis and one on antithesis, evoke the circularity of the spider's existence and the frustration that results. *De sa substance* (out of her substance) is inverted from its natural syntactical order to reinforce the sentence turning on itself. And the series of reflexive verbs (*s'affamer/se nourrir; s'épuiser/se refaire; se maigrir/s'engraisser*) adds the impression that the circle never stops. The spider's fate is ironically analogous to the freak of injustice set up by a materialistic society—the lottery. The word "lottery," not just an association with a game of chance, mobilizes a whole structure of cultural symbols. Michelet found a way to link the practice, supposedly imported with the Medicis, to the "fatalistic" forces of the church, for "the original name of the lottery at Genoa was

---

recently proliferated) seem to have a similar movement in mind: a contrast, incompatibility associated with it must be *traversed*, must be legitimized linguistically. Each subject alters, stretches, rearranges its semantic field so that passage or overlapping is somehow made possible. Max Black describes the operation as filtering and demonstrates it with the statement "man is a wolf": "The effect, then, of (metaphorically) calling a man a 'wolf' is to evoke the wolf-system of related commonplaces. If the man is a wolf, he preys upon other animals, is fierce, hungry, engaged in constant struggle, a scavenger, and so on. . . . Any human traits that can without undue strain be talked about in 'wolf-language' will be rendered prominent, and any that cannot will be pushed into the background" (*Models and Metaphors: Studies in Language and Philosophy*, Ithaca, 1962, p. 41). Jean Cohen, a French critic who tries to study the action of metaphor as scientifically as possible, delineates a similar transposition based on an initial *écart* ("distance") or semantic impertinence and a consequent reduction of that *écart*. Mallarmé's "*solitude bleue*" is used by him as an example. The *signifié* of blue focuses upon the feature of color, which cannot, at first glance, be reconciled with the central meaning of solitude. When, however, one considers all the various "codes," or the "system of related commonplaces," that surround solitude—what Cohen calls a "second signifié" Se_2—junction occurs. Within the semantic code of blue lie, for instance, the *semes* isolation, infinity, and purity, because of an association with sky. The result is an actual shift of meaning on the primary subject "solitude" as well as on the secondary subject "blue"; both undergo a linguistic metamorphosis.

Giuoco del Seminario" (*Histoire de France*, XII, 297). Later the term connoted the military and diplomatic strategy of Waldstein, Richelieu, and Mazarin, all great gamblers; thus, it meant risks that would ruin the people. But the disasters of national warfare could still not compare to the final apotheosis of the lottery in the eighteenth century—the stock market: "All of this was nothing in comparison to what happened as gambling, the lottery, the love of speculation reached the entire population" (*Histoire de France*, XV, 32). Mindful of these sociohistorical resonances, the reader should realize that the spider fights not "prey" but "the system."

The fatality of the spider's natural environment (meshed with the code of capitalistic society) is compounded by the destiny of its anatomy:

> Le pis, pour ce pauvre animal, c'est qu'il est laid foncièrement. Il n'est pas de ceux qui, laids à l'oeil nu, se réhabilitent par le microscope. La spécialité trop forte du métier, nous le voyons chez les hommes, atrophie tel membre, exagère tel autre, exclut l'harmonie; le forgeron souvent est bossu. De même l'araignée est ventrue. En elle la nature a tout sacrifié au métier, au besoin, à l'appareil industriel qui satisfera le besoin. C'est un ouvrier, un cordier, un fileur et un tisseur. Ne regardez pas sa figure, mais le produit de son art. Elle n'est pas seulement un fileur, elle est une filature. Concentrée et circulaire, avec huit pattes autour du corps, huit yeux vigilants sur la tête, elle étonne par la proéminence excentrique d'un ventre énorme. Trait ignoble, où l'observateur inattentif et léger ne verrait que gourmandise. Hélas! c'est tout le contraire; ce ventre, c'est son atelier, son magasin, c'est la poche où le cordier tient devant lui la matière du fil qu'il dévide; mais, comme elle n'emplit cette poche de rien que de sa substance, elle ne grossit qu'aux dépens d'elle-même, à force de sobriété. Et vous la verrez souvent, étique pour tout le reste, conserver toujours gonflé ce trésor où est l'élément indispensable du travail, l'espérance de son industrie, et sa seule chance d'avenir. Vrai type de l'industriel. "Si je jeûne aujourd'hui, dit-elle, je mangerai peut-être demain; mais si ma fabrique chôme, tout est fini, mon estomac doit chômer, jeûner à jamais." [Pp. 202–3]

(The worst part, for this poor animal, is that it is basically ugly. It is not like some things, ugly to the naked eye and restored through a mircroscope. The overspecialization of a trade, we see it among men, atrophies one limb, overdevelops another, prevents harmony; the blacksmith is often hunchbacked. The spider, likewise, is potbellied. With her, nature has sacrificed everything to a job, to need, to the industrial apparatus satisfying this need. She is a worker, a ropemaker, a spinner, and a weaver. Do not look at her features, but the finished product of her art. She is not only a spinner, but a spinning mill. With a concentrated and circular form, eight legs around her body, eight eyes always watching from her head, it is astonishing to see her off-centered by the bulging of an enormous stomach. A vulgar physical trait the inattentive and frivolous observer would interpret only as gluttony. Alas, it is the exact opposite; this belly is her workshop, her store, the pocket where the ropemaker can keep in front of him the material for the cord he unwinds; but, since she fills this pocket with nothing but substance from herself, she fattens only at her own expense, because of her sobriety. And you may see her, emaciated everywhere else, always keeping this treasure swollen for the indispensable element of work, the hope of her industry, her only chance for the future. A true form of industrialist. "If I fast today," she says, "perhaps I will eat tomorrow; but if my factory is idle, everything is over, my stomach will be unemployed, empty forever.")

Michelet must begin by confronting the description of the spider, which has been fixed not by scientific observation, but by language usage and literary history.[4] In actuality, the

[4] Black particularly emphasizes the dispensability of an irrefutable *reference* in the metaphorical operation: "The important thing for the metaphor's effectiveness is not that the commonplaces shall be true, but that they should be readily and freely evoked" (p. 40). The role of reference in figurative expression, however, is still highly controversial: "It comes down to the difficult question of reference. Certainly poetry, unrealistic (nonrealistic, surrealistic...), does not refer to things one by one; but this distraction as far as a demonstrable reality is concerned is not the same thing as the pure and simple absence of reference. Linguistics (cf. Jakobson) legitimately emphasizes

viscous substance that composes the spider's web does not come from the stomach at all, but from spinnerets whose operation is anatomically independent. Nevertheless, it is not to Michelet's advantage to question a myth that had long been handed down about how the spider *seems* to spin. Ovid's Arachne was no exception, and even her ugliness—her body dominated by belly—is the echo of a tradition in which Michelet can be included:

> . . . and [Arachne's] head
> Was shrunken, and the body very tiny,
> Nothing but belly, with little fingers clinging
> Along the side as legs, but from the belly
> She kept spinning
>
> [*Metamorphoses*, tr. Rolfe Humphries (Bloomington, 1961), p. 133]

The adjective, *ventrue* (potbellied), seems unavoidable in the semantic context of the noun "spider," radiating other unpleasant associations; the *Grand Dictionnaire universel du XIXe siècle* includes in its list of negative arachnid modifiers: *ventrue, laide, difforme, affreuse, sale, repoussante.*[5] By the

---

the poetic function as centralizing on the message, but what poetry corresponds to by means of objects . . . is unknown, misunderstood, perhaps inevitably, by the science of poetics" (Michel de Guy, "Vers une théorie de la figure généralisée," *Critique*, no. 25, October 1969, p. 855). Cohen confesses, in an article published after his *Structure du langage poétique*, to this unavoidable problem: "Because admittedly the referent of 'fox' is concrete, that is, tangible, whereas that of 'tricky' [*rusé*] is not, must you conclude that you cannot understand the phrase 'that man is foxy' without precisely imagining the animal? Nothing is less certain" ("Théorie de la figure," *Communication*, no. 16, 1970, p. 25).

[5] The entire list of modifiers suggests numerous metaphors and values: "agile, subtile, vive, prompte, rapide, adroite, habile, industrieuse, ingénieuse, savante, laborieuse, vigilante, patiente, suspendue, fileuse, filandière, tisseuse, ménagère, ventrue, laide, difforme, affreuse, sale, repoussante, vénimeuse, vorace, carnassière" (*Le Grand Dictionnaire universel du XIXe Siècle*, Paris, 1867, Vol. I).

end of Michelet's passage, horror at the sight of an odious monster is converted into pity and sympathy.

If the spider participates in an economy, she has a trade. After preparing his *metaphore filée* (metaphor-thread)[6] by distributing aspects of its code into the text—*métier* (trade), *forgeron* (blacksmith), *appareil industriel* (industrial apparatus)—Michelet feels free to level it to its essential elements: "C'est un ouvrier, un cordier, un fileur et un tisseur." This series—again four elements—also divides into distinctions, not equivalents. *Ouvrier* is the general term most expected, and *fileur* (spinner) has been adequately prepared for by *filet* (thread) used twice previously in the text to refer to the spider's web. *Fileur* engenders *tisseur* (weaver) in the logic of spinning followed by weaving, and *cordier* (ropemaker) seems a poetic suggestion, which reinforces the idea of individual craftsmanship, of industry still as *métier*. Only after Michelet has established the fact that the spider's stomach is her workroom; that she by metonymy is a complete spinning operation, a primitive mill; only after he has diverted all attention away from the spider's appearance to its use, its art, does he move in swiftly with a most picturesque portrait of the deformed creature. Without the aid of a microscope, hyperbole makes us exaggerate the size of the spider—after all, she was just previously compared to a spinning mill. It's like seeing a picture of a spider without knowing its perspective and, therefore, being astonished by the huge domelike stomach and sinister mass of eyes (*yeux vigilants*). At this point Michelet gives the reader no exit but agreement; none of us will admit to being the superficial observer. We are made to understand,

[6] See Riffaterre's article "La Métaphore Filée dans la poésie surréaliste," *Langue française*, 3 September 1969: "What is called a metaphor-thread is in fact a series of metaphors tied one to another by syntax—they are a part of the same sentence, narrative structure, or description—and by meaning: each one expresses a particular aspect of the whole, object or concept, represented by the first metaphor in the series" (p. 47).

by contrast, that Michelet is the attentive and serious commentator par excellence, but is scrupulous too about how he reveals his observations. Do we allow him to become, beyond a doubt, our reliable narrator?

Confident in his maneuvers, Michelet seems next to seize upon a private poetry that he may have been planning since the word *cordier* or that may have simply emerged of its own inevitability. The stomach-workshop becomes a pocket, which is rich in connotation: it is the ropemaker's apron as well as the marsupial's pouch, and it also recalls in French the *poche* (*des eaux*), an image of birth.[7] Finally, a faint but probable resonance comes from the original image associated with the lottery: "The Italian governments were generally lotteries or names put in a sack, *imbursati,* drawn by the magistrates" (*Histoire de France,* XII, 5). As the spider takes on the vaguest notions of tender maternity—*grossit* (fattens), *gonflé* (swollen) —and as the social system grows pervious to economical miracle, *trésor* (treasure), the bitter corollary is exposed. The individual worker, the artisan in the small shop (*fabrique*), is never free from the fear of a shut-down (*chômage*). Michelet has already evolved the significance of the chapter's title "L'Araignée, L'Industrie, Le Chômage" and is beginning to show why the spider—actually an archetypal insect ("great destroyer and fabricant, the industrialist par excellence, the active worker of life," p. viii)—is also an irresistible object for his observation.

Once Michelet begins to address the spider, the tone of the text turns immediately personal. The identity he has created for the spider releases a wellspring of memory: "My first

[7] "Poche (des eaux): saillie que les membranes de l'oeuf, détachées de la matrice et poussées par les contractions utérines, font à travers le col dilaté" (when the egg membrane, detached from the uterus and rejected by its contractions, bursts through the dilated cervix) (*Dictionnaire de la langue française,* ed. Littré, Paris, 1863–1869, II, part one).

contact with a spider was very agreeable. In the poverty of my childhood, when I worked alone (as I have said in *The People*) at my father's printing press, ruined and deserted at the time, the shop was temporarily in a sort of cellar sufficiently lighted since it was the cellar on the boulevard side where we lived but the ground floor on the rue Basse" (*L'Insecte*, pp. 203–4). So far, Michelet's introduction of the spider has carried him directly from naturalism into myth, and this first effort at documenting his actual *contact* with a spider had already entered the fictions of literature. Michelet remembers he had once mentioned this particular companion of his printing duties in *Le Peuple;* some of the same phrases that seemed apt for depicting this crucial time and place in his childhood return almost untouched: "The place of my work, our shop, was scarcely less dark. For a while, it was a cellar in relation to the boulevard we lived on, the ground floor on the back street. There I had for company sometimes my grandfather when he came, but always, very devotedly, a busy spider who worked near me, and harder than me, I am sure" (p. 18; written in 1846).

As early as 1846, much of the biographical specificity had been lost, though it can be partially revived in an even earlier, first notation of the same setting, but without the spider: "The shop, located in a kind of celler level with the rue de Bondy, was very cold and dreary. It was there that I learned to *compose*. It was there that my poor grandfather, who worked the press as well as he could, tried to teach me how to sing the scale" (*Ecrits de jeunesse*, p. 188; written in 1820–1822). The exact date (varying from 1808–1813) and circumstances of the passage recorded in *L'Insecte* can still not be documented with absolute certainty since some further biographical confusion exists, but it is clear that Michelet in this third version exaggerates the sad solemnity of his office and its unmitigated solitude and desolation. Grandfather is conveniently eliminated, he who in the *Mémorial* was the one to play the heroic solitary role: "My grandfather printed, sometimes with Papa, sometimes alone, God knows how!" (p. 199).[8] A strange effect is also created (one wonders if this is a printing error) when *Basse* is capitalized, so as to indicate the street name.

[8] In *Le Peuple*, Michelet explains that Napoleon had by 1800 already cut down on Michelet père's potential business: certain newspapers were outlawed. *Ma Jeunesse* mentions the suppression of the *Courrier des armées*, one of Michelet père's clients, as particularly damaging (see also Viallaneix' notes to the *Mémorial*, *Ecrits de jeunesse*, pp. 382–83). Although Michelet insists that his father was not overtly political, the latter had obtained the favor of the Jacobins and was doing some of their important publications in 1795–1796. Napoleon, therefore, had no reason to spare him. On 5 February 1810, Napoleon decreed that only sixty of the largest Parisian printers would be allowed to continue operations. Michelet père's important contracts must have dwindled before that; he was sent to debtor's prison in 1808, and in 1809 when the family moved to the boulevard Saint-Martin (where the passage in *L'Insecte* takes place) Michelet learned to print, but business was not lively. Already he and his grandfather worked together on publications of little intellectual or political value, on *ouvrages de ville*. Michelet would have been about eleven years old. After 1810, the situation became bleak. Evidently the press continued to print a book (or books) that legally "belonged" to Michelet's father (see Viallaneix, *Ecrits de jeunesse*, p. 390), although only immediate members of the family—grandfather, mother, and son—were allowed to work. "My sick mother stitched, cut, folded. As a child, I set type [*composai*]. My grandfather, very weak and old, had the hard job of the press, and he printed with trembling hands. The books we printed and which sold well enough, contrasted noticeably by their futility with these tragic years of considerable destruction. They were banalities, mundane games, social amusements, charades, acrostics" (*Le Peuple*, 1974 ed., p. 66). One particular contract (to print Fabre d'Olivet's *Savant de société*) stood out in Michelet's mind as one of his worst ordeals; the book's profits were all to go to the usurer Vatard. Though it is hard to pin down the dates of this experience, it might have furnished a source for this passage in *L'Insecte*. In the *Mémorial*, Michelet remarks that the edition was being finished in 1811; but in one of the copies of Fabre d'Olivet's book he wrote that the work took place in 1812–1813: he would have been, therefore, between thirteen and fifteen years old. "I set the type for most of this book. . . . When I got home from M. Mélot's and finished my little bit of homework, I put on my apron and intrepidly set my twelve or fifteen pages" (*Ecrits de jeunesse*, p. 199).

Certainly the word *cave* (cellar) and all its damp, dark, secretive connotations continue to echo in *Basse* (*Bondy* being a ludicrous alternative), and the ominous atmosphere grows in preparation for the spider's appearance:

Par un large soupirail grillé, le soleil venait à midi égayer un peu d'un rayon oblique la sombre casse où j'assemblais mes petites lettres de plomb. Alors, à l'angle du mur, j'apercevais distinctement une prudente araignée qui, supposant que le rayon amènerait pour son déjeuner quelque étourdi moucheron, se rapprochait de ma casse. Ce rayon, qui ne tombait point dans son angle, mais plus près de moi, était pour elle une tentation naturelle de m'approcher. Malgré le dégoût naturelle, j'admirai dans quelle mesure progressive de timide, lente et sage expérimentation, elle s'assurait du caractère de celui auquel il fallait qu'elle confiât presque sa vie. Elle m'observait certainement de tous ses huit yeux, et se posait le problème: "Est-ce, n'est-ce pas un ennemi?"

Sans analyser sa figure, ni bien distinguer ses yeux, je me sentais regardé, observé; et apparemment l'observation, à la longue, me fut tout à fait favorable. Par l'instinct du travail peut-être (qui est si grand dans son espèce), elle sentit que je devais être un paisible travailleur, et que j'étais là aussi occupé, comme elle, à tisser ma toile. Quoi qu'il en soit, elle quitta les ambages, les précautions, avec une vive décision, comme dans une démarche hardie et un peu risquée. Non sans grâce, elle descendit sur son fil, et se posa résolûment sur notre frontière respective, le bord de ma casse, favorisé en ce moment d'un blond rayon de soleil pâle. [Pp. 204–5]

(Through the grating of a large basement window, the noon sun came in at a slant and brightened a little of the dark case where I was setting tiny lead letters. Then from the corner I clearly saw a prudent spider coming toward the case, figuring the ray of sun would lure some absentminded gnat looking for lunch. The sunbeam, whose angle did not hit her but fell nearer me, was an obvious temptation for her to come closer. Despite a natural disgust, I admired the steady measure of the shy, slow, and careful testing she used to find out about the character of the person to whom she was about to entrust her life. She most assuredly watched me with all eight eyes and considered the problem: "Is it an enemy or not?"

Without looking closely at her face, nor making her eyes out very well, I knew I was being watched, observed; and apparently the observation turned, in the long run, totally in my favor. Perhaps because of some common instinct for work (so strong in her species), she sensed that I was a peaceful worker and as busy as she was, weaving my web. For whatever reason, she skipped the small talk, the precautions, with a sharp decisiveness, as if taking a daring and risky move. Not without grace, she descended her thread and stopped resolutely at our respective border, the edge of my case enhanced at this moment by the blond streak of pale sun.)

The *cave* is converted by the presence of a *soupirail grillé* (grating) into a prison and its lonely inhabitant seems to be working a heavy penance as if for an angry king (or father). The printer slowly assembles his letters; the historian builds up the years of his documented pyramid; the writer weighs his words. Yet it takes some time for the spider to recognize a burdened fellow worker: at first he looks to her like a giant competitor, some monster of another world who has her life in his hands, some terrible Claude Frollo in his laboratory. Michelet, we know, is the opposite; he has become like his fictive specimens, a nervous victim of observation. He waits under the eerie impression that all eyes are upon him, until at last a triumphant chiasmus of metaphor occurs. Various reversals of roles make both realize that at the center they are the same. Both are mutually monstrous and frightened; both *défiant* and *prudent*. The boy-printer is metaphorically a spider (*à tisser ma toile*), and the spider is like an invisible childhood companion. In *Le Peuple,* Michelet reminisces about the fantasies of these quiet hours: "Never, it seems, did my imagination travel so far as while I stood immobile at this case"

(p. 16). Through imagination the boy was a burgeoning alchemist, and the golden sunlight, which seemed the compensation for—or the last stages of—his work with lead, unfurls the magic, threadlike ladder from a supernatural universe, the *fil* (ironically, *filets* in printing terminology are the metal pieces used to make borders and edges). His lugubrious workshop becomes the antrum that opens as a disguised gateway to another realm; both representatives of their worlds—chosen perhaps because of their superior instinct for work—meet at the intersection, the *frontière respective*, *bord de ma casse*, and perform both a mystical and social pact:

> J'étais entre deux sentiments. J'avoue que je ne goûtai pas une société si intime; la figure d'une telle amie me revenait peu; d'autre part, cet être prudent, observateur, qui certainement ne prodiguait pas sa confiance, était venu là me dire: "Eh! pourquoi ne prendrais-je pas un tant soit peu de ton soleil?... Si différents, nous arrivons cependant ensemble du travail nécessiteux et de la froide obscurité à ce doux banquet de lumière.... Prends un coeur et fraternisons. Ce rayon que tu me permets, reçois-le de moi, garde-le.... Dans un demi-siècle encore, il illuminera ton hiver."
>
> Comme la noire petite fée le disait en son langage, bas, très-bas, on ne peut plus bas (ainsi parlent les araignées), j'en gardai l'effet vaguement. [P. 205]

> (I was of two minds. I admit I did not relish that intimate a society; the face of such a friend hardly appealed to me; on the other hand, this careful, observant creature who certainly did not lavish her confidence had come out to say to me: "Well then! Why shouldn't I get a little of your sun?... Though different, we both come from lowly work and cold obscurity to this sweet banquet of light.... Take heart and let us form a community of brothers. This sun you give me, take it back and keep it.... A half-century from now, it will light your winter."
>
> Since the tiny black fairy said this in her own language, speaking softly, so softly, almost impossible to hear (spiders speak that way), I can only vaguely remember what happened.)

The female guardian angel who comes down from on high (related to the initially repulsive medusa, oversensitive orchid, and timid haliotis) is, as usual, ambiguous: she is a fairy but black—therefore good or bad? The negative connotations surrounding the first solitary spider, "envious, defiant, exclusive," begin to fade since these traits of a previously savage egotism can describe, with a slight twist of phrasing, a timid, overly cautious individual. When the two protagonists, printer and spider (observer and observed, writer and subject, reader or writer and text), can merge perspectives, there can be nothing pejorative in their attitudes, and any antagonism is only caution preparing the more trustworthy discussion that breaks all barriers.

Both protagonists play the combined roles of good, but ugly, fairy (*fileuse*) come to save the girl or boy in dire straits with no hope of relief: such is the plot of many fairy tales, which now can include in their lineage genres as foreign as history and natural history.[9] Michelet is a reverse Rumpelstiltskin, spinning not grain into gold for the miller's daughter, but gold into grain—some wayward fly—for the spider. Or the spider is like one of the Three Spinning Fairies. All three had horrible deformities: one a huge foot, one a protruding lip, one a swollen thumb (Michelet's witch has an enormous stomach). The Three Fairies (in French, "Les Trois Fileuses") spin flax into gold so the poor girl cannot be harmed by the wicked queen; the spider gives the boy courage to get out his fifteen pages before supper. But her gift is also more farsighted;

[9] As in all comparative folklore, the archetypes are profoundly ambiguous. The spinner can be a lovely maiden or an old hag; the old hag can also execute a miraculous boon, turn a simple error into misfortune, or bode evil. *Fey Morgane* in Adam de la Halle's *Le Jeu de la feuillée* and the wicked fairy in Sleeping Beauty pronounce curses on their disrespectful hosts. According to Walckenaer's edition of Perrault's "Sleeping Beauty," the witch is only a *bonne vieille* who was out of touch with the law of the land and "had not heard that the king had prohibited the use of spinning wheels" (*Les Contes de Charles Perrault, suivis de la dissertation sur les contes de fées par le Baron Walckenaer*, Paris, 1876, I, 8).

she brings an eternal inner light—the cliché, ray of hope. Without this ambiguous Joan of Arc, this muse of times of misery, the boy would become discouraged; the future historian would lose faith in history. Or, as Michelet writes in *L'Oiseau*, in the questionable moments of life, a kind of shudder of strength goes through us and, like the nightingale who sings, "our soul at these indecisive hours of dusk, finds again its inner light" (p. 374).

Michelet's spider is almost a symbol, almost an incarnation of the apocalypse we can all share—albeit an ambiguous symbol. And yet she fails. She is nowhere up to the kilowatt power of Hugo's equivalent figures: Stella, Lux, the Angel Liberty who turns black Satan transparent. Satan in Hugo's *La Fin de Satan* started out as a lonely, yet invidious spider: "Comme la tarentule au centre de ses toiles, / Le vaste malheureux et le vaste méchant [Like a tarantula in the midst of its web, / Vast in its evil and vast, its unhappiness]." But his redemption is total and without afterthought; his resurrection eternal: "Satan est mort; renais, ô Lucifer céleste! / Viens, monte hors de l'ombre avec l'aurore au front! [Satan is dead; live, o heavenly Lucifer! / Come, climb from the shadows with dawn on your face!]." Although Hugo and Michelet share final visions, Hugo focuses on that moment when "night dissolves" all at once and "the whole universe is one united family" ("Lux," *Les Châtiments*). A curious quote from the *Histoire de France*, expressing an opinion against the clarity of language, reveals the historian's ambivalence toward utopia and apocalypse and recalls, instead, his nostalgia for beginnings, for the "unorganizable" of time: "No place of rest without shadows. No more mystery, and no more obscure sanctuaries. The divine Night (of Homer) is abolished" (XII, 291). *Le Banquet*, written contemporaneously with *L'Insecte*, deals with present states of gray, and not just with light. Michelet's star is unlike Hugo's and Dante's and his writings do not always burst forth, but sputter like a ship's lamp: "I will pass by, if necessary, like an unknown beacon that saves someone at sea who does not know his own name. If only from evening to morning my light shines evanescent but helpful, I will be grateful! I will have done my part for the banquet!" (Conclusion to *Le Banquet*). Michelet's banquet is dim and frugal, perhaps because its hostess and its guest do not break out of time like Hugo's figures; for the historian, every apocalyptic moment is susceptible to the fading of time; he knows it beforehand and meanwhile. The spider's voice was quiet, no *clairon.* The effect was so vague he almost forgot it: "But this slept within me. Then it woke for a short while in 1840 but disappeared again in sleep until the day of 15 May 1857, when I finished explaining it for the first time, writing it down" (*L'Insecte*, p. 205). The "pure" memory of his childhood–although already ambiguous–reappears in different, but related, forms to give him confidence. Not like Musset's souvenir, untouchable and buried forever ("*O la plus chère tombe et la plus ignorée*"), nor like Baudelaire's excruciatingly heavy memory ("*j'ai plus de souvenirs. . .* ") Michelet's recurring image resembles Proust's consoling sonata composed by Vinteuil. But, perhaps also like Proust, Michelet cannot remain content with the momentary joy of recognition but must ex-plain, must write. Somehow neither the expanse of time from memory to memory nor its instantaneous collapse exists if it is not captured in a chapter, in a book. Tragically, this obsession to document each recurrence and the long, tediously temporal preparation (Michelet emphasizes this more than Proust perhaps) finally undercuts any effort to create a symbol, to find transcendence through a unique and burning timeless figure, because a text, unlike a cry or a note, is not closed off and must go on somewhere else.

Donc, en 1840, après une perte de famille, je passai les vacances à Paris, et seul me promenais tout le jour dans mon petit jardin de la rue des Postes. Les miens étaient à la campagne. Je me mis machinalement à regarder les belles étoiles concentriques que les araignées faisaient autour de mes arbres, qu'elles raccommodaient, refaisaient sans cesse avec une louable industrie, se donnant une peine immense à garder le peu que j'avais de fruits, de raisins, me soulageant aussi moi-même de l'importunité des mouches et de la piqûre des cousins. Elles rappelèrent à ma mémoire la noire araignée domestique qui, dans mon enfance, entra en conversation avec moi. [P. 205]

(So, in 1840, after a death in the family, I spent my vacation in Paris, and walked about alone all day in my little garden off the rue des Postes. My immediate family was in the country. I automatically began watching the marvelous concentric stars the spiders were making in my trees, stars they mended constantly, and remade with remarkable industry, taking great pains to protect what few fruits or grapes I had, keeping me, as well, free from the annoyance of flies and gnat bites. They brought to mind the black domestic spider that had broached a conversation with me when I was a child.)

There is no single spider like Hugo's Stella, who heralds the "giant light," but a spider subjectively special to Michelet, surrounded perhaps, certainly followed by, innumerable spiders, each with her own *star*, her own potential light: the word *étoile* is a brilliant find, right for linking the solitary spinner (*fileuse*) of his childhood to the garden spiders of years later. The narrator is still lost in memory, although he has moved forward perhaps twenty-eight years from the first deep reverie. He is still alone and totally preoccupied with himself, or his troubles. The text does not indicate his personal trouble: was the *perte de famille* the death of a distant relative or the traumatic loss of his first wife, Pauline?[10] The

[10] The exact date or month when this experience could have occurred is impossible to verify in the *Journal*. Michelet visited the Père Lachaise cemetery many times during 1840. He mentions spiders once but his children, allegedly absent at the time the memory was transformed into literature, are present: "Visited cemetery with my children. Never absent before for so long a time: the crowns [were] changed, the spiders as on a tomb that belongs to solitude" (I, 328). There was a funeral for a friend, Daunou, the same year (I, 329).

text portrays a man distracted, watching and yet not *observing* the diverse activities of spiders around him, spiders who seem to be working for him, protecting and consoling him like loyal servants. The first person is the textual center of the passage—"*je* passai . . . seul *me* promenais . . . *mon* petit jardin. . . . Les *miens*. . . . *Je me* mis . . . de *mes* arbres . . . fruits que *j'*avais . . . *me* soulageant aussi *moi*-même." This tone of intimate (and absolute) possession that Michelet often uses is poignantly conveyed in the affectionate "mon *petit* jardin," the surprising "*mes* arbres." Everything circles and returns to its one owner. And yet, mindless of the gardening and trapping of insects around him, what he is specifically watching are stars. This *étoile* is embedded in the sentence and (according to the principles of transformational grammar) present (in the "deep structure") like an echo—"[*étoiles*] *qu'elles raccommodaient*, [*étoiles*] *qu'elles refaisaient*"[11]—and it fulfills the little black fairy's promise. The act of memory shakes Michelet from his torpor, and he begins once more to observe. The *étoile* becomes the key transition from *fil* (thread) to *toile* (web), and Michelet notices that his new friends are not the old one:

> Celles-ci étaient fort différentes. Filles de l'air et de la lumière, toujours exposées, toujours sous les yeux, sans abri que le dessous d'une feuille où il est aisé de les prendre, elles ne pouvaient avoir les réserves, la diplomatie de mon ancienne connaissance. Tout leur travail était visible, tout leur petit mystère au vent, leur personne à discrétion; elles n'avaient de protection que la pitié ou les services si positifs qu'elles rendent, l'intérêt bien entendu. [P. 206]

(These were very different. Daughters of air and light, always exposed, always in sight, with no safety except a leaf's underside

[11] See Richard Ohmann's article, "Generative Grammars and the Concept of Literary Style," in Glen Love and Michael Payne, eds., *Contemporary Essays on Style: Rhetoric, Linguistics, and Criticism* (Glenview, Ill., 1969), especially his breakdown of Faulkner's sentence, pp. 141–42.

where it is easy to surprise them, they could not afford to have the reserve, the diplomacy of my old acquaintance. All their work was visible, all their little mystery out on the wind, their entire person dependent; they had no protection besides pity or the positive services they render, with interest of course.

Michelet returns to the stance he took at the beginning of the chapter; the first person drops out, and the business of re-evaluating the spider continues. Each metamorphosis has centered upon a metaphor with a particular adjectival aura: the aura has undergone the change of value. At first the spider was "envious, exclusive, defiant, egotistical, ugly, potbellied, savage"; then, by extension the adjectives were softened. The Solitary Spinner was "timid, vigilant, careful, observant"; now she is said to have been "reserved, diplomatic." Finally, a third set of associations surrounding the spider is created by antithesis. Whereas the Solitary Spinner was the daughter of the damp dark, a furtive shadow in the cave's corners, the garden spinners are "daughters of air and light." The domestic house spider stared at Michelet with her terrible eyes, while the ones outside must submit themselves to other eyes, to the observer's again, to any predator's. They seem to be even more the victims of fate than the original solitary savage; they have only a leaf, the hunter has the underbrush. But these new spiders are not without guarantees; they are protected by pity or, even better, by an exchange of services—by *interest.* The economic vocabulary returns, and it seems the spiders are gaining in sophistication. They are servants of sorts to their patron Michelet, the garden's planter, but they hold an unwritten contract based on personal interest. They know they will be allowed on the windows and in the trees, for Michelet would have neither harvest, nor peace, without them.

A parallel evolution continues to link Michelet's autobiography, the developing economy of the spider society, and the professional writing of history. The tools and materials of the young apprentice, his methods for setting type, were straightforward and simple: single lead letters composed each line, which would, with endurance on his part, lead to a text. The fairy spider let herself down on a single thread, and their spontaneous agreement was more like the supernatural granting of a wish. The garden spiders, emerging capitalists, learn to bargain with their work as a commodity. They do not drop down in their celestial machines to the dinner table but, like sailors, tilt their canvas into the winds, always adjusting it to changing directions, holding forever to a heeling vessel that functions, like history, between man and nature, myth and economy, autobiography and sociology, soft speech and business deals. "The web [*toile*] does not fall straight [*ne tombe pas d'aplomb*]: that would give it only one current; the spider, an expert sailor, slants it wide [*lui donne une grande obliquité*] so it gets two or more currents" (p. 207).

The obliquity of the *toile* or text, the woven thing, suspended between two or more currents, introduces further divisions. Between the realms of lead (what falls straight, *un fil à plomb*) and gold (the sun), lies the infinite diversification of textiles. The spider, something between mother and machine, secretes a cloud from her *filières* or *mamelons:* "From the bottom of its stomach, four spinnerets or nipples, able to extend or withdraw (in the fashion of a telescope), squirt forth, in their motion, a very small cloud which grows from minute to minute" (p. 207). The substance, threaded through a *filière* or screw-plate, a *mamelon* or breast, might appear to be one thread but it is actually a cord twisted from "four thousand threads," variable in consistency and strength. Certain stickier fibers are used for the warp; others, a tough cotton, for instance, for the egg's cocoon. The slightly digressive metaphor of the sailor is again harnessed to the technical code of weaving, and the reader is given a detailed demonstration of the process. One forgets that "she" represents the body of an animal and reads (obliquely) the gestures of a woman explaining how to operate her loom.

Quand elle a fourni un jet suffisant de fils pour entreprendre la toile, d'un point élevé elle se laisse glisser et dévide son écheveau. Elle y reste suspendue, et de suite remontant au point de départ à l'aide de son petit cordage, elle se porte vers un autre point, et continue traçant ainsi une série de rayons qui partent tous du même centre.

La chaîne ourdie, elle s'occupe à faire la trame en croisant le fil. Courant de rayon en rayon, elle touche chacun de ses filières qui y attachent le fil circulaire. Le tout n'est pas un tissu serré, mais un véritable filet, de telle proportion géométrique que toutes les mailles du cercle sont toujours de même grandeur. [Pp. 207–8]

(When she has furnished a sufficient spurt of thread to start the web, she slides off a top point and unwinds her skein. She stops, suspended, and quickly ascending back up to the starting point with the help of her little cordage, she moves to another point and continues tracing in the same way a series of spokes all taking off from the same center.

The warp finished, she applies herself to making the woof by crossing the thread. Running from spoke to spoke, she touches them with her spinnerets each time, attaching the circular thread. The whole is not a close-knit fabric, but a true net with such geometric proportions that every link of the circle is always the same size.)

The web's texture, the intricate blending of spokes like sun rays widening on a circular axis, describes Michelet's own writing: neither the apparent cloudiness or indivisible thread, a long line (*fil* of the argument), made of thousands of fibers, moves in and around itself, measured in symmetry, constructing chains (*mailles*) that create the illusion of a circle and the whole artifice hung, out of kilter, in the air. The final design is not a *tissu serré* (tight weave), an opaque cloth, but *un véritable filet* (a true net-work).[12]

[12] Judgments of Michelet's style have been astonishingly varied, as if he were a Dr. Jekyll/Mr. Hyde writer. Lucien Refort, in an extensive, conventional study of the historian's style, divides it chronologically into three groups, which have, oddly enough, probably influenced

This part of the chapter begins to retrieve images left incomplete in the very beginning section, to "explain" them, to keep rounding them out. The *jet suffisant* reminds one of the maternal references still only partly developed—the *mamelons, poche des eaux*, and *cordier*'s sack. It was back in the beginning of the chapter that Michelet asked us to suspend judgment—"Do not look at her features, but at the finished product of her art"—and now he answers our anticipation by proving the near perfection of the web. The chapter "L'Araignée, L'Industrie, Le Chômage," following on the heels of an ecstatic parade of "insect arts," does, after all, fit into the book's greater project. In the previous chapter, Michelet was dazzled by the brilliant insect colors and by the form and structure of their bodies and their products, which could even provide models for human ornamental and architectural techniques. Under the microscope he found that wings revealed "unexpected designs, sometimes vegetable curves, slight branching, sometimes striated, angular figures . . ."

later critical tastes. Refort implicitly prefers the early "poet" of the *Moyen Age* in the *Histoire de France* and of the first sections in the *Histoire de la Révolution française;* after that, the "polemicist" invades the poet; and finally, in *Les Temps modernes* the "sectarian" begins a definitive decline (*L'Art de Michelet dans son oeuvre historique (jusqu'en 1867*), Paris; Champion, 1923, p. 21). Refort criticizes Michelet's disruptive style: "His sentence gives one the impression of not having been, from the beginning, thought out and organized as a whole but rather as consecutive elements added together while the thought developed, each one joining onto the one preceding somehow or another" (p. 109). Charles Bruneau, in "L'Epoque réaliste," vol. XIII, *Histoire de la langue française*, ed. Ferdinand Brunot (Paris, 1953), also saw a similar development in Michelet from "sincere" writer to pure rhetorician: "Going too far, the historian ceases to be that man who revived the past, and is only an author calculating his effects" (p. 179). Michelet admitted to the Goncourt brothers that he thought "with pen in hand," but also impressed upon them how important it was to correct the *écriture émue* of a first version. In my own study of the manuscript of *La Montagne*, I have come across both examples: passages almost unreadable with corrections and deletions and moments of what look like writing with ease, if not copies from another worksheet.

(pp. 191–92). The circle was always a magical figure for Michelet, and the spider's web of intricate proportions approached the ideal, something abstract artists would try to re-create with compass and ruler.

At first, the adjectival *concentrée et circulaire* added to the spider's pejorative portrait as pure stomach. Anyone familiar with Michelet's work will, however, suspect a reversal of value, since the circular sea urchin and crab were enviable for the same reasons:

> Cette toile, sortie d'elle, vivante et vibrante, est bien plus qu'un instrument, c'est une partie de son être. Circulaire elle-même de forme, l'araignée semble s'étendre en ce cercle et prolonger les filaments de ses nerfs aux fils rayonnants qu'elle ourdit. C'est au centre de sa toile qu'elle a sa plus grande force pour l'attaque et pour la défense. Hors de là elle est timide; une mouche la ferait reculer. Cette toile est à la fois pour elle un télégraphe électrique qui sent le tact le plus léger, lui révèle la présence d'un gibier imperceptible, presque impondérable; et en même temps, comme elle est quelque peu visqueuse, elle lui retient cette proie, retarde même et empêche de dangereux ennemis. [P. 208]

> (This web, growing out of her, alive and trembling, is much more than an instrument, it is a part of her being. Circular in form herself, the spider seems to reach out into the circle, prolonging the filaments of her nerves as the spokes of thread she weaves. It is at the center of her web that she has the greatest offensive and defensive force. Outside of that area she is timid; a fly would make her cringe. First, the web is for her an electric telegraph, sensitive to the slightest touch and able to reveal the presence of her game, almost imperceptible, barely imaginable; and, at the same time, since it is slightly viscous, the web also holds her prey for her, or even slows down and impedes dangerous enemies.)

Metonymy, of which Michelet is fond ("*la maison, c'est l'être*"), operates, in the end, the spider's supreme metamorphosis. This particular tack used to transform beast to beauty is again linguistically motivated: *araignée* literally comes from the form *araneat* (what is "spidered") rather than the animal itself (*Dictionnaire de la langue française*, I). Otherwise, the older *aragne* (used by La Fontaine) would have survived. The viscous silver design is a manifestation of the same being as the round, repulsive body. It is as if the fine nerves—a quality the spider has in common with all Michelet's superior females—were exteriorized into a web. The insect wears his skeleton outside as his house, his coat of armor, his bedizened robe; the spider wears her nerves and is metamorphosed herself into a star (*fils rayonnants*). Michelet has redefined the spider by dramatically switching the tonality of the word *cercle*. And yet this switch has been a matter of careful gradation, a metaphorical journey that has proceeded from morpheme to morpheme. *Fil* (*fileuse*, *filature*) has grown into *toile* through the mediation of *filet*, the links, or *mailles du cercle*. *Filaments*, the final addition to this cluster of *fil*-formed words,[13] has spread into *toile-étoile*. If this were Hugo, the next step would be: "Car Dieu, de l'araignée, avait fait le soleil" (For God, from the spider, made the sun) ("Puissance Egale Bonté," *La Légende des siècles*). But Michelet is not halfway through his paragraph before the sour note is sounded, the relentless ambiguity let in. When Michelet's spider is in the center of its web, unlike Hugo's tarantula-Satan, the gesture is one of imminent attack or defense. The clash of codes that opened the chapter returns, only heightened, and the pejorative connotation of circle reasserts itself. The spider is a hunter who must watch for her game, seize her prey, and she is also part of a highly evolved technical society where messages are sent by telegraph.

The chapter starts its descent by sharply delineating the

[13] Whitman also calls the spider's thread a "filament": "A noiseless patient spider, / . . . / It launch'd forth filament, filament, filament, out of itself,/Ever unreeling them, ever tirelessly speeding them" (*Leaves of Grass*).

dialectics of the original metaphorical proposal (Nature/Culture), by drawing conclusions and generalizing them until the result seems all-engulfing:

Tout vit de proie. La nature va se dévorant elle-même, mais la proie n'est pas toujours achetée et méritée par une industrie patiente, qui mérite d'être respectée. Aucun être cependant plus que celui-ci n'est le jouet du sort. Comme tout bon travailleur, elle lui fournit double prise, et son oeuvre et sa personne. Une infinité d'insectes, le meurtrier carabe, la demoiselle, élégante et magnifique assassine, n'ont que leurs corps et leurs armes, et passent joyeusement leur vie à tuer. D'autres ont des asiles sûrs, faciles à défendre, où ils craignent peu de dangers. L'araignée des champs n'a ni l'un ni l'autre avantage. Elle est dans la position de l'industriel établi, qui par sa petite fortune, mal garantie, attire et tente la cupidité ou l'insulte. [Pp. 209–10]

(Everything lives on prey. Nature moves on by devouring herself; but prey is not always purchased and earned through patient industry, which ought to be respected. Nothing, however, is more the plaything of fate than the spider. Like any good worker, she is worth a double catch, both her work and person. An infinite number of insects, the murderous carabus beetle, the dragonfly, an elegant and refined assassin, have only their bodies and weapons and joyously spend their lives killing. Others have safe places, easy to defend, where there are few dangers to fear. The field spider has neither of these advantages. She is in the position of the established industrialist, who by his small fortune, poorly guaranteed, attracts greed or insult, makes them tempting.)

The first sentence is a knell; how different from the winding syntax of the sentence tracing Michelet's edenic, star-scaped reverie.[14] The reflexive construction of "*la nature va se dévorant*" takes up where "*elle s'épuise pour se refaire*" left off. The text reinforces the fatality beyond anatomy, that of

[14] Edmund Wilson was struck by what he recognized as a sharp, more cursory vigor in Michelet's "late style": "Here Michelet's chief literary vice, a kind of romantic verbiage, had entirely faded away; the influence of Tacitus, from his earliest reading one of Michelet's great admirations, seems to assert itself. Here he anatomizes politics

society (and perhaps history), which is now so intimately wrapped up with the movements of the universe as to be indistinguishable from them. The sentence "prey is not always purchased and earned through patient industry" refers directly to the spider whose hard work has not been justly rewarded. The double code, society/nature, makes us immediately interpret the outburst against the carabus beetle and dragonfly and against those who escape the fray as explicit social satire. Two classes are exempt from the worry of work and reward: hired soldiers and freeloaders, *rentiers* living off their pensions. In contrast, the spider is caught like a worker whose factory shuts down, or like a small manufacturer whose capital cannot carry him far enough and whose profits are slim.

Such a close social analogy represents a considerable development from the first spiders—primitive hunters of the forest, simple artisans, and the solitary spinner of some medieval castle tower or cellar. The first spiders emerged from the vagueness of time: the critic can more or less fix a date corresponding to Michelet's childhood for the appearance of the domestic spider, but Michelet offers no such date. He would as soon leave us with the impression of early civilization whose history is legend and myth. But when the garden spiders catch his attention, Michelet assigns them a historical situation: 1840. And as the chapter progresses, so does civilization until France is in the midst of an accomplished Industrial Revolution. In 1840, France had not developed to the extent of Great Britain. The garden spiders could still be suspended in a period of benign paternalism, when "contracts" could be informally worked out to everyone's advantage.

Michelet knew, however, that this could not last. He had been to England in 1834 and seen horrors that awoke again the trauma of his childhood—*chômage*. Viallaneix captures this moment of both terrible memory and foresight: "[The trip]

---

and intrigue in a style which grows more and more incisive and terse and with a caustic coldness like Stendhal's" (*To the Finland Station*, p. 30).

brutally reveals to this son of an artisan the servitude of the industrial civilization. Considering the condition of workers as Michelet precociously knew it under the Empire, nothing was worse than unemployment" (*La Voie royale*, p. 40).

Le Peuple (1846) was Michelet's prophetic cry to France that all classes would be equally dehumanized and demoralized by a materialistic society (his view of mutually dependent classes is not as dialectical as Hegel's master/slave but reminiscent of its fatalism). Michelet (unlike Marx), however, divided his sympathies between the proletariat and the small merchant and manufacturing class (petite bourgeoisie). The small businessman, it seemed to him, was particularly doomed—and he perhaps had risked the most: "The small factory owner thinks he is launched; he pushes, shoves, runs down men and things, workers and machines; the industrial Bonaparte of 1820 reappears for a moment; then he is weighed down, goes under, must sell at a loss" (*Le Peuple*, p. 84). By the time Michelet wrote his chapter for *L'Insecte*—he documents it to the day, 15 May 1857—France's textile industry under the Second Empire was at last able to compete with England's: the era of the small *fabricant* was fading, and large companies became more profitable.

Michelet then expands the bestiary of the hunt while elaborating a more complicated economic hierarchy:

Le lézard d'en bas, l'écureuil d'en haut, donnent la chasse au faible chasseur. L'inerte crapaud lui darde sa langue visqueuse qui le colle et l'immobilise. C'est le bonheur de l'hirondelle, dans son cercle gracieux, d'enlever sans se déranger l'araignée et la toile, et tous les oiseaux la considèrent comme une grand friandise ou une excellente médecine. Il n'est pas jusqu'au rossignol, fidèle, comme les grands chanteurs, à une certaine hygiène, qui, de temps en temps, ne s'ordonne, pour purgatif, une araignée. [P. 210]

(The lizard from below, the squirrel from above hunt down the frail hunter. A motionless toad snaps out his viscous tongue that glues it to the spot and paralyzes it. The swallow, circling gracefully overhead, is delighted to carry off both spider and web without much effort; and all the birds consider her a rich delicacy or excellent medicine. There is not even a nightingale, faithfully following, like all great singers, a certain regimen, who, from time to time, does not prescribe a spider for himself as a laxative.)

The undercurrent of the socioeconomic code has been so thoroughly established by this point in the text that Michelet does not need to make his metaphor explicit. Diderot, whose relentless dance and pantomime ("*la grand branle de la terre*") in *Le Neveu de Rameau* strikingly resembles Michelet's schema, enumerates each analogy. Michelet invites us to use our imaginations. The lizard and squirrel are competitors on the same vertical scale with the spider; the lizard is perhaps another *fabricant* who snaps up the same orders; the squirrel, a larger enterprise that corners the market. The toad evokes the government, which alone has the power to paralyze by taxes or by decree. The most sublime hypocritical roles are reserved for the swallow and nightingale—the creditor and the usurer. The swallow was the spider's archenemy in La Fontaine's fable: the scene is almost synonymous with Michelet's except that La Fontaine's impenitent spider—a *filandère* or spinner (La Fontaine carries the word play one farther)—is punished for her egotism:

> Ainsi, d'un discours insolent,
> Se plaignait l'Araignée autrefois tapissière,
> Et qui, lors étant filandière,
> Prétendait enlacer tout insecte volant.
>
> . . .
>
> La pauvre Aragne n'ayant plus
> Que la tête et les pieds, artisans superflus
> Se vit elle-même enlevée.
> L'Hirondelle, en passant, emporta toile, et tout. . . . [15]
>
> [*Fables,* X, vi]

[15] Using speech with an insolent ring,
The spider bred choler, though once court embroiderer—
Now a mere speck in her swaying snare
Woven for what she could trap on the wing.

. . .

When the element of fable surfaces in the *Histoire de France*, the swallow signifies death or a change of ministers; the web is swept away in one fell swoop: "Outside, this grand system of alliances, this web tediously built, taken away in one blow" (XI, 134).

Free indirect discourse depicts the commentary of the two stuffed shirt birds, the sparrow recommending in falsetto a spider as a "*grande friandise ou une excellente médecine*," the nightingale confiding, in turn, his health's delicacy, his need for a *purgatif*. And yet they are both sinister: *chanteur* suggests blackmail, and *cercle gracieux* conjures up the hawk's flight pattern or crows hovering over the bed of the dying. The play *Les Corbeaux* was a symptom of the nineteenth century's obsession with money-grabbers. Michelet's little comedy combines humor with a strangely personal tone of bitterness. He had identified so closely with the lonely spider, the hard worker, that surely he felt the bile rise when he met again the figures out of the past who symbolized his family's ruin: their L'Heureux or Gobseck–Vatard. How different is the nightingale of *L'Insecte* from the *artiste* of *L'Oiseau* who sings sorrowfully at dusk and trembles in fear at night. But, ultimately, it is a matter of perspective in the round dance, the "*pantomime des gueux*."

As if the atmosphere of fatality were not heavy enough, Michelet brings up anatomy for one last time:

> Ne fût-elle gobée elle-même, si l'instrument de son métier périt, c'est la même chose. Que la toile soit défaite coup sur coup, le jeûne un peu prolongé la met hors d'état de fournir du fil, et bientôt elle meurt de faim. Elle est constamment serrée dans ce

---

> The souring spinner, groaning like Job,
> Merely got head and feet; but never worked, so was one to rob.
> Our swallow on a certain raid
> Carried off flies in silk of the spiderweb,
> With the spider dangling like a fob.
> ["The Spider and the Swallow," *The Fables of La Fontaine*, tr. Marianne Moore, New York, 1954, p. 243]

cercle vicieux: pour filer, il faut manger; pour manger, il faut filer. Ce fil, c'est pour elle celui de la Parque, celui de la destinée. [P. 210]

(Whether she is gulped down herself or not, if the instrument of her trade is destroyed, it is all the same. When the web is torn down time after time, a slightly longer fast makes it impossible for her to produce thread, and soon she starves. She is forever being enclosed in the vicious circle: to spin, one must eat; to eat, one must spin. This thread for her is the thread of the Three Fates, the thread of destiny.)

At the beginning of the chapter, the image of the belly—with just so much substance to spin—suggested a circle: the rhetorical device used was epanalepsis. Here the word *vicieux* (vicious) is pronounced for the first time, although, as usual, we have heard it coming on slowly and softly. Before, the fabric was not so closely woven; now the net tightens. The phrase following *vicieux*, called antimetabole or *antimetamorphosis* (repetition of words, in successive clauses, in reverse grammatical order), linguistically conveys paralysis as closely as possible. The words cancel one another out: "*pour filer, il faut manger; pour manger, il faut filer.*" The text seems to stand still for the second time: it stopped first in the epiphany of communion when boy and spider met, and now it turns in place at a point of despair. The spider and narrator find themselves in a trap that, although it stalls the text for a moment, must be resolved if only by the very narrative necessity of moving on.

Michelet finds a mythological figure to express, and thereby to overcome, the predicament, but it is, as always, an ambiguous one. The perfect solution would be to substitute *Parque* (also the name of a particular spider) in another one of Michelet's magic formulas: "*L'homme est son propre Prométhée*" (man is his own Prometheus); "*La femme est sa propre Parque*" (woman is her own Fate). If we could each measure and cut the *filet de nos jours* (thread of life), our freedom would be absolute—we would be God. But though we spin our own "days," make our own lives and our very beings, we are constantly fighting Fate. Michelet's tone vacillates in this passage between a statement of courage, which emphasizes man's creativity as curse and survival, and a jovially sinister irony that both undermines and rises above ideology.

After such uncomfortable philosophical speculations, the text turns abruptly to an anecdote: "We once tried the experiment of tearing down a spider's web three times in a row" (p. 210). What sounds like a royal we, one realizes later, refers to Michelet and Athénaïs. The narrator passes from a previously intense involvement to the statements of an apparently professional naturalist. Although Michelet, like the spider and worker, must have recognized his place on the wheel of fate, he also began to take his distance. He could stand back and see the whole system turn. It was then perhaps easier to take on the informative voice that echoes the one at the chapter's beginning. But Michelet's distance does not quite succeed. As if out of nervousness and guilt for this distance, he resorts to all the old saccharine codes to make the reader feel for a female figure: "Three things combine to wear her down: her zeal for unceasing work, her nervous and exacerbated sensitivity, finally, her double respiratory system." The hyperbole will lead to the inevitable sigh, and whatever the subject, it will be discovered to have a soul . . . or this time, a heart: "Just by seeing its movements, you know it is more than an insect; the flow of life must rush through in a rapid circulation, the heart must beat differently than in the housefly or butterfly" (p. 211). But the outcome—operatic as usual—is interestingly curious:

Advantage, but danger. The insect braves with impunity the unhealthy odors of the putrid swamp. The spider cannot hold up. Suddenly struck, she falls into convulsions, trembles, and dies. I saw it one day in Lucerne; the chloroform, whose effects the stag beetle endured for ten days before dying, immediately, upon first contact, struck down the spider. She was basically strong, and I watched her eat a gnat. I wanted to observe her so I poured a drop on her. The effect was terrible. A human suffocation could not have been more awful. She fell back, got up again, then collapsed. Nothing would help her up and the joints of her limbs gave way. There was a particularly pathetic thing about it, in this supreme moment her breasts were fertile. In the agony of death, her mammillae let out a little cloud of webbing leading you to believe she was going to keep on working even as she died. [Pp. 211–12]

The passage turns on the familiar dialectic of vulnerability or sensitivity, a quality characterizing the highest form of moral and physical development as well as the point of greatest mortal danger. But this death outdoes even the rape of the ant nymphs in pathos. Again the reader loses the perspective of the animal subject—it is as if Michelet was afraid of the anthropomorphic effect here when he reminds one, before the worst part, that this is, after all, a spider, thus not "real," not a "human suffocation." It doesn't help much; in fact, it only heightens the horror. The modern reader cannot keep Kafka's metamorphosis out of mind—the image of the dying insect touches our deepest fears: lying helpless on one's back, kicking.

Michelet plays for the melodrama; his personified dying animal is a mother. All during the chapter we have been waiting for this obsessively recurrent metaphor to receive more than a passing nod. It comes to the fore, of course, as a "*jolie morte*." She was struck down in her prime. Certainly, the nineteenth-century reader had several vivid models to project upon Michelet's dying spider—Atala, Nana, and especially Julie and Emma. *La Nouvelle Héloïse* stood for motherhood in all its suffering and splendor. When the collapsing spider struggled for her life, she was succumbing in the same exaggerated fashion as Julie. Like Michelet, Rousseau's narrator, M. de Wolmar, looks on in shock and impotence: "Coming into the room, I found her totally out of her mind, unable to see or hear, recognizing no one, rolling about the room wringing her hands and gnawing the chair legs" (Pt. 6, XI). Still, there is not in Rousseau the final touch. We know that at the moment of death anything may come out of the contracting body organs. The black ooze running from Emma's lips, after the arsenic, like chloroform, took its toll, is perhaps the most ghastly example. Michelet intended for the milk seeping from the involuntarily swelling breasts to be sublime, and yet, in the context of the romantic aesthetic, that also means grotesque.

Michelet differs in one crucial way from M. de Wolmar: Michelet killed his female victim. And yet one still has the feeling that it was all out of his control. While intimately identified with the solitary spinner, Michelet could only be helpful to her; even as patron to his garden spiders, he was beneficent. But as naturalist, he finds his subject almost automatically growing cold. And as writer, a writer of history, perhaps he thinks he kills it. His chloroform is ink. His dreams, projects, and prophecies, the repulsive spider he redeems, all fade on the page. It is as if the chapter literally unwinds at the end, as if the cotton cloth decomposes into a thread which is a thousand minute threads, and then a viscous cloud: "I felt very sad and, in the hope that the air would perhaps revive her, I put her on my window sill; but she was no longer herself. I do not know how it happened, it was as if she had disappeared and was nothing more than an anatomical model. Her substance vanished, leaving but a slight shadow. The wind carried it toward the lake" (*L'Insecte*, p. 212). "Explained," "written," she is not herself, but merely the bare imagined outlines. But what was this "self"? A subject appeared, it metamorphosed from one dialectic to the other, from one metaphor, one set of adjectives, through numerous transformations into their opposites.[16] A savage huntress, a monster, became an

[16] Riffaterre studies in some detail the aesthetics of metamorphosis with reference to Hugo and his techniques: "In poetry as a whole, one

artisan, a solitary spinning fairy, an industrial worker, and a small businessman, changing again into one of the three Fates and, finally, into a mother. The puffed, ugly, selfish one turned into a selfless skeleton. The metaphor seems to have run its course. But one has the feeling, because of the lake, which is like an eternally renewable sea for the spider, that the process could start over again, that the rhetoric could continue to hold its own reality.

---

of the most frequent themes of this dynamic becoming is naturally the passage from one form to another, the dissolution of forms. To evoke, for example, a man who is absorbed, assimilated by a hydra (*Travailleurs . . .*), reminds one of the decomposition of Mr. Valdemar in Poe. The theme is, of course, not limited to horror; rather, we are actually dealing with a particular aesthetic created *ad hoc*, that of metamorphosis. . . .

"This technique allows poetry to make use of the pathos peculiar to the transformation scenes of productions with elaborate stage effects. Thus, it dramatizes by accelerating any evolution that would be an imperceptible gradation in nature. Affinities, secret analogies, which reality [*le réel*] hides from view, are revealed by substituting one for another the elements that a fundamentally rational vision would continue to separate. This is the mechanism of metaphor. But metaphor is a transfer that has been completed, a substitution already accomplished: one does not see the revealing steps bringing it together, one sees only the result [*on ne voit du rapprochement révélateur que le résultat*]. Hugo's technique, though, by focusing on the very process of substitution is finally a metaphor in movement [*métaphore en mouvement*], ... it is a tool to probe the *universal analogy;* from image to image, form to form" (*Essais*, pp. 232 and 234). The capacity of a word to transform within its system of associations into its own contradiction suggests, as well as the universal analogy, the total relativity of confusion.

10 Language at Sea: Infinite Motion in Place

L'Oiseau (1856) is followed closely by *L'Insecte* (1857), but four years separate *L'Insecte* from *La Mer*. More than a lapse, this is a passage into another stage. Michelet's narrative voice is changing. The crisis and agitation of the 1850s were subsiding; the disappointments and serious health setbacks had been reckoned with. In the *Histoire de France*, the violent days of 1793, the vigorous years of the Renaissance were over. A true exile began, the exile shared in spirit with Victor Hugo and Edgar Quinet, the slow receding of the self from everything it had once depended upon. No more classes, no limelight, letters instead of students: this alone would have been a difficult adjustment, but family and closest friends seemed to be leaving, too. Alfred Dumesnil, Michelet's son-in-law and protégé, and the younger circle of friends around him, felt awkward about the historian's second marriage, and after the death of his daughter Adèle, there was little or no reason for more than a formal relationship. The Quinets too were personally and ideologically drifting away from their former colleague and friend. Michelet's *Journal* becomes more and more devoted to the body, his and his wife's. But as life draws in around him and Athénaïs, his vision enlarges; from the moralistic counseling of *L'Amour* and *La Femme*, Michelet turns to more openly mythic subjects, *La Sorcière* (1862), *La Bible de l'humanité* (1864), and to the cosmos, *La Mer* (1861) and *La Montagne* (1868).

These last books are excessive in their ideological persistence.

The tripartite design—statement, opposition, return of statement; paradise, fall, regain—forces, each time, a moral comeback: in *La Sorcière*, the grandiose early witch dissipates into false fragments of herself and yet she remains the model for the future; in *La Bible de l'humanité*, the religions of light give way to those of the dark but the original strain will emerge again. In *La Mer*, Michelet literally begins with the genesis of the sea and primitive man, encounters the modern betrayal of man and sea, but discerns signs of reunion, promoted in the last chapter, called *vita nuova*. No longer a question of "revaluation," the scene is one of a cosmic epic battle. Michelet's previous nature books essentially were to present one protagonist, one Insect, one Bird, but this is difficult since the diversity of the species demands that a writer deal with them separately as frigate, petrel, carabus beetle, domestic spider. But the sea can stand on its own as a general concept. It has a long literary history that practically ignores distinctions like Black, Mediterranean, Atlantic. . . . And this tradition, initiated by Homer, almost unanimously condemns the sea. A man venturing out on the sea because he had to survive by fishing, or because he was condemned to wandering (Ulysses), was punished with the greatest of misfortunes: "The sea, in fact, is that state of barbaric vagueness and disorder out of which civilization has emerged and into which, unless saved by the effort of gods and men, it is always liable to relapse. It is so little of a friendly symbol that the first thing which the author of the Book of Revelation notices in his vision of the new heaven and earth at the end of time is that 'there was no more sea.' "[1] The romantics were to change the tonality of tradition. Hugo, in the last line of *Les Travailleurs de la mer*, proclaims the stark difference: "*Il n'y a plus rien que la mer*" (There is no longer anything but sea).

Michelet and Hugo had to start, nonetheless, with the preconceived Homeric image of the sea: "Its meaning appeals

[1] W. H. Auden, *The Enchafèd Flood* (New York, 1967), pp. 6–7.

naturally to the imagination as a huge sterile and deserted surface; Homer's *pontos atrugetos*, the *vastum mare* in Latin, the Scandinavian's vast or *voest*, actually referring to the desert . . . also, *maru*, in Sanscrit, means desert" (*Grand Dictionnaire universel du XIXe siècle*, XI). The etymological meaning of *atrugetos* in Greek is linked more precisely with the idea of "unharvested,"[2] but the word actually evolved toward its negative pole "barren." Michelet wanted to cultivate this most extreme point of the definition before operating his shift in meaning:

L'eau, pour tout être terrestre, est l'élément non respirable, l'élément de l'asphyxie. Barrière fatale, éternelle, qui sépare irrémédiablement les deux mondes. Ne nous étonnons pas si l'énorme masse d'eau qu'on appelle la mer, inconnue et ténébreuse dans sa profonde épaisseur, apparut toujours redoutable à l'imagination humaine.

Les Orientaux n'y voient que le gouffre amer, la *nuit de l'abîme*. Dans toutes les anciennes langues, de l'Inde à l'Irlande, le nom de la mer a pour synonyme ou analogue le *désert* et la *nuit*.

Grande tristesse de voir tous les soirs le soleil, cette joie du monde et ce père de toute vie, sombrer, s'abîmer dans les flots. C'est le deuil quotidien du monde, et spécialement de l'Ouest. [*La Mer*, pp. 3–4]

(Water, for anyone on land, is an unbreathable element, the element of suffocation. Fatal and eternal barrier, irrevocably separating two worlds. It is not surprising if the huge mass of water we call the sea, unknown and dark in its deep thickness, has always been frightening to the human imagination.

The Orientals see in it only bitter depths, the *night of the abyss*. In all ancient languages, from India to Ireland, the name of the sea is synonymous with or analogous to *desert* and *night*.

Such sadness every night to see the sun, joy of the world and father of all life, sink and be swallowed up by the waters. It is the daily mourning of the world, and especially of the West.)

[2] *Atrugetos*, the negation of a root which suggests the harvest of the grain crop, literally means "unharvested."

The use of repetition, tautology, accumulation, and hyperbole leaves us with the feeling, shared by the first men on earth, that nothing can change this almost sacred separateness of the sea. Repetition sometimes represents slight variation (*fatale / éternelle; inconnue / ténébreuse*), sometimes precision, and thus gradation in intensity (*l'élément non respirable*, *l'élément de l'asphyxie*), but often it is the simple accumulation of synonyms: *gouffre* (depths) / *abîme* (abyss). Several modifiers add nothing but emphasis and exaggeration to the sense of their nouns: *énorme masse* (huge mass), *profonde épaisseur* (deep thickness). Finally, to complete his purposely overbearing image, Michelet evokes a scene that harks back to the time when words were a sensory and emotive experience, when the sea was not a concept but the daily disappearance of the sun. According to Vico, this was when all men were poets. The latter draws upon the same example of "night" understood literally as sun-sinking-into-the-sea to illustrate the phenomenon of primitive language: "*The ancient Germans*, said Tacitus, *understood night as the sun which passes under the sea from West to East*" (*Oeuvres choisies de Vico*, tr. Michelet, Paris, n.d., p. 382). Sea, therefore, was not yet an arbitrary sign, but a metaphor before the fall into catachresis, or at least as close as any verbal translation could come to experience.

Yet "desert" and "sea" with their particular systems of associated commonplaces are both the same and opposite:

> As places of freedom and solitude the sea and the desert are symbolically the same. In other respects, however, they are opposites; e.g. the desert is the dried-up place, i.e., the place where life has ended, the Omega of temporal existence. Its first most obvious characteristic is that nothing moves; the second is that everything is surface and exposed. No soil, no hidden spring. The sea, on the other hand, is the Alpha of existence, the symbol of potentiality.[3]

[3] Auden, p. 19.

Michelet's task, then, will be to engineer not simply a shift in value, but the linguistic containment of opposites into one, and of the many into one: to find a single image or, better yet, a word that would embrace the Alpha and Omega and everything in between.

The Homeric code is, therefore, slowly subverted in the text until it becomes a kind of skeletal sketch for Michelet's own vision, characterized by light, movement, and life, instead of darkness, stasis, and death. Michelet, whose true predecessor is probably Buffon, immediately becomes the model proponent of the revised "life-giving" bodies of water.[4] Yet only by magic can opposites be successfully dissolved, and usually it is a question of the clear triumph of one over the other: "The drama is not the union of opposites but the suppression of opposition, by the transformation or distinction of one of the antithetical terms."[5] As a way of refusing a solution, Michelet's imagination—and language play—compensates by a heady verbal proliferation. The sea does not deny its night, but its heavens glow with the various antics of live constellations or any form and matter suggestive of shine: "Bronze crabs, brilliant sea anemone, snowy porcelain-shells, golden eels, undulating whorls, everything lives and moves" (*La Mer*, pp. 107–8). Finally, this half-world lingering between *Nox* and *Lux* resorts, for its definition, to verbal compromise. Michelet extracts the adjective from his more Homeric phrase *mer ténébreuse* and reinserts it into his own personal concept: *fécondes ténèbres* (fertile shadows). The night of the abyss (*nuit d'abîme*) is spun around on the axis of abyss to form a new expression, *abîme de vie*, without the negative connota-

[4] *Le Grand Dictionnaire universel du XIXe siècle* quotes Michelet's statement: "The fertile Sea vivifies the earth with its vapors." In Littré's *Dictionnaire de la langue française*, Buffon represents the same point of view: "[The sea] is not a cold and sterile element, it is a new empire as rich, as peopled, as the former one [the land]" (II, part one).

[5] Jean Cohen, "Théorie de la figure," *Communications*, no. 16 (1970), p. 14.

tions of something black and bottomless. A final grouping, derived from the earlier *profonde épaisseur* (deep thickness), hesitates between antithesis and a kind of miraculous logic—*épaisseur transparente* (transparent thickness)[6]—for such depth as the ocean's cannot help sooner or later but fade into opacity.

Nevertheless, Michelet still wants to find one word or syntagma that will state the contraries of the sea. Antithesis with maximum tension might compel a fusion of meanings, so Michelet falls back on the oxymoron. The sea is verbally captured as a *flot solidifié* (solidified flow). Whereas *épaisseur transparente* is imaginable, *flot solidifié* is by definition impossible. No contortion of associations can make noun and modifier meet. Only in the linearity of a text can they stand side by side. But oxymoron is still not union. In the chapter "La Mer de lait" Michelet thinks he finds single-word possibilities for embodying the impossible couple. *Mucus*, for instance, includes the opposites beginning/end, inorganic/animal, solid/liquid: "What you best come to understand in the *mucus* of seawater is that it is at the same time an end and a beginning" (p. 114). Variations on the root *gelée* (*eau gélatinisée*, *gélatineuse*, *la gélatine;* cognates of jelly, gelatin) also express the lingering linguistic moment between life and death that is the sea. *Gelée* carries in French both the positive and negative nuances of its etymology, from *gelare:* to freeze and to congeal. *Gelées végétales* or *animales* were used in earlier times as medicine or had medicines added to them and were therefore considered beneficent, whereas frost, the other meaning of *gelée*, can deaden any organism. Gelatin, the thickening agent in jelly, is still used in drugs. The semisolid substance, *gelée*,

[6] "Dans ses *fécondes ténèbres*, la mer peut sourire elle-même des destructeurs qu'elle suscite, bien sûre d'enfanter encore plus. . . . Je parle du monde infini d'atomes vivants, d'animaux microscopiques, véritable *abîme de vie* qui fermente dans son sein. . . . La mer, dans son *épaisseur transparente*, doit en être, ici et là, fortuitement illuminée. Elle-même a un certain éclat, je ne sais quelle demi-lueur qu'on observe sur les poissons et vivants et morts" (*La Mer*, pp. 107–8, my emphasis).

was once even imagined, like *mucus*, to be a kind of original amorphic germ in the creation of higher life forms. The nineteenth-century Littré *Dictionnaire de la langue française* refers to Bonnet's *Lettres diverses* as its source for this more fanciful extended definition: "Such was the primary force of the majestic oak and powerful rhinoceros; they were in the beginning only a drop of jelly and even less so" (I, second part).

Michelet seems to be looking for what Freud called primal words with an antithetical sense–whose very concept has, in the twentieth century, been called into question.[7] In *La Mer*, he has lost patience with the slow-moving metaphor that needs a chapter for completion. There are hints of the same inspiration that infused the passage on the spider, but they are dropped or scattered in *La Mer* over a series of barely related pages. The metaphor of seawater sustains a gamut of material possibilities that progress in a logic expanding with the space of the sentence: "How much more you have this impression when you find, in their early stages of formation, the yellow-white ribbons where the sea is working on the soft beginnings of its solid fucus algae, called laminaria, which upon turning brown achieve finally the solidity of hides and leather" (pp. 112–13). Under the skin, inside the diaphanous coat, hidden

[7] "It is therefore *a priori* improbable—and a close look confirms it—that these languages, however archaic they are supposed to be, escape the principle of contradiction assigning to one expression two mutually exclusive or contrary notions. . . . Suppose a language exists where "large" and "small" are both said in the same way, this would be a language where the distinction between "large" and "small" has literally no sense and where the category of dimension does not exist and not a language that includes a contradictory expression of dimension" (Benveniste, *Problèmes de linguistique générale*, p. 82). Freud's own article, "Antithetical Sense of Primal Words," is based upon the ideas of the German philologist Karl Abel: "If everything that we know is viewed as a transition from something else, every experience must have a double meaning, or else for every meaning there must be two names" (Freud, *On Creativity and the Unconscious*, ed. Benjamin Nelson, New York, 1958, p. 60).

in a bulbous drop of water, is a world of activity, but what interests Michelet is names, more than appropriate images: "This drop, will it be an infusorian, the primitive monad that, by wriggling and vibrating, soon becomes a vibrion? . . . This drop, what will come of it, will be the vegetal thread, the soft silky down that you would not take for a living being and already is no less than the firstborn hair of a young goddess, a strand of hair with the sense of touch, expressing so well: *Venus'-hair?* This is not a fable, it is natural history" (pp. 116–17). From the mystical drop of water whirls into life a cilium that anticipates the coming of its mistress, Venus, as out of a shell or foam. This hair, the goddess's herald, waits patiently, sublime, but also somewhat grotesque because, after all, disembodied. It resembles Lautréamont's fantastic hair of God: "The stick was, then, not made of wood! I noticed next it rolled up and back out with the ease of an eel. . . . I began to watch it more and more closely and saw it was a hair!"[8] Michelet does not arrive at his hair through visual association, but by verbal links. The inorganic drop of water begins to show capacities for life as the duplicitous *monade*, a word whose meanings allow it to hover between inorganic and organic realms. Monad, a philosophical term, can refer to the irreducible, elemental unit of any larger system (as in Leibniz). Meaning "unity" in Pythagorean terms, it was, for Democritus, more precisely an atom propelled with eternal movement and, thus, the symbolic origin of all nature. *Monade* is, at the same time, the name of an infusorian. From *monade*, the form modulates into a vibrion, a bacillus providing the elusive link to the next step in the shaping of life—the hair.[9] But the final

[8] *Les Chants de Maldoror*, p. 147.

[9] Hair is a conventional image used to describe microscopic plant life, bacteria, or algae. When passages from Michelet are compared with those in Darwin, one finds that almost identical images are used, and yet the comparison only serves to emphasize the final poetic effect of Michelet and the scientific journalism of Darwin: "The water was slightly stained as if by a red dust; and after leaving it for some time

verbal association—after thread, down, and hair—is unmotivated by meaning; a maidenhair fern (Venus'-hair, *cheveu de Vénus*) has no place in a chapter on microscopic algae or *animalcules.* One could surmise that after multiple jumps in creation from microscopic vibrion, a final result might be a fern, but, in this case, the sound of signifiers held priority over semantics.

Michelet cannot hide his nervousness; he does think he has gone too far in pure linguistic gymnastics, so he reassures the reader that everything is strictly scientific: "This is not a fable, it is natural history." The fact is, and he has complained of it in *L'Insecte* as well as in *La Mer*, Michelet has entered a new world where "his" language is not spoken: "Having fallen from the sky to the entrance of the somber realm, in the presence of the mysterious and mute sons of night, what language can I invent?" (*L'Insecte*, p. vi). This world, as his self-consciousness tells us, may be closer to fable, to the legendary times described by Vico, than to natural history.

In reality, Michelet chose the perfect context, in which fable and science merge.[10] The nineteenth century marks the serious scientific discovery of the sea, not only by global exploration, but also in laboratory investigation. Marine biology

---

quiet, a *cloud* collected at the bottom. With a lens, that has one-fourth of an inch focal distance, small hyaline points could be seen darting about with great rapidity and frequently exploding. Examined with a much higher power, their shape was found to be *oval*, and contracted by a ring around the middle, from which line curved little *setae*" (Darwin, *Journal of Researches*, p. 17, my italics).

[10] Whereas I have been more concerned with the ideological breakdown as revealed through Michelet's language searching for its own content, Michel Serres, philosopher and historian of science, whose insights of dynamic structure have passed from mathematics to art, builds a case using both *La Mer* ("Michelet, La Soupe," *Revue de l'histoire littéraire de la France*, Sept.–Oct. 1974, pp. 787–96) and *La Sorcière* (in *Hermès* (*La Communication*, I) Paris, Éditions de Minuit, 1968, pp. 219–32) for Michelet's full comprehension and use of the sciences of his time and of their history.

and zoology were new frontiers. Unimaginable species were showing up every day and had to be named. Sometimes a latinate term would be chosen but more often the scientist, reverting back to the instincts of his primitive forefathers, simply said what the strange creatures looked like. The scientists, like the first poets, could speak only in metaphors: *mer de lait*, *étoile de mer*, *éléphant de mer*, *orient de la perle*, *écumeur de mer*, *fleuves de la mer*, *voies lactées*, *ceinture de Vénus*, *piqueur de pierres*. Coming upon the new vocabulary of the sea was like discovering a rare language of ready-made poetry. And the excitement of names generates, in turn, an entirely different text. Starting in *La Mer* (and continuing in *La Montagne*), Michelet breaks up his chapters into poetic pieces with an important white space (*blanc*, as he indicates in his manuscript) between them. This superficial change reflects the internal splintering energy. Michelet's aesthetic becomes more violent. Either he will collapse two opposing words together or he will let the verbal possibilities explode. A passage is composed of zigzags, leaps, and reversals whose only coherence is the flexible code of language. Such an endeavor (or discovery) brings Michelet closer to Rimbaud, where he belongs. Rimbaud's letter to Demeny echoes Michelet's deepest preoccupation: "He [the poet] is infused with humanity, with *animals* even; he should make his inventions felt, caressed, heard; if what he brings back from *over-there* has a form, he gives it form; if it is formless, he renders it without form [*informe*]. To find a language" (*Oeuvres complètes*, ed. Suzanne Bernard, p. 347). In the context of the sea, whose primitive life, *molle et demi-organisée*, made it the formless state par excellence, Michelet loosens his language and forgoes connections. It is no wonder that the section of chapters, "La Genèse de la mer," that deals with the changing, sometimes amorphous forms of sea beasts from protozoan and polyp to whale and siren is longer than the two last sections, in which man plies the seas, killing its wealth, and people begin to crowd beaches.

The language of the *informe* is put to the test in the chapter on corals, "Fleur de sang" (blood-flower coral, another found metaphor). Readers (and writer perhaps) are pleasantly at a loss while minute inhabitants and geographies file by, transforming as they go. Technical terms are easily scattered among familiar phrases. To plot the metaphoric mélange the reader must proceed from word to word, since almost every one is stylistically marked and resonates with one or more crisscrossing poetic codes: the passage tests our tolerance (and language's) of figurative writing. There is a central metaphorical pattern operating loosely in the larger context of the chapter. The general topic, anthozoans, provides two immediate metaphorical subjects in its etymology: animal/flower (plants, trees). "The soft gelatinous plants . . . seem to want to deceive us, so we think they are animals" (pp. 139–40). A basic dialectical grid is also set up to control ensuing passages, at least minimally: eternity/ephemerality, solid/vapor, straight/curved: "Some have the firmness, the quasi eternity of a tree. The others unfold, then fade, like a flower" (p. 140). Thus some structure does exist, but it is drowned in distracting or fragmenting notions, as exemplified especially in the instance of the alcyonarian.

What Michelet notes about polyps can be applied to his own language: "Each branch holds a world" (p. 144):

Bien autrement variable, le protée des eaux, l'alcyon, prend toute forme et toute couleur. Il joue la plante, il joue le fruit; il se dresse en éventail, devient une haie buissonneuse ou s'arrondit en gracieuse corbeille. Mais tout cela fugitif, éphémère, de vie si craintive, qu'au moindre frémissement tout disparaît, rien ne reste; tout en un moment est rentré au sein de la mère commune. Vous retrouvez la sensitive dans une de ces formes légères; la cornulaire, au toucher, se replie sur elle-même, ferme son sein, comme la fleur sensible à la fraicheur du soir. [P. 140]

(Variable in another way, the proteus of the seas, the alcyonarian polyp, assumes all shapes and colors. It plays the part of a plant or fruit. It stretches up and out into a fan, becomes a bristling hedge, or curves into a graceful basket. But all this, so fleeting and ephemeral, from such a timid thing that it all disappears with the least ripple, nothing is left; in one instant everything returns to the common mother's womb. You also find there a sensitive one among the delicate forms; the cornularia curls up at a touch, shuts its womb like the sensitive flower at the evening's cold approach.)

The opening phrase provides more than an adroit transition; it launches directly into the spirit of the text. The phrase refers back to a description of how the anemone reproduces and, immediately thereafter, "melts," "evaporates." It infers that the *alcyon* will do likewise in its own manner. Yet the phrase also acts as a general introduction, for every individual to follow will be "*bien autrement variable*" from the one just preceding. The appositive, proteus, *protée des eaux*, which acts as a second transition to the true subject of the sentence, *l'alcyon*, should be helpful when it is actually confusing–a false turn before the reader gets his bearings. Proteus seems the perfect analogy in the natural world for the polyp; moreover, he vividly represents Michelet's own quest. Like Aristaeus or Odysseus, when Michelet asks each creature to explain its mystery, he must maintain his grip on the fickle captive throughout its numerable metamorphoses. The problem with using Proteus in this particular context is that *protée* serves as the name for many types of infusorian, similar in shape to polyps but not related to them. Before the reader is given a chance to recognize the main subject, Michelet has already completed one metamorphosis: a coelenterate into a simple protozoan.

Despite initial confusion, the kernel sentence of the opening lines is a simple topic sentence: "*L'alcyon prend toute forme et toute couleur.*" But the one word *alcyon* immediately releases a mythological code because it is spelled the same (in French, not in English) as the word for the imaginary bird Halcyon, which came into being through traditional metamorphosis

(Ovid).[11] *Alcyon* is already encumbered with too many mutually exclusive associations–a protean protozoan, a class of polyps, a bird that rules over calm. The next sentence tells us that a game of high comedy is involved. This *alcyon* is a mime, instead of a divine incarnation. Starting off with generally related objects–plants or fruit–"*il*," the actor, plays the role of a fan, bush, or basket at will. The metaphoric suggestion is produced by the verb (with no effort at eventual resolution into explicit statement as happens with the spider–"*c'est un ouvrier*"). The reflexive verb *se dresser* (straighten, stretch up) and the verb "become" emphasize the transitive state of metamorphosis. "He" is not, like the classical Ovidian notion, changed by *fiat*, but remains in constant motion, going from one form to another. The short repetitions of uninterrupted subject-verb (*il joue . . . il joue*), an unusual pattern for this particular text, builds into the release of a third extended (right-branching) sentence: the alcyonarian expands and swells as the phrasing rounds. *Buissonneuse*, an onomatopoeic modifier for the hedge, is a tautological adjective and serves only as poetic filler. *Gracieuse* echoes *buissonneuse* and continues the function of making the sentence grow slowly in order to heighten the contrast that follows.

The polyp-bloated basket deflates, like a jellyfish or a pompous octopus, into nothing. It beats a hasty retreat to the womb. The effect is comical, as if our impressive Proteus was a child showing off, playing *Matamoros*, swashbuckling his bushes. *Mais* signals the withdrawal, which is quickened by the imperceptible absence of "is"–"But all this, so fleeting. . . ." The ellipsis (common in Michelet) prepares for a forceful,

[11] Halcyone's lover Ceyx was killed at sea. After a dream, she realizes that he is dead and she goes down to the shore to find that his body has washed up on land. In her grief, she throws herself into the sea but is saved by being metamorphosed into the Halcyon Bird. The story is told in Ovid's *Metamorphoses*, Book XI, ll. 731ff.: "She ran along it [a jetty], leaped into the sea— A marvel that she could—and never fell, But seemed to skim the surface, like a bird."

double-verb phrase: "Everything disappears, nothing is left." The intransitive sense of *rentrer* (return)—"tout . . . est rentré au sein"—is stylistically marked because it contrasts with the continuous action of *devenir* and the reflexive verbs. The door of mother's womb has slammed shut. But, though the scene is comic, Michelet offers his usual sympathy. He calls the trembling, timid, basically formless mass "*la sensitive*" as a term of endearment. This affectionate characterization is general enough to cause a kind of merging of all the individuals in the paragraph. *La sensitive* could refer back to the insecure actor at the beginning, but since the same designation fits the *cornulaire*, who also doubles back into the womb, one gets the impression that everything has been the metamorphosis of a creature vaguely called "*la sensitive.*" Michelet cleverly allows the adjectival noun to portray polyp and delicate female before specifying at the end his underlying simile, animals like flowers: "*comme la fleur sensible à la fraîcheur du soir.*" *Cornulaire*, linked through *sensitive* to *alcyon*, is scientifically misleading, since it is not a true equivalent but a genus under the subclass Alcyonaria. Why would Michelet have chosen this word except that it rhymes with *légères* and evokes a cornucopia closing in upon all its fruits and plants, swallowing up the text that made it?

Michelet's discovery of the polyp vocabulary preserves the sea's mystery, while describing it, more successfully than the easy metaphors, *mer de lait* or *cheveu de Vénus*. Although the passage confines itself at first to Alcyonaria, Michelet begins to mix the genera of different classes:

Lorsque d'en haut vous vous penchez au bord des récifs, des bancs de coraux, vous voyez sous l'eau le fond du tapis, vert d'astrées et de tubipores, les fungies moulées en boules de neige, les méandrines historiées de leur petit labyrinthe dont les vallées, les collines, se marquent en vives couleurs. Les cariophylles (ou oeillets) de velours vert, nué[12] d'orange, au bout de leur rameau

[12] *Nué* is correct according to the Hachette and Flammarion

calcaire, pêchent leurs petits aliments en remuant doucement dans l'eau leurs riches étamines d'or. [Pp. 140–41]

(When you lean out over the reefs, the banks of coral, you see under water a carpeted floor, green with tubipora and astraea, you see fungi rolled into snowballs, meandrine narrating their stories in tiny labyrinths whose valleys and hills are the bright areas. Caryophyllia (or carnations), of green velvet blended with orange, from the tip of their chalky poles, are fishing little morsels by slowly waving in the sea their rich stamens of gold.)

Marine microbiology was a young science and the nature of polyps had only recently been confirmed as animal, not vegetable, but surprising headway had already been made. The *polypiers actiniaires* (not related, as Michelet knew, to jellyfish) were said to comprise two "*tribus*":[13]

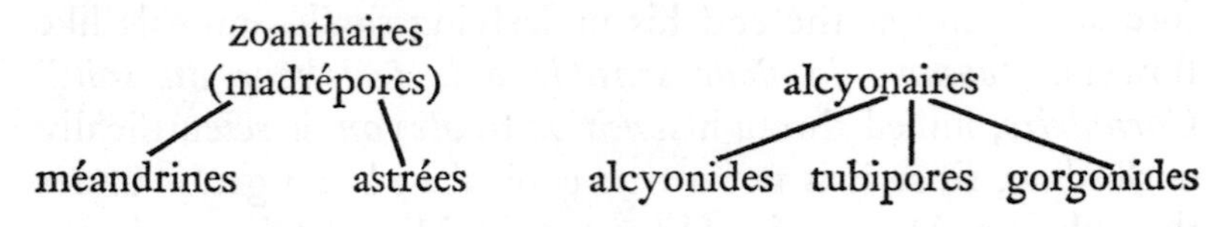

This nineteenth-century grouping largely corresponds to a more complete modern classification:

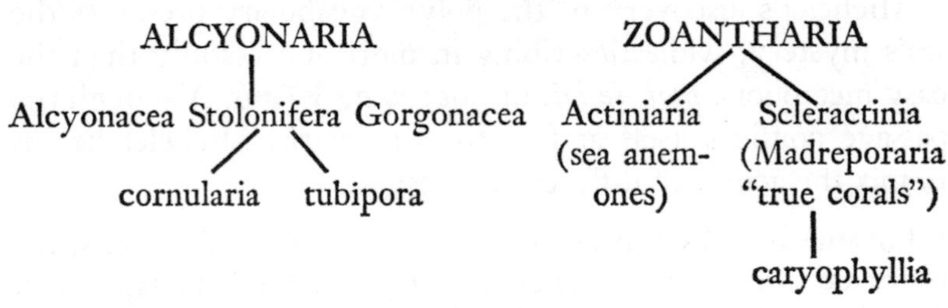

editions of *La Mer*. If this is not a printer's error, Michelet is using, not a noun form for clouds, but the verb *nuer* (to match, blend colors in wools, silks). The proximity of *velours* only partially motivates this unusual usage.

[13] *Le Grand Dictionnaire universel*, vol. XII. In 1727, Peysonnel de-

Michelet cares less for the proper class distinctions than for the evocative names, thus imitating the effect of a foreign language where we catch a phrase here and there and remain content, for the most part, with the phonetic flow.

The metaphorical twists created by the series of names lead literally into a labyrinth. Ironically, Michelet is playing guide, as if we were in a glass-bottom boat and pointing out the corals; he takes a distanced tone, "Vous retrouvez . . . vous vous penchez . . . vous voyez." He is a special guide of the imagination taking the reader through three different fantasies in one sentence. Down on a green carpet, one sees stars (*astrées*), strewn around the organ pipes (*tubipores:* organ-pipe coral) that rise like a sunken cathedral. From here one emerges into a winter scene, for Michelet transforms mushroom coral into snowballs. Finally, the travelers wander off or "meander" into a strange Minoan architecture, reading the history and legends (*méandrines historiées*) of a microscopic populace sculptured in bas-relief against the walls. The already minute world shrinks again, and, squinting into the sculpture, one sees that the rippled forms are actually valleys and hills, a whole new countryside with invisible inhabitants. This one sentence conveys the infinite regression (always an unimaginable grandeur on some scale) of the polyp metropolis, surpassing the bee, ant, or termite cities.

The rest of the passage can be analyzed only in terms of sheer linguistic delight. Logic cannot comprehend the cariophyllia: both velvety and calcareous, it is a fishing pole (*rameau calcaire*) with other pliable poles growing out of it, also fishing. The only way the sentence or "verset" coheres is through rhythm, sensuality, and sound.

---

clared that the "flowers of coral" were animals, but science was slow to accept his discovery. Michelet must have been, again, in the forefront among writers to use the polyp as a theme, for he is quoted twice in *Le Grand Dictionnaire universel's* article on madrepores (and Toussenel once).

> Les cariophylles (ou oeillets) de velours vert,
> nué d'orange, au bout de leur rameau calcaire,
> pêchent leur petits aliments
> en remuant doucement dans l'eau
> leurs riches étamines d'or.

Alliteration, rime, and a slowly descending last octosyllabic line—repeated *ã*'s resolving in *o*'s—make a reader wonder if he is discovering a "Fêtes Galantes" written in poetic prose or one of Baudelaire's hymns to his "green paradise."

Slowly the reader, who was leaning from above, finds himself enmeshed in a vision from below; he has been trapped in the exotic kingdom:

> Sur la tête de ce monde d'en bas, comme pour l'abriter du soleil, ondulant en saules, en lianes, ou se balançant en palmiers, les majestueuses gorgones de plusieurs pieds font, avec les arbres nains de l'isis, une forêt. D'un arbre à l'autre, la plumaria enroule sa spirale qu'on croirait une vrille de vigne et les fait correspondre ensemble par ses fins et légers rameaux, nuancés de brillants reflets. [P. 141]

(On top of this world down below, as if to shade it from the sun, undulating like willows or lianas or swaying like palms, the majestic gorgonacea, several feet tall, form a forest with the dwarf trees of the isis. From tree to tree the plumaria winds a spiral you would think the tendril of a vine, and its tiny thin branches glimmering in brilliant hues make it all correspond together.)

Huge (in microscopic perspective) *gorgones*, recalling the menacing Gorgon sisters, have been tamed into slaves. They wave palm branches above the head of little Isis, the Egyptian princess. Rich sonorities and balanced rhythms lull to the end:

´ ´ ´   ´ ´ ´   ´ ´   ´ ´ ´   ´ ´ ´
"par ses fins / et légers / rameaux, / nuancés / de brillants /
´ ´
reflets."

The passage concludes in the cage of dialectics that inspired the departure in the first place: "quasi-eternal" trees (gorgonacea) are intimately linked with the evanescent flower-delicacy of rootlets. Rocks and hardwood seem to have the same consistency as velvet and snowflakes. Our traditional sensory responses are foiled and we are defined by the measurements of the text. This same textual relativity could be dangerous: Michelet knew that the dimensions of the *Histoire de France* were false and that the medium itself imposed an ideology: "I appreciate the microscope and use it. . . . In history, it has its dangers. It makes you believe that moss and mold are tall forests, makes you see the least insect and imperceptible infusorian at the same height as the Alps. All the petty characters of this impoverished time are amplified in our historic microscopes" (*Histoire de France*, XI, 177).

When Michelet spoke often of history as fiction, he meant "unbelievable" but he also realized that representational reality could hardly avoid distortion. His style reflects the fact that he did not depend upon *vraisemblance* to define history or science, and this rejection of normal definitions confused his critics: "Are not these associations of things," wrote Charles Bruneau, "that are stunned to find themselves in each other's company, totally spontaneous like Hugo's? It must be instances like these that Sainte-Beuve was thinking of when he criticized Michelet for 'primping until he was flamboyant.' "[14] The Goncourt brothers also saw in Hugo and Michelet an obvious opportunity for comparison: "Michelet! the genius who has risen above everything and everyone these days: there is something of *La Mer* in Hugo's 'Travailleurs.' "[15] But did this fraternal alliance between, as the Goncourts called them, the "somnambulist of the sea" and "the historian of dream, somnambulist of the past" not work to the latter's disadvantage? Michelet could then be called an unreliable historian, a frustrated poet.

[14] Bruneau, "L'Epoque réaliste," p. 190.

[15] Edmond and Jules de Goncourt, *Journal: Mémoires de la vie littéraire, 1851–1896* (Monaco, 1956–58), VII, 177 (orig. pub. 1887–88).

The subjects that interested Michelet and Hugo became curiously parallel at the end of their careers:

Les Châtiments	*Histoire du XIXe siècle*
Les Contemplations	4 naturalist books
La Légende des siècles	*Bible de l'humanité*
La Fin de Satan	*La Sorcière*
Les Misérables	*Temps modernes*

It may also help to remember how the mature work of the two older literary statesmen compared to the work being done by their younger contemporaries: *Les Fleurs du mal* was published the same year as *L'Insecte*, and *Madame Bovary* the year before. *Les Poèmes barbares* (Leconte de Lisle), the first translation of *On the Origin of Species*, *Salammbô* (Flaubert), and *La Sorcière* all appeared in 1862. Finally, Rimbaud composed his frequently quoted letter (*du voyant*) the same year Michelet wrote his last and most misunderstood work, his history of Napoleon. These contemporary writers were all striving for a heightened sense of "reality," whether in everyday experience, drugs, or dreams. Hugo spoke of hallucinations; Rimbaud prescribed his programmatic sensory distortions: his *raisonné dérèglement de tous les sens.*

Certainly, Michelet's polyp world reproduces a kind of undersea experience similar to Henri Rousseau's *Dream.* Michelet himself went so far as to call the other-worldly feeling "phantasmagoria." But unlike the contemplative ecstasy Hugo's *mages* anticipate under a rushing sky (*"l'évanouissement des cieux"*), Michelet's deformed reality depends almost solely on changing sensual perspectives. "Phantasmagoria" can refer to things seen or imagined, but the word also includes optical illusions, fluctuations that do not mean modifying substance, but surface—color, shape, design, shading. Michelet significantly uses the word, not in a context of the occult, but with reference to the writings of the empirical scientist Darwin: " 'On land our prairies and forests,' said Darwin, 'seem deserted and empty, if you compare them to the sea's.' And in fact, people who travel across the transparent seas of India are surprised by the phantasmagoria the ocean floor offers" (*La Mer*, p. 139).[16]

The polyp colony was not actually progressing, but going through every kind of contortion while remaining in place—swelling, disappearing; rocking back and forth or trembling; twisting or stiffening. Even static, the polyps metamorphose as passing lights and colors play on parts of their bodies. Michelet's polyps, in contrast with his spiders, do not reflect a relatively ordered linear evolution, but as incarnations of a proteus present a problem for language: how to represent infinite, spontaneous change in a temporal medium. Michelet sensed that he could not really capture the polyps in words: "Who can be their interpreter? And what word translates them? . . . You spell out, think you understand. Then the light leaves you and you hold your forehead in frustration" (p. 143). None of the arts, as far as Michelet could tell, neither painting nor sculpture, had yet contrived a way of incorporating the complexity of nature, especially of the eclectic sea. At these times, when the great, euphonious voice of the sea seemed lost, obscured by the maze of foreign tongues, Michelet was frustrated and thought he had failed. But his failure was, in essence, his success. Like Proust, his obsessive search for the truth, straining with a knowledge of inevitable fading and change, led to complicated syntax, a "*surimpression*"[17] of images and

[16] Darwin and Michelet express two opposite temperaments; Michelet's reaction to the coral civilizations was to a sensual extravaganza. Darwin's is rational and matter-of-fact: "I am glad we have visited these islands: such formations surely rank high amongst the wonderful objects of this world. It is not a wonder, which at first strikes the eye of the body, but rather, after reflection, the eye of reason" (*Journal of Researches*, p. 553). Northrop Frye in *The Well-Tempered Critic* (Bloomington, Ind., 1963), pp. 57ff., compares Darwin's prose with Gibbon's, and concludes that stylistic devices used by the naturalist were accidental.

[17] Gérard Genette has well summarized the same conflicts and ironic victories in Proust: "Proust's writing [*écriture*], between con-

codes, and (illusory) subversion of the text's temporality. Michelet's verbs, again like Proust, are infrequent in the density of swollen, modifying clauses (for contrast, they can be interrupted by a rare abrupt short statement). Such a heavily nominal and adjectival prose (supposedly a modern stylistic trait)[18] does not even tend to "spatialize" the text in compensation for the loss of temporality because the diverse impressions obey no hierarchy and, by continually qualifying and contradicting one another, they end by leveling everything.

There are definitely two different kinds of accomplishment in *La Mer*. One is the poetry of harmony. Michelet senses the rise and fall of the sea in his own breathing: "L'Océan respire comme moi" (p. 21). He coaxes the thousands of tiny mute voices into chorus and orchestrates the surge into a single cosmic hymn. From the Ocean arises the great poem of dialogue and desire: "Since it is the rich crucible out of which creation arises to build its power, it naturally has a living eloquence. It is life speaking life. Living beings born of it by the millions, by the billions are words. The sea of milk they

---

scious intention and real completion, falls prey, therefore, to a singular reversal: setting out to free essences, it ends up constituting, or restituting, mirages; designed to reunite, by the substantive depth of the text, the profound substance of things, it results in an effect of phantasmagoric superimposition [*surimpression*] where depth crosses itself out, where substances devour each other" ("Proust-palimpsest," *Figures*, Paris, 1966, I, 52).

[18] Stephen Ullmann, *Style in the French Novel* (Cambridge, 1957), has signaled this "style substantif" as a modern development and studies it, in detail, as used by the Goncourt brothers. Ullmann judges that this style answered to perceptual and psychological needs of the time. The substantive style could, he proposes, evoke chaotic experience without having to sort it out and could present an "impressionistic" view of reality. Josephine Miles's historical, statistical study of three major styles—predicative, balanced, and adjectival—documents the modern preference for the adjectival style. Her study includes nineteenth-century contemporaries of Michelet in the following order, based on the degree to which they used the adjectival style: Macaulay, Ruskin, Pater, Carlyle, and Darwin (in Love and Payne, eds., *Contemporary Essays on Style*, pp. 198–99).

emerge from, the fertile jelly of the sea, even before being formed, a white froth, speaks. All this flowing together is the massive voice of the Ocean" (p. 400). Since Michelet's *La Mer*, perhaps only Saint-John Perse has met his eloquence and "by huge upsurges of humours and intumescent language, by images in bold relief and luminous shadows sloping off" defied the poetic challenge of the moving, viscous sea, "la Mer mouvante . . . la Mer gluante . . . " (*Amers*). But, as Perse also knew (veiled in his title, *Amers*), there is the bitter side of the sea—a poem of violence and alienation, of relentless change at times unpredictable, destructive, chaotic beyond the powers of linguistic coding. Michelet did not recognize that the total synthesis, which he yearned to achieve in (natural) history, could only be hinted at by confronting its impossibility.

Perhaps Michelet's verbal vision seems more modern than his professed theory (as with Proust). By the time he had written *La Montagne*, Michelet must have suspected that language was beyond good and evil, since the sole reality of words derived from a literary context. Michelet must have seen that his phrases were substitutable in almost any context, that his literary subjects were only slots to be filled by sonorous words. *La Montagne* represents, in a sense, a crisis for Michelet, for it "should have been" the ultimate personal union of himself with nature when both speak in unison. But it was also the inevitable backlash of a language that had received and exercised considerable freedom in *La Mer*. If he had succeeded in metamorphosing the sea's image with rhetorical tricks, these devices would return to flip the reversible words over again on their dark sides.

In *La Montagne*, Michelet has reached the breaking point: either proceed with his marriage to nature as planned, or listen to the warnings of his own words. Perhaps, in many ways, he was already anticipating Rimbaud's call for a new vision and a new form. Moments in *La Mer*, *La Montagne*, *Nos Fils*, and the *Histoire du XIXe siècle* are much closer to the *Illumina-*

tions than a Baudelaire sonnet; but Michelet, the bizarre bourgeois, would not admit to the joys of abandoning himself to the alchemy of language. There is a kind of time-lag between his Rimbaudian expression and his acceptance of responsibility for such liberated texts. Were Michelet to declare, "I alone hold the key to this savage parade," his very *raison d'être* would be subverted. Were he to admit to such tampering, both the historian, who follows the dictates of events, and the naturalist, who supposedly submits to the initiating experiences of the earth, would be disclosed as the creatures and creation of linguistic parody.

11 The Multiple Discourse of *I*

I enters any context in Michelet, at any time. But the pronoun is difficult to pin down, for it attempts to encompass every person permitted by the text; apparently oriented around the empirical personality of the nineteenth-century author himself, it is also the first-person subject emanating from a resurrected time, one that combines many voices, often unspoken, misquoted, already deformed as Michelet within himself re-deforms them, naming it re-creation. Moving in from one subjective point—his own space and time, his own peculiar temperament or anecdote, biography—Michelet proceeds toward a mythical conjunction of passions, where event would speak for itself in its proper proportions, and from there, back out again to the subjectivity of his text and style. Ideally, there should be no disparity between a specific, faithful language and open communication, or, at best, distances are bridged by illusion, authority, or knowledge, but sometimes the gaps are irreparable.

The historian's aggressive or seductive first person forces an immediate intimacy calculated to build the unity projected, yet this intrusion has usually been received by a modern public as something curious or dubious: "Michelet's absorption in his history, his identification of himself with his subject, carried him to singular lengths. His emotions and the events of his own life are always breaking through into his narrative; and, conversely, the events of history seem to be happening to him."[1] There is something ludicrous about this director who "leaps onto stage, rebukes and encourages the performers, interjects asides to the audience."[2] Michelet himself was irritated by the Jesuits' subjective methods, which he called "biographical amplification"; he criticized Loyola's *Exercitia*, saying, "He brazenly mingles himself in it, with absolute familiarity. . . . An enormous extension of the self, of its human personality" (*Histoire de France*, IX, 53).

Although Michelet's presence in the text, comparable to the Jesuits', colors his interpretations, he cannot be exempted from professional standards that are, not objectivity, but the depth, breadth, and honesty of source work. Despite "certain prejudice and hardly pardonable stubbornness,"[3] Michelet's reputation is being rehabilitated, not only as an ethnographer, but as a serious historian as well. The textual surface of his works would, however, dissuade anyone who recognizes history by an air of objectivity. As the *Histoire de France* progressed, Michelet delighted in responding to critics that he was avidly "partial": "Would that history emerged from the false and unfair impartiality it has upheld until now" (*Histoire de France*, IX, 210). His interpretations of the seventeenth and eighteenth centuries were regarded as a breach of good taste, but this may have pleased the author: "History, the judge of the world, has as its first obligation to lose respect" (X, 300). Designated as a kind of shock treatment, Michelet's method suggests that reason and gradual education alone do not bring about change. Objectivity connotes false security. The excessive anal-compulsive themes of the last volumes seem silly to

[1] Edmund Wilson, *To the Finland Station*, p. 24.

[2] George Peabody Gooch, *History and Historians in the Nineteenth Century* (Boston, 1959), p. 172.

[3] Maurice Bouvier-Ajam, "L'Histoire cent ans après Michelet," *Europe*, 51 (Nov.–Dec. 1973), p. 173. See also Jacques Le Goff's preface to the fourth volume of the *Oeuvres complètes* (Paris: Flammarion, 1971).

sophisticated readers, sick to others, but Michelet had not abandoned his method: "It would be too convenient for tyrants if history spared them their horrible memories. . . . So much the better if you are upset, if your cold heart finally feels something" (XII, 280). The whole point of the Louis saga was to portray the gross inequities of attention: the King's bowel movements and menu came before the people's hunger. It is, however, almost impossible either to separate with accuracy or to bring together what is meant by Michelet's *I*. Did he become obsessed with his own and Athénaïs' bodily functions because of Louis or vice versa? The question "who is speaking," often behind contemporary critical investigation, answered by "I" continues to throw the question back on itself.

Michelet is most recognizable in two particular uses of the first person: a naive form of "Madame Bovary, c'est moi" ("La France, c'est moi"), and the intrusion of a martyr-historian. Both lend themselves to irony: the first because of its insinuating ring of "l'état, c'est moi," and the second because perfectly expressed in Proust's parody: "At the high point of Louis XIV's reign, when absolutism seemed to be destroying all freedom in France, for two long years—more than a century—(1680–1789), each day unexplainable headaches made me think I would have to interrupt my history."[4] Certainly, the crux of Michelet's authenticity as a historian, as far as he was concerned, depended upon the success of his identification with the people. *Le Peuple* is based on that moral credibility: "Do not be surprised, if, knowing as much as anyone about the historic precedents of the people, also, having myself shared in their life, I feel an urgent need for the truth when one speaks of them" (p. 4). The extreme, however, of this identification leads, not to Louis XIV's image, but to its opposite, to a Christ, a child-genius, a figure of the people. Such is Jacques, medieval man: "Good God! is this my father? medieval man?...'Yes.

[4] Marcel Proust, *Pastiches et mélanges* (Paris, 1947), pp. 40–41.

. . . See what has become of me! Witness a thousand years of sorrow!...' The pain, I felt it at that moment rise in me from the depths of time.... It was he, it is I (same self and soul) who suffered all that" ("Préface de 1869," p. xxviii).

Distinctly varied uses of the "I" take the *Histoire de France* from illusory intimacy to apparent textual distance. The historian enters the text as several personae in addition to the suffering symbol of the people. Since most of the later volumes deal with the court of the Louis', testimony is recorded by a spectator who resents his participation in the drama: "I shudder when I hear from the mouth of Louis XIV: I give her three months; then, *she will go to the Hospital Prison*" (XIII, 253). Michelet seems like a voyeur or an impotent observer irreparably cut off from action by the translucent wall of time. He is like the husband in *La Sorcière* who is drugged so he cannot speak and who must watch his wife, drugged as well, participate in her own rape. When the historian tries to overcome this barrier through the sympathy of his own experience, the effect draws the reader's attention to the ever present breach of time; the reality of a galley is supposedly rendered by a contemporary and personal analogy: "Those who, for nights, long feverish nights, stayed motionless, crowded, uncomfortable, as, for example, we used to in public carriages (I was in one once for a hundred straight hours), they alone can imagine something of this terrible life" (XIII, 246). This contemporary persona is, finally, readily identifiable, as a working historian; suggesting little of mythic proportions, Michelet is a middle-aged man researching archives: "I was hoping to find in the prison records something about these martyrs, but searched in vain" (XIII, 244). Though Michelet may have hoped the historian would take on the same universal significance as the peasant or factory worker, ultimately he infused into the text, balancing or counteracting the heroic figure, the character of the writer.

A curious and much quoted passage of *La Montagne*,[5] "La Bollente. —Acqui," has always appeared to be the triumph of "I" over all that is "not-I," the one personal apocalypse beyond the tensions of history. What makes the incident crucial, unlike any other central event in either the histories or natural histories, is that Michelet is, for once, the subject and narrator combined. The passage is almost "overdetermined" by the many roles assumed by the subject: tour guide, spiritual instructor, pagan or Christian hero. Yet the real drama of the "I" works toward a final consciousness of its grammatical (im)-possibilities.

The narrative structure of myth and ritual would seem to effect, by its own momentum, the resurrection of the bather, Michelet, or first person. The Italian setting is overlaid with Egyptian resonances. The subject is introduced as a fatigued historian enclosed in the "*énorme pyramide*" of his own construction. The *fangarolo*, who prepares the bath, doubles as a kind of Egyptian slave; he is described as a "*sculpteur habile dans le genre égyptien.*" Covered with mud ("a funereal drape"), the bather will resemble a dead king carved on the lid of his sarcophagus. Even a touristic summary of the buildings becomes a warning to the frivolous vacationer who forgets he is in the most sacred of spots. One is transgressing, as in the virgin forests, on hostile territory; the Bormida river, "*insoci-*

[5] All the criticism of Michelet's later work needs rethinking; the natural histories, in particular, were too easily dismissed as simplistic and of little empirical interest to positive science, as in Robert Van der Elst's *Michelet naturaliste* (Paris: Delagrave, 1914). *La Montagne*, the last and one of the most curious of the natural histories, was considered by Claire-Eliane Engel as the end of a slow decline: "What can one say about it [Michelet's *La Montagne*]? A few admirable pages emerge from the midst of insipid declamations. A very simplistic philosophy, an unfortunate essay on the social explanation of mountains, a complete indifference to the new aspects of the problems of Alpine life and science, all this helps make this volume a hybrid, disconcerting work. . . . As for the landscape at Saint-Gervais, at Grindelwald, at Samaden, he apparently never raised his head" (*La Littérature alpestre*, Chambéry, Librairie Dardel, 1930, p. 239).

able, inhospitalière," flows through a sinister countryside where a bull rams its horns, without any noticeable reason, up against a horse, where the sulfurous soil permeates the atmosphere with its odor, and where one meets on an ordinarily fine day the convoy of a funeral. The "*Mère commune,*" the earth herself, seems to keep hundreds of streams trapped under the surface, and they turn and stretch like someone "badly buried." It is understood that they await, as in Chrétien de Troyes' bewitched land of *Logres* (*L'ogre*), their deliverer.

Finally, Michelet describes the last bath of his cure in fifteen-minute episodes, but so much detail seems to invite the frustration of the main myth. The narrator hopes to overcome the distinct identities of present writer and former patient by calling them both *I;* he, in fact, changed the original account of the same bath in the *Journal*, where he had used the impersonal *vous* form: "*elle* vous *pénètre . . . ;* vous *réagissez sans doute . . .* " (II, 274). A tension is evident already in the first stage of immersion, because of the slips in and out of the present tense. The traditional historical present, frequent especially in the *Histoire de la Révolution française*, achieves the heightened sense of drama it is supposed to.[6] But this is the present of reflection: "For the first quarter hour, quietude. My mind was still free to wander. I turned my thoughts to myself, my bad side, its origin. I accused myself alone, my undisciplined will, my excessive efforts to relive by myself the life of all mankind. The dead I conversed with [*conversai*] for so long beckon me [*m'attirent*], would like me [*me voudraient*] on the other shore. Nature still holds me [*me tient*] here, wants me [*me veut*] on this one" (*La Montagne*, p. 76). The reader is confused at this point about whether the subject is drawn

[6] "A blacksmith, an old soldier, without wasting time in idle talk, set [*se mit*] bravely to work. He marches forward [*s'avance*], hatchet in hand, leaps [*monte*] upon the roof. . . . The crowd rushes [*passe*] over it, and enters [*est dans*] the court. The firing began [*on tirait*] at once from the towers" (*History of the French Revolution*, ed. Wright, p. 171; *Histoire de la Révolution française*, I, 154).

back into the emotional impact of the past or whether the experience of fourteen years earlier lives on until the present. The resulting blur of the event—whether I-present or I-past is speaking— (similar in passages of Constant's *Adolphe* or Rousseau's *Confessions*) contributes to the narrator's unreliability. Whereas this ritualistic marriage with the earth must be effected with lyricism, that is, with as little distance as possible, the confession begins, in an unstable text, to seem artificially contrived, whether it is or not. The confession other than the historian's official one is already a sign that the baths were the healing of a past or imagined moment: tension is what is expressed in the present.

The narrative line continues toward the *fiat* of oneness; marriage and return to the womb: "In the second quarter hour, her power increased. My thoughts disappeared in the profound absorption. The only idea that stayed with me was *Terra Mater*. I felt her very presence, caressing and compassionate, bringing warmth to her injured child. From outside? From within as well. For she penetrated with life-giving spirit, entered me and combined her self with mine, infusing me with her soul. The identification between us was complete. I could no longer tell myself apart from her" (*La Montagne*, p. 76). The text is essentially driving toward the annihilation of "I" into "it" or "her." Dialogue has been revealed for what it is: the exchange between first and second persons depends simply upon the perspective of the person speaking, who automatically becomes *I*. The intimacy of address is perhaps too obvious a *tour de force;* channels of communication already exist between you and me. "What defines Michelet's voice," Gaëtan Picon has explained, "is that there is always a second person: the imminence or presence of the vocative. Strange doubling of the voice, of the viewpoint: a constant displacing of borders between the inside and outside, within the closed field of their confrontation; ventriloquism."[7]

[7] Picon, Introduction to *L'Etudiant*, pp. 38–39.

Conversation with the nonperson is, on the other hand, linguistically excluded.[8] Victor Hugo attempted to cast his voice beyond what speaks, to make silence echo. After his exile on Guernsey and Jersey,—because of either a closeness to death, or "being," and absolute solitude—all he had conversed comfortably with before (*je/tu*) transformed into a cosmic overvoice, a speaking void, the *bouche d'ombre*, and he entered into a different, awesome self-dialogue (*je/on*).[9] Michelet was experimenting in his writing with the same union: the *Terra*

[8] See the fifth section of Benveniste's *Problèmes de linguistique générale*, "L'homme dans la langue." " 'I' and 'you' are reversible: the person 'I' defined as 'you' can think of himself and be reversed into 'I,' and 'I' (me) become a 'you.' The same relationship is not possible between one of these two persons and 'he, she, it,' because 'he, she, it' in themselves designate no one or nothing in particular" (p. 230, from the chapter "Structure des relations de personne dans le verbe"). The discussion, following Jean Starobinski's talk reproduced in *Literary Style: A Symposium*, ed. Seymour Chatman (New York, 1971), poses this problem of identity in autobiography: "As for the 'I' of autobiography, there is no other definition of 'I' than the one who calls himself I. This is essentially a 'shifter' definition (to use Jakobson's term): the autobiographical 'I,' the *auto in autobiography*, is the exorcising substitute for the linguistic tautology that 'I' is the one who says 'I.' It tries to exorcise the tautology, to divert it, to substantivize and deformalize it. Thus it is a process of 'deshifting' the shifter. How? By filling this 'I' who says 'I' with an image, that is, someone of veracity and sincerity; he is, of course, no less imaginary than any other character in narrative. This ontologically empty 'I' is filled by Rousseau with a figure possessing desire, pride, and intelligence. The autobiography is something which fills that which is unfillable at the level of language" (p. 296; the same talk was published in Starobinski's *La Relation critique* (1970), without the discussion).

[9] See Pierre Albouy's "Hugo ou le Je éclaté," *Romantisme*, 1–2 (1971), pp. 153–64: "The *I/you* becomes *one* [*on:* you, we, they, one], in these cosmic weddings after death, and the *one* acquires the virtues of *I/you*, that is love and sexuality" (p. 62). "An *I* continues to appear beyond all precise determinations of person and nonperson, height that is depth, depth, height: exterior interiority and interior exteriority" (p. 63). "Thus, it is impossible to reduce the poet's *I* to *me* or *not-me*. It is *I* and *one*, it is the *I* and its very transcendence lived out by death, taken on by voice" (p. 64).

Mater was like Humanity, the People, the mutes of history's sea. But these interlocutors are actually abstractions, there is nothing personal about them, for they represent, in the end, what Michelet most feared, what he called, quoting Goethe, the *grand Tout.*[10] Thus, despite the jubilant tone, Michelet's marriage to the earth was riddled with anxiety and was finally symbolically avoided by a last-minute, almost instinctive refusal. When faced with the situation, the *I* could not totally dissolve itself into its negativity, into the nonperson *She:*

> A ce point qu'au dernier quart d'heure, ce qu'elle ne couvrait pas, ce qui me restait libre, le visage, m'était importun. Le corps enseveli était heureux, et c'était moi. Non enterrée, la tête se plaignait, n'était plus moi; du moins, je l'aurais cru. Si fort était le mariage! et plus qu'un mariage, entre moi et la Terre! On aurait dit plutôt *échange de nature.* J'etais Terre, et elle était homme. Elle avait pris pour elle mon infirmité, mon péché. Moi, en devenant Terre, j'en avais pris la vie, la chaleur, la jeunesse. [P. 77]

> ([Absorbed] to the point that by the last quarter hour, what she did not cover, what stayed free, my face, bothered me. The buried part of my body was happy and this was me. Unburied, the head was complaining and it was no longer myself; at least I thought not. So absolute was the marriage! and more than a marriage, between myself and the Earth! You might say, instead, an *exchange of natures.* I was the Earth and she was man. She took on my infirmities, my sin. As for me, once I became the Earth, I received her life, warmth, and youth.)

Something unnamable continues to complain, to speak. It is as if the self has split into the dialectics of what it is not; neces-

[10] Hugo did not choose the easier alternative by any means. Although he became preoccupied with the "beyond," that autonomy and enigma of the other, rather than with exchanges, marriages, and compromises, he had to describe this void without relying on cliché, repetition, monotony, and abstraction. See Jean Gaudon's *Le Temps de la contemplation* (Paris, 1969), especially "Architectures d'ombre."

sarily simplifying by using Freud's terminology: the ego seems to drop out between the superego of history and nature and an unclaimed unconscious.

The narrative structure, acting as the ego, persists with the resurrection. "Années, travaux, douleurs, tout restait dans le fond de mon cercueil de marbre. J'étais renouvelé. Sorti, j'avais sur moi je ne sais quelle lueur onctueuse" (Years, work, pain, everything settled to the bottom of my marble tomb. I was remade new. After I emerged, I had an unctuous glow around me) (p. 77). Beginning with the child-hero's fear for his life in a land ruled by an evil spirit, the ritual ends in the luminosity of a risen god. The reader does not have to know that Louis XIII passed through the same rites without emerging victorious[11] or that Michelet himself was no closer to a cure. The medical result of the bath was negligible; he wrote in the same *Journal* entry that contains the source material for his chapter (28 July 1854): "Storm, and psychic storm; pain in my left hip, for a minute very sharp" (II, 274).

A parenthetical expression that represents, in Michelet, a constant, irrepressible urge to interrupt, shatters the magical atmosphere with its reminder to the reader: "Elle m'avait grandi de vie et de puissance. Puisse-je en être digne (disais-je), y puiser ses torrents, et d'un coeur plus fécond, entrer dans son unité sainte!" (She elevated me in life and power. If only I could be worthy of it [I said], if only I could draw from her torrents, and with a more creative heart, enter into her holy unity!) (p. 77). The scene reverts immediately, through this parenthesis, to the past; the *I* of 1854 steps back from the *I* of 1867; the writer stands away from the god. It is like the stages of conscious distancing that span from joy to journal as they filter through the opening of Wordsworth's

[11] Louis XIII "*se croit rené*" (thinks he is reborn) when he rises from the sickbed after another close call with death and sees the shining Provençal blonde, Madame de Hautefort, "this beautiful light of life that Nature adorns for the dead who are resuscitated" (XII, 43).

Prelude: "Oh there is blessing in this gentle breeze . . . " begins in the midst of fiction. "For I, methought, while the sweet breath of heaven / was blowing on my body, felt within / A correspondent breeze . . . " The syntax and thought have begun to turn in already upon their different selves. Finally, the full journey to the written text is documented in the most complex sentence:

> Thus far, O Friend! did I, not used to make
> A present joy the matter of a song,
> Pour forth that day my soul in measured strains
> That would not be forgotten, and are here
> Recorded [46–50]

The last sentence of Michelet's chapter "La Bollente. –Acqui" leaves the ambiguity intact: "L'*Oiseau*, la *Mer*, l'*Insecte*, en vinrent, avec la *Renaissance*, et celui qui les fit, et qui fait tout: l'*Amour*" (The *Bird*, the *Sea*, the *Insect* came [from this unity] as well as the *Renaissance*, and the one who made them, and who makes all: *Love*). The publication dates of the three natural histories embrace the publication of *La Renaissance* (1855) in the *Histoire de France*, which preceded by months the writing of the first paragraphs of *L'Amour*. But Michelet is playing as well on his titles as substantives themselves: his personal renaissance in nature gave him the strength to start his series of natural histories, and love was always the muse and driving force behind his whole work. According to one reading, the production of books is a closed but fertile circuit; according to the other, life and morality remain the justification for art. As an odd twist to this seemingly sleight-of-hand punctuation, the conclusion of *La Montagne* reverses the book-to-act (referent-to-text) relationship; the title is not italicized as if it is already reality: "I see beyond my book another one beginning: The Regeneration of the Human Species [Régénération de l'espèce humaine]."

In the chapter following "La Bollente. –Acqui" is another

apparently small stylistic detail that discloses the writer's other voice, the one that thinks "*avec la plume.*" A familiar tic of Michelet's style, the first person inserted at the junctures of clauses in a *dis-je* or *disais-je*, a *je vois*, reveals his definition of himself as writer-orator, as writer-observer, or, more precisely, voyeur. In "La Montée de la Terre. –L'Aspiration," the same narrator who joined in matrimony with the earth watches, immediately thereafter, a compensatory torture scene replete with the usual autoeroticism and a ritualistic suicide. The earth, separated as ever from the sun, "aspires" toward him, pushing through layers of rock, submitting herself to every mechanical and chemical transformation possible, to geological metamorphosis:

Penché sur le limon brûlant, bouillonnant, cette miniature des grands travaux de la Terre, assistant à tous les efforts que la vertu intérieure fait pour sortir et monter, j'imaginai aisément tout ce dont elle est capable pour se rapprocher de celui que toujours elle regrette, et vers qui, par tous ses arts, elle tend éternellement. Les procédés mécaniques, les combinaisons chimiques, filtration, trituration, expansion, éruption, fermentations qui dépassent la portée du minéral, elle fait tout, l'impossible même. Elle réussit à percer. Elle finit par monter. . . . Car la vie croît par la vie, l'obstacle et le frottement. [P. 80]

(Leaning over the burning, boiling mud, this miniature of the vast work of the Earth, watching all the effort that interior virtue exerts to emerge and climb, I easily imagined everything she would do to get closer to the one she always regrets and toward whom, by all arts, she is eternally attracted. The mechanical processes, chemical combinations, filtration, trituration, expansion, eruption, fermentations which go beyond the range of minerals, she does it all, even the impossible. She succeeds in breaking through. She finally ascends. . . . For life thrives on life, obstacle, and friction.)

The rock that undergoes pressure, that liquefies, boils, and vaporizes, finally emerges as the "powerful elixirs of life," or more precisely, as blood: "This is perfectly natural; for it is the blood of our Mother who opens her veins for us." The revealing clue to the sacrificial murder is "*j'imaginai.*" The narrator means both that he thought about, pictured, the inner workings of the earth and that he imagined the whole drama.

Clearly, the imagination represented for Michelet one of the most ambiguous of presences. A passage in *L'Oiseau,* hidden under the guise of a condemnation of the imagination, is a strange self-fulfilling prophecy of what books the "bewitched" author will write:

The powerful fairy who performs for man most of what is good and bad, the imagination, plays at disguising nature in a hundred ways. In all that surpasses his forces or offends his sensibilities, in all necessities commanded by the harmony of the world, he is tempted to see and blame a malevolent will. A writer composed a book against the Alps; a poet foolishly placed the throne of evil on these beneficent glaciers, the water reserve of Europe, which pours into its rivers, assuring fertility. Others, even more thoughtless, have cursed the polar ice fields, misunderstood the globe's marvelous economy, the majestic balance of alternating currents that are the life of the Ocean. They have seen war and hate, the wickedness of nature in these rhythmic movements, deeply peaceful, of the universal Mother. [Pp. 73–74]

The writer, foolish poet, and "others" are the present and future forms of Michelet's first person. The historian criticized, for example, Byron's inhuman image of the Alps, and yet, the same year that *L'Oiseau* was published, "Michelet" writes in his *Journal:*

Manfred, Byron. The stupidity of this sublime young man is not to have wanted to resemble Faust and, for that reason, to have imagined a crime, a criminal Manfred. Weak invention: we are all criminals, all troubled without knowing why.

Modern man does not need crime to be tragic. He is so by the enormous questions he is asked. Enormity I can only compare to the hundred blue vaults, so transparent and yet secret, a monstrous glacier carries in its belly. But our human glacier is always moving, constantly changing its vaults and crevasses. And at the slightest movement, it crushes a million men. Destroyed, we should give our blessing. There is no Arcinane, no Nemesis, no evil power in this, there is, instead, universal order and the greater will, love guiding the world and killing only to give birth. [II, 311; 1856]

The logical extension of Michelet's ideology is finally a sinister, truly chilling, rationalization of evil. Modern history has witnessed the kind of perversity applied to language by politics, the way any expression can become a slogan of totalitarian control. Analyzing the methods in literature for establishing value, Kenneth Burke concluded that any such aspiration is liable to create its opposite, an immorality; Michelet exercised both of the methods Burke exposes: "The first would try to *cut away*, to *abstract*, all emotional factors that complicate the objective clarity of meaning. The second would try to derive its vision from the maximum *heaping up* of all these emotional factors, playing them off against one another, inviting them to reinforce and contradict one another, and seeking to make this active participation itself a major ingredient of the vision. . . . In their ideal completion, they have a certain superficial resemblance, in that both are 'beyond good and evil' " (*The Philosophy of Literary Form*, New York, 1957, pp. 128–30).

The historian was mindful of the narrow area in which one wrote to avoid, on both sides, a moral apathy. He could never leave his observations, especially in the *Histoire du XIXe siècle*, to their own relativity, and yet he knew that a "philosophy of history" like Hegel's would defeat the very faith in rational discourse and argument he espoused: "But to interject into the detail, the combat of the world, this fatal opium of the philosophy of history, these circumspections [*ménagements*] of a false peace, is to put death in life, is to kill history and morality, to let the indifferent soul reply: 'What is evil? What, good?' " (X, 300). It is logical that advanced age brings on a multiple vision that has seen everything become its opposite; still, Michelet must have felt bitter about the betrayal of the grand words that had sustained him, sustained his oratory and the flame that almost led to action. In the *Histoire du XIXe siècle*, Michelet meditates on the ironic history of the word "liberty":

All Europe knew the secret; the name alone of *liberty* produced this miracle.

Liberty against Napoleon, that is the universal slogan. . . . Could Austria, until then the stronghold of despotism, the center of the retrograde party, change roles and language, take as her rallying cry such an odious word as one borrowed from France, from the Revolution? They tried it with success in Tyrol against the Bavarians. They even dared to use it in Italy; people thought they were organizing hotbeds of insurrection. All this, lacking grace, with little success, in a visible fear of succeeding all too well.

What would it be like, the archdukes said among themselves, if all our barbarians along the Danube were to understand and repeat this fatal Shibboleth! Austria, while pronouncing the word, was afraid of it herself, like the magician, who trembles at his own incantations, at his appeals to the infernal powers. [III, 283]

The dialectics of all things depended finally upon the balance of white and black magic, on the perspective one could believe or impose as belief.

Still, Michelet praised the imagination. This "good fairy," the "*imagination solitaire*,"[12] was, he admitted, the only faculty on which any artistic representation could rely. Neither maps nor a trip in a balloon nor the fantastic "georama" could

[12] Edward Kivie Kaplan's "Michelet's Poetic Vision: The Structure of his Philosophy of Nature and Man" (Diss. Columbia University, 1970), studies Michelet's epistemology as a parallel to his order of beings. The "free (solitary) imagination" or "pure vision," which is the final and highest means of gaining knowledge, belongs to the most evolved creative man, and to God or the God-in-man. "Pure vision, unimpeded by space and substance, presents a separation from the spectacle while, at the same time, perceiving its totality" (p. 239).

render the earth in its mystery and variation: "But no representation conveys reality. Nothing expresses relative heights and depths. . . . In this, our senses betray us: It [the earth] is too grandiose; everything escapes us. . . . But with thought, with the solitary imagination, far from all distractions, you can embrace this huge and beautiful being, infinitely more complicated than any living thing born of its own womb" (*La Montagne*, pp. 88–89). The historical perspective, ranging among the people-infusorian, the courtier-insect, the king-emptiness, the Revolution-everything, could not be translated by the leveling text, but only by imagination.

Finally, the "solitary imagination" becomes a kind of universal first-person, an I/it or *je/on*, dissolved in the fabric of linguistic action. During the appearance of the aurora borealis, Michelet fulfills in his own way Flaubert's dictum that the writer "must be like God in the universe, present everywhere and nowhere visible" (*Correspondance*, III, 62, 1852):

The first persons to see them [the lights], our old seamen, thought it was a formal ball. To the sharp eye, the heart more attuned to the emotional state of nature, it is pure theater. You cannot mistake the trembling of captive souls, their troubled heartbeat. Then, alternatives, calls, strident replies, yeses, nos, threats, fighting, victories, and foundering. Sometimes tender moods, like the way the daughter of the sea feels, flashing at night, the Medusa, when her lamp glows red, languishes, and pales, off and on.

A highly emotional witness takes an active part in the drama, the compass needle. By its movements, it visibly corresponds with and attends to it all, expressing the phases, crises, and peripeteia. It seems anxious, terrified, *crazy* (the word the sailors use).

In fact no one is calm watching this. Such prodigious activity without noise seems more like magic than nature.[13]

[13] "Les premiers qui les virent, nos vieux navigateurs, croyaient y voir un bal. Pour un oeil pénétrant, un coeur plus attentif aux émotions de la nature, c'est tout un drame. On n'y peut méconnaître le frémissement d'âmes captives, leurs profondes palpitations. Puis des

When one learns to recognize Michelet's voice, one hears it everywhere. Thus, if he does not personally speak, he finally succeeds in lending a voice, his voice, to those subjects whose history most interested him, to the mute and dumb spectators of time.

The "old seamen," potentially objective spectators or mythical questers, could become the center of the narration, but Michelet ultimately rejects them. The universal heart, "*un coeur plus attentif*," is closer to the interpreter he wishes. The ubiquitous "you" (*on*) further confirms that the witness of the scene is larger than the men huddled on shore. The sailors mistakenly take the cosmic phenomenon too lightly—as a dance. To create the proper atmosphere—melodrama, suspense, fear, terror—someone else is needed. The compass (*aiguille*) is chosen to guide our response. It is a kind of pen without a visible guiding hand, like René Char's "*marteau sans maître*," whose "master" needs no introduction. Another vague no one (*personne*) reflects the *aiguille*'s excitement until the tension grows. While the proper spectator is schooled in his attitude, a grandiose theatrical performance is building to its climax. But this is eerie entertainment. Everything does happen as if by magic; no one is seen moving props or heard whispering cues. "It is eleven at night. The fighting stops in harmony. The lights have battled enough. They agree with each other, grow peaceful and share a mutual love. They ascend together in glory. They are transfigured into a sublime fan, a dome of

---

alternatives, des appels, des répliques violentes, des oui, des non, des défis, des combats. Des victoires et des défaillances. Parfois des attendrissements, comme ceux de la fille des mers, qui flamboie la nuit, la Méduse, quand tour à tour sa lampe rougit, languit, pâlit.

"Un témoin tout ému paraît prendre à ce drame une vive part, l'aiguille aimantée. Par ses agitations elle correspond visiblement et s'intéresse à tout, en exprime les phases, les crises, les péripéties. Elle paraît troublée, effarée, *affolée* (c'est le mot qu'emploient les marins).

"Mais personne n'est calme à voir cela. Un si prodigieux mouvement sans aucun bruit, cela paraît moins nature que magie" (*La Montagne*, pp. 103–4).

fire, like the crown of a divine hymen." Active verbs are almost all dropped in a passage dominated by reflexive verbs: "Elles [*lumières*] *s'entendent, se pacifient* et *s'aiment.* Elles montent ensemble dans la gloire. Elles *se transfigurent* en sublime éventail, en coupole de feu, sont comme la couronne d'un divin hyménée." At the last moment, everything knows the role that nobody taught, and the finale is perfectly orchestrated by nobody.

The aurora borealis converges in one moment of unison the reality that four nature books have gradually imposed upon the reader as constant transition and imbalance, as definable only by "alternatives, calls, replies, yeses, nos." Michelet's aurora is the act of a poet who still insists on leaving (and finding) the world in a state of marriage no matter what methods, preparations, and aftermath are involved. He is careful not to mar the effect of the aurora's transfiguration: no temporal or personal gaps are given a chance to slip in. The first person stays out; the vision is not relegated to a past separated from the present. In a world of metamorphosis, where slipping and sliding, even if by dialectics, is still disquieting, where the simultaneous impression of flinging back and forth between Yes and No could produce a tired Maybe, epiphany must be seized whenever the opportunity arises or the poet feels up to it. It is as if Michelet had been able to take the advice of Wallace Stevens, who had long meditated on how he could confront the ambivalent power of nature with words and the imagination. It is appropriate that the poet be instructing someone like himself, called a rabbi, someone also like Michelet in that he is a kind of sacred historian of a people who must hold to a minimal religion:

> Read to the congregation, for today
> And for tomorrow, this extremity,
> This contrivance of the spectre of the spheres,

Contriving balance to contrive a whole,
The vital, the never-failing genius,
Fulfilling his meditations, great and small.

In these unhappy he meditates a whole,
The full of fortune and the full of fate,
As if he lived all lives, that he might know,

In hall harridan, not hushful paradise,
To a haggling of wind and weather, by these lights
Like a blaze of summer straw, in winter's nick.

["The Auroras of Autumn"]

12 Conclusion: The Dead and the Wooden Doll

Language is both a divining rod and a magic wand. One part of the self, blind and knocking about, depends upon the shock of energy sent from somewhere outside. The other part of the self boasts of its omnipotent ego. The range of Michelet's voices grew almost to the limit of madness, at least the madness a text can afford. Truly something else was speaking through the ever-present *I*, a Third Person not accounted for in the script, the unconscious forcing itself into whatever degree of consciousness writing implies. Sometimes history, like a diabolical presence, must be appeased: "The shocking account you will read is taken textually from her three depositions (so naive, of undeniable truth). We would have liked to have abridged, to make it less painful. But then it would have lost importance and usefulness. History, justice command. We must obey. Here it is: . . . "(*La Sorcière*, Paris: Garnier-Flammarion, 1966, p. 244). But often something irresistible is drawing Michelet on–like La Cadière's final confrontation with Father Girard in *La Sorcière*–often a void leading away from the Revolution opens to history and he must follow: he would have preferred to pursue the forces of liberty, the Protestant martyrs, but history pointed elsewhere: "History would not allow it. . . . They are accessories, drawn into their present position under the sovereign influence that will also bear them away. . . . This influence is the Spaniard" (*Histoire de France*, IX, 47).

The different voices grow farther and farther apart, yet Michelet keeps drawing larger circles of another overvoice saying again that everything is as it should be: one persona undermines underneath, while the other repairs, scaffolds, and entertains above. Part of the historian confesses a growing confusion and yearns for the good, simple days of the sixteenth century (which had been relatively complicated compared with the fifteenth century): "I could no longer find the sharp outline and frankness of my sixteenth-century men (whom I still miss). . . . Situations also are complicated and confused. Neither men nor things are amenable now to the absolute and systematic solutions we used to give them" (*Histoire de France,* XI, 306, note 1). A debate opens in the notes or echoes in prefaces as Michelet considers for himself the problem of contradiction. A discussion of methods usually leads to both an apology for, and a retraction of, the same techniques. A note in the volume on the seventeenth century is boldly entitled "Mes contradictions," yet the preface introducing the eighteenth century reminds the reader that these digressions are only the practical inconveniences of giving previously obscure history its due hearing and that the historian still remains faithful to his "simple principle."

The mask of "simple principle" hides a wealth of confession. The naive ideologue lets another spokesman play the role of subtle critic; an attack on someone else is often so passionate that it reflects directly and vengefully back on Michelet, the attacker, perhaps without his realizing. The historian would willingly incarnate Romme, Danton, Vergniaud, or Diderot, but Richelieu, Louis XIV, the Inquisitioner Spengler, the King's Jesuit confessors, all the diabolical influences of history also had to pass through his ego, mixing theirs and his. Michelet's analysis of Richelieu is an invitation to the critical counterreading his naive ideologue should try to avoid, the reading that would lead to the opposite of what Pierre Albouy defined as the goal of myth: "the collective action of exaltation or defense." This automatic, almost involuntary undermining of his own text sustains, however, a tension and energy, the essence of open form, an ever pregnant sentence that myth oversimplified could not condone; Albouy goes on to enlarge his definition: myth "expresses a particularly complex state of mind or being,"[1] the minimal coherence of madness and health, the medicine man's translation of his silent client.

Richelieu represents the man searching for water who said upon finding or not finding it that he knew what the outcome would be all along; he is the simple heart dragging a hidden cape of sinuous evasions behind: "He is careful not to admit that these mistakes were imposed upon him. He claims them as his own, wants always to have ruled, to possess and lead everything. . . . It is useful for these great actors to compose in this way their own heroic portrait, to crown themselves with laurel, to gather, if they can, all their curves into an ideal straight line. But it is up to history to retrace their sinuous steps, their twists and turns under the pressure of events, without taking into account the prearranged systems by which they wish continually to dominate opinion and dupe posterity" (*Histoire de France*, XI, 109). A slight manuscript revision, like makeup, enlivens Michelet's portrait of himself, adds a little radiance to the darker lines. The conclusion of *La Montagne* undergoes a subtle lift and leaves courage where there had been disappointment: "If I had followed only man alone, his savage history, *I would have faltered in sadness*" replaces the more acidic "*I would perhaps have gone lower* [baissé] *because of chagrin and bitterness.*" "If I had followed Nature without alternating, *I would have fallen* (*like many I know today*) *into the nonchalance of right*" removes the

[1] "Je définirais le *mythe littéraire* comme l'élaboration d'une donnée traditionnelle ou archétypique, par un style propre à l'écrivain et à l'oeuvre, dégageant des significations multiples, aptes à exercer une action collective d'exaltation et de défense ou à exprimer un état d'esprit ou d'âme spécialement complexe" (*Mythes et mythologies dans la littérature française*, p. 301).

physical sensation of the anxiety in "*I would perhaps have grown soft with indifference*" (my italics).[2]

As Michelet's "*marche sinueuse*" became more apparent, the text grew in nervousness, the justifications increased in stridency but the undermining only accelerated, so that the emotional impact of these later works is inevitable. Written a year after the publication of *La Montagne*, the Preface of 1869 to the *Histoire de France* is the inevitable sequel to a growing consciousness. Its text is a syntactical battle between Michelets. The *I* is as much on the defensive as Nietzsche's first person in *Ecce Homo* or Rousseau's paranoiac of the *Dialogues.* Not just the usual romantic image of self-genesis, this repetition of *I*'s is more serious than infantile: "No one penetrated into the infinite detail of the diverse development of (France's) activity. . . . No one had yet embraced her living unity in one sweep. . . . I was the first to see her as one soul and person." And later: "I saw her first as one soul and one person." The litany of *I*'s is unremitting: "Here again, I am forced to say, I was alone too. . . . " "I had only one advantage, the savage virginity of my opinion. . . . " "I saw what was clearly there but . . . I must say, I also had merit. . . . " The echo to Nietzsche's chapter titles is poignant: "Why I am so wise," "Why I am so clever," "Why I write such good books."

Interrupting the self-praise, Michelet sets about to review the two cornerstones of his method that have steadily been eroding and carrying his identity with them. First, the Preface of 1869 admits to tampering with the vast lines of history, but the historian restricts his example to the history of the Middle Ages. He realizes that his irrepressible urge for unity led him to build an illusory image, "a lugubrious harmony, a colossal

[2] From Michelet's notes for *La Montagne* (*fonds Michelet,* Bibliothèque de la ville de Paris): "J'aurais peut-être baissé de chagrin et d'amertume" crossed out for "j'aurais faibli de tristesse"; "j'aurais molli peut-être dans l'indifférence" becomes "je serais tombé (comme plus d'un aujourd'hui) dans l'insouciance du droit."

symphony," but, instead of pursuing the implications of this discovery, that is, what other misrepresentations had occurred, he dismisses the error as adolescent: "these juvenile lines, light-headed if you will, but excusable, of course, because straight from the heart" (*Histoire de France*, I, xii). In the space of a few pages, Michelet turns his argument in such a way as to conclude, finally, that the disproportions had their own truth. Like that of Richelieu, the mask of the naive ideologue claims that no truth could have surpassed these "errors." Again, Michelet describes exactly what he himself does, in terms of what Spain does or the underhanded Catherine de Medici: "They present the lowly spectacle of a tournament of blind men, armed with clubs, who strike out without seeing. They walk at random and fall, then swear, getting up, that they meant to fall" (*Histoire de France*, IX, iii).

The Preface of 1869 also considers the thorny problem of subjectivity, whose dangers Michelet articulated with his usual defensiveness: "My life was in this book, entered completely into it. . . . But is it not dangerous to identify book and author? And are a person's works not colored by his feelings and his time?" (p. vii). The influence of one's biography is inevitable and underlies the emotion any contemporary historian can lend to the past, but Michelet knew he went a step farther, that he expected history to operate literally as a family: "The son made the father. If it [my history] emerged first from me, from the storms of my youth (still there, somewhat), it gave me in turn so much more strength and light, creative energy, the true power to resurrect the past. If we resemble each other, so much the better" (p. ix). A transference occurred, in the psychoanalytic sense, for Michelet did use history for therapy: "So I continued along my way . . . strengthening my faith by my losses and hopes, drawing closer, as my home broke apart, to the home of my country" (*Histoire de la Révolution française*, I, 8).

The young historian had insisted he would obliterate his

"vile self" in history, and yet the ego is everywhere. Perhaps, like Proust's Marcel, he hoped to create a more acceptable self by giving it an apparently secure past and present.[3] The effort was self-defeating, for language cannot reconcile the self's ambivalence, and by merely reflecting the split, insists, ironically, on its inescapable presence.

Michelet knew that a writer's solitary profession forces him automatically into a private world—"I had my own world inside myself" ("Préface de 1869," p. xi)—and that, with time, a separation from the "outside" world would increase. Like many writers, he was both tempted by this singular life and afraid of its isolation. In 1841, he recognized his destiny to be literally metamorphosed into a book: "An invisible will, some hidden force, chance or Providence, rules that I give nothing of myself to my personal life, that I be, not a man, but a book" (*Journal*, I, 357). Yet he could not sustain this unnatural pressure indefinitely: "Away from reality for so long, exiled in a world of papers, return, my soul and daughter, return to your beginnings. . . . You will become a man; you will be less a book; less a scribe, less a shut-in, a dreamer, less vain and subtle" (*Journal*, I, 679). The paradox of creativity parallels that of the house: "We surround ourselves with our books, our acquisitions, we triumph in growing large like this. But sometimes we realize that our personality is no longer lightweight. We are disappearing under what makes our richness. We find it heavy, and then we begin to groan" (*La Montagne*, p. 86).

One's work can be the opposite of rejuvenating. Not only does it overburden the historian, it tortures, drains, burns him out. "I was my own world. I had my life, my renewals and and productivity within myself; but my dangers, too. Which

[3] See Leo Bersani's *Marcel Proust: The Fictions of Life and of Art* (New York, 1965), especially p. 19: "The conflict between the narrator's desire to possess a permanent image of himself and his conviction that value adheres only to what is not recognizable as belonging to the self creates a continual and unresolved tension between two kinds of literary works."

ones? my heart, my youth, my method itself, and the new condition imposed upon history: no longer to recount and nothing more, or to judge, but to *conjure up*, *remake*, *resurrect* the ages. To have enough flame to warm ashes that had been cold so long, that was the first point, not without peril" ("Préface," p. x) Michelet's method depended upon passion and tension, but such energy is not everlasting; like his spider or nursing mother, he weakened as he worked at his best. The conclusion to the Preface of 1869 is a love song to his vampire wives: France and her history. At this point, the *I* seems totally displaced: "Always pushing farther in my ardent pursuit, I lost sight of myself, went out of myself. I passed alongside the world and took history to be life" (pp. xxxvii–xxxviii).

At first, the image of the brave Sisyphus, the martyr of France, the sacrificial victim, enhances the historian as he moves from the line of traditional heroes to take his allotted place behind the silent toilers of time. But one glance in the mirror, one lapsus of rhetoric, reveals the other side; Michelet, like Mary Shelley's Frankenstein, has become his own monster: as doubles, the creator and his awful progeny are also confused for one another. Michelet has outdistanced his very devils; more persistent than the Jesuit father confessor, more curious about his own urine than Louis was of his, more prolific than the hated Spengler and Del Rio, rolling ever greater volumes together to perpetuate the evils of the medieval society he abhorred—the world of the word: "Words! Words! This is all their [the Church's] history. They were in the end *a language* [*une langue*]. Verb and verbalism [*verbalité*], that is all. One name will remain for them: *Speech* [*Parole*]" (*La Sorcierè*, p. 301). Published the same year as the Preface of 1869, *Nos Fils* contains one of the most frequently quoted and poignant passages in Michelet's long underground plaint about the disappointments of language: "O problem! To be old and young at the same time, to be knowledgeable and a child! I pursued these thoughts in my mind all my life. They rose before me and crushed me. In them I felt our misery, the impotence of those who are educated, the clever. I despised myself" (Paris: Librairie Internationale, 1870, p. 363).

Ironically, this is exactly what happened: Michelet the child, the lightheaded youth, began a dialogue with the sophisticated skeptic. Candide entertained Sade. Out of the mouths of kings and heroes came the obscenity of farce. Hope spoke of decadence. Another current, moving in history alongside the Revolution, was the mime troupe specializing in massacres and coups under the cloak of authority: the well-known production of Saint Bartholomew's Day, better than the inferior Sicilian Vespers and the antics of Cesare Borgia, came close to falling on its face during the *Eighteenth of Brumaire*, but was saved by the grotesqueries of an empire. Always they had the same actor: Jupiter steps forward to recite the lines of Scapin.

The historian is drawn closer to his most hated double, who is actually only a slip of a letter away: *Totus mundus exercet histrionem* (X, 271). It does not take much to turn the text inside out, and the reality it reproduces: the *trompeurs* (deceivers) are eventually *trompés;* the *menteurs* (liars) are caught in their own traps; "les spectateurs étaient le spectacle" (*Histoire de France*, XII, 97); the historians are history and the writer remains his own subject.

Crisis rolling toward chaos becomes continuity again; the slight touch unbalancing a pair starts the fission on its way to confusion; the weather vane of politics looks like the circling earth. Yet anything beyond this is off limits for history, which must move through two simultaneous channels of epic and farce, of mystic republicanism and anarchy,[4] of myth and miracle, and all the gradations between.

[4] Hayden White's chapter on Michelet in *The Historical Imagination in Nineteenth-Century Europe* (Baltimore, The Johns Hopkins University Press, 1973) gives Michelet's text and ideology the space it needs in which to move; his reading of the *Histoire de la Révolution française* is a long-awaited revision.

Outside is the realm of Alibi. Both pejorative and attractive, as is everything and every word in Michelet's universe, *alibi* is literally the *ailleurs*,[5] the elsewhere, like Baudelaire's "any-where but out of this world," that pretends to cut its contact with time. It is either of the extreme dialectical sides trying to deny the pull of the other. The *Histoire de France* represented one edge of history tipped as far as it could go toward night-mare. France was embodied in everything it was not; the King, descended from a long line of Italians or Spaniards, closed himself off in the receding world of Versailles' royal chamber, a cell like the living death of the *in-pace*, and surrounded him-self with surrealistic figures. Louis XVI, culminating the antihistory of France, lived "in a complete alibi, in perfect ignorance of the country he ruled" (*Histoire de France*, XVII, x). The empty imagination increased every day in voracious-ness and fed on its self: "They had to continue, at any price, augmenting the alibi the king lived in" (p. 68). The nature books, on the other side of the *Histoire de France*, offered the opposite but identical alibi, which is poetry. In *L'Oiseau*, while Michelet was still under the hopeful influence of an ideal regenerative nature, the warbler, though encaged, sang from a life that was entirely somewhere else: "An all-powerful *alibi* kept her far away, in her native woods, in love's nest" (p. 38). A step just before this radical departure, when the Revolution is just springing forth and history is eternally new, is where Michelet would locate the eccentric center of his work, which he would call the "natural sublime": "The sublime never leaves nature" ("Préface de 1869," xxxi). But, of course, this reality is short-lived, and even alibi is implicated in the dialec-tic, for one place is always another's absence, another's escape: writing as life, ideology as action. . . .

Michelet needed the confines (though elastic to almost

[5] For a more complete discussion, see my article "L'Alibi, ou l'autre discours de Michelet: *La Montagne*," in *Michelet cent ans après*, pp. 63–74.

infinity) of history. Poetry, the nature of contemplation and, perhaps, the true nature of Revolution, like the isolated alibi, was difficult for him to deal with, ambiguous, even frightening. He needed the dialectic of the other and of no one, to polarize and define his all-encompassing I; he could not have sustained Hugo's ego on the lonely promontory or Danton's at the tribune but had to be moving, always moving between. His final stance, which is not unity or the golden mean (what he called a "cold" *milieu*), is the rhetorical and philosophical expression of irony. Again, the word splits into its positive and negative connotations, which cover from one extreme—a mechanical, lifeless abstraction, the rictus—to the other—the abundant comedy of change. "Irony: art is also an irony. There would be too much sadness if we could not, in our turn, make fun of nature. The great comedians are sad, unless they have a clever word. They go then their particular way, knowing there is one fixed thing in the world: change" (*Journal*, I, 355). Much of Michelet's later discourse juxtaposes what one would identify today as Nietzschean with a hold-over from early utopian socialism and a constant unextinguished hope for progress.

Both the villains and true heroes of Michelet's work appear in the guise of irony. Napoleon withdrew from the hissing of his audience, and "retrenched into a laugh, an abominable irony" (*Histoire du XIXe siècle*, III, 344), but the same word metamorphoses radically to describe the child. A recurrent image seems to satisfy Michelet in his search to explain what writing is, what any useful fiction is; he speaks of the consummate artist as a young girl playing with her doll. The girl or writer calls the representation "my daughter" and smiles knowingly and not-knowingly. "Such is the essential condition of creativity. It is love, but also the smile" ("Préface de 1869," xxii). Behind this smile is a consciousness at ease with itself, a naiveté that is wiser than it knows. The girl is like the historian who binds himself just enough to his own voices of self-consciousness so that he can maintain his sublime rhetoric, so that neither a degrading farce nor a transparent lyric can drown out, literally swallow up, the other. He (and she) are both fools and experts of ruse. "France was, was not a dupe. The two things are perhaps true, and complement each other well. The child is serious while rocking the doll in her arms (even sincere), she kisses and loves it, but knows very well it is made of wood" (*Histoire de France*, XII, 290–91). Michelet, historian of Resurrection, frequently confessed that the dead would never be other than dead.

The "demi-hypocrite" (Lancaster) and the "sincere charlatan" (Law), like the naturalist and the historian, are alternatives and combinations of health and madness. Rousseau, who elicited Michelet's instinctive sympathy and a consequent ambivalence, is profoundly afflicted: his effort to adopt two complete and apparently contradictory visions dramatizes what Michelet was close to becoming, his temptation and greatest fear: "He wants us to follow *Nature*, wants us to return to *Nature*. But simultaneously he admits the existence of *Anti-Nature*, of miracle" (*Histoire de France*, XVII, 65).[6] Reading Rousseau gave Michelet the same impression one has in reading the *Histoire de France*, the mythologies (*La Sorcière*, *La Bible de l'humanité*), and the natural histories today: they are the work of a man possessed with conflicting powers: "A damned man, it is that very thing. He carried at this moment a Hell of discord; demons fought within him. He was great with his children *Emile*, *Julie*, and the *Contract* (three books in two years)" (p. 51). But from fission to fusion Michelet

[6] See Paul de Man's chapter on Derrida and Rousseau in *Blindness and Insight* (New York, 1971), especially: "The awareness of distance, in Rousseau, is at times stated in a blind, at times in a semi-conscious language, and the same applies to the awareness of presence. Rousseau truly seems to want it both ways, the paradox being what he wants wanting and not-wanting at the same time. This would always assume some degree of awareness, though the awareness may be directed against itself" (p. 118).

could not let anything rest; the magic wand covers over what the divining rod disclosed. Rousseau is at his *fond du fond*, at some (arbitrary) bottom, allied with the diabolic Anti-Nature: "He stays in the bastard middle which suits the crowd, half-reasoning, half-Christian. But what is he at heart [*au fond*]? Christian" (p. 66). And Michelet would be the other bastard, the hesitating medusa, that would lean toward the side of nature, Rousseau's double, the mask of his mask.

Still, neither Michelet can excuse the other. He will never be Marx; he will never be the founder of a social science. He will never be Hugo. His rhetoric will both exasperate us and lead us into the complexities where his real interest is to be found. Any one of his individual works is an introduction into the labyrinth, but he should not be long exiled from his entire edifice. More than a totalitarian dream, his work is an endless investigation (a history) which an obsessive curiosity surely helped rather than hindered; his words are bait. He spins the reader around in front of many mirrors and refuses categorization so that the simple principles, as blatantly corrupt and contorted as they are, are at least and at most a place to come back to.

could go. In one long essay [illegible] what [illegible] the divinity [illegible] Rousseau [illegible] some (rather [illegible]) [illegible] "He stays in the [illegible] middle which [illegible] crowd, half-[illegible] [illegible] the [illegible] nature. Rousseau [illegible] in the [illegible].

Only rather, Michelet can [illegible] he will never [illegible] be the founder [illegible]. He will [illegible] Hero. His rhetoric will [illegible] exaggerate [illegible] lead us into the [illegible] where [illegible] interest is to be found. [illegible] of his [illegible] is an introduction into the labyrinth [illegible] should [illegible] his [illegible]. More than a [illegible] his work is an endless investigation [illegible] history which [illegible] rarely helped rather than hindered [illegible] are built. He [illegible] and refuses [illegible] and comforting as they are [illegible] at least [illegible] a place to come back to.

Bibliography of Michelet's Works and Related Criticism

Works of Jules Michelet

L'Amour. 4th ed. Paris: Hachette, 1859.

Le Banquet. 1st ed. Paris: Calmann-Lévy, 1879.

Bible de l'humanité. Paris: Chamerot, 1864.

Des Jésuites. With Edgar Quinet. Utrecht: Pauvert, 1966. Orig. pub. 1843.

Du Prêtre, de la femme, de la famille. 3d ed. Paris: Hachette, 1845.

Ecrits de jeunesse: Journal (1820–1823), Mémorial, Journal des idées. Ed. Paul Viallaneix. 2d ed. Paris: Gallimard, 1959.

L'Etudiant. Ed. Gaëtan Picon. Paris: Seuil, 1970. Orig. pub. 1877.

La Femme. 15th ed. Paris: Calmann-Lévy, 1885.

Histoire de France. 17 vols. Paris: Librairie Internationale, 1876. (Editor who first published the entire series with Michelet's "Préface de 1869"; subtitles began with Vol. VII as follows:) VII: XVIe siècle, *La Renaissance;* VIII: XVIe siècle, *La Réforme;* IX: XVIe siècle, *La Ligue et Henri IV;* XI: XVIIe siècle, *Henri IV et Richelieu;* XII: XVIIe siècle, *Richelieu et la Fronde;* XIII: XVIIe siècle, *Louis XIV et La Révocation de l'Edit de Nantes;* XIV: XVIIe siècle, *Louis XIV et le Duc de Bourgogne;* XV: XVIIIe siècle, *La Régence;* XVI: XVIIIe siècle, *Louis XV (1724–1757);* XVII: XVIIIe siècle, *Louis XV et Louis XVI.*

Histoire de la Révolution française. Ed. Gérard Walter. 2 vols. Paris: Gallimard, 1952. Orig. pub. 1847–1853.

Histoire du XIXe siècle. 3 vols. Paris: C. Marpon et E. Flammarion, 1880.

History of the French Revolution. Trans. Charles Cook. Ed. Gordon Wright. Chicago: University of Chicago Press, 1967.

L'Insecte. Paris: Hachette, 1858.

Introduction à l'Histoire universelle in *Oeuvres complètes.* Ed. Paul Viallaneix. Vol. IV. Paris: Flammarion, 1971–. Orig. pub. 1831.

Jeanne d'Arc et autres textes. Ed. Paul Viallaneix. Paris: Gallimard, 1974.

Journal. Ed. Paul Viallaneix. 2 vols. (Vol. I, 4th ed.). Paris: Gallimard, 1959 and 1962.

La Mer. 2d ed. Paris: Hachette, 1861.

La Montagne in *Oeuvres complètes.* Vol. XXXIII. Paris: Flammarion, 1893–1899.

Nos Fils. 2d ed. Paris: Librairie Internationale, 1870.

Oeuvres choisies de Vico. Paris: Flammarion, n.d.

Oeuvres complètes. 26 vols. Paris: Flammarion, 1893–1899.

Oeuvres complètes. 20 vols. when completed (5 vols. to date). Paris: Flammarion, 1971–.

L'Oiseau. 9th ed. Paris: Hachette, 1867.

Le Peuple. Ed. Lucien Refort. Paris: Didier, 1946. Orig. pub. 1846.

Le Peuple. Ed. Paul Viallaneix. Paris: Flammarion, 1974.

La Sorcière. Ed. Paul Viallaneix. Paris: Garnier-Flammarion, 1966. Orig. pub. 1862.

Michelet Criticism

Allen, Gay Wilson. "Walt Whitman and Jules Michelet." *Etudes anglaises,* 1 (May 1937), 230–37.

L'Arc, no. 52 (n.d.). "Michelet" issue. Articles by Jacques Le Goff, Roland Barthes, Linda Orr, Claude Mettra, Pierre Malandain, Robert Mandrou, Pierre Nora, Paul Viallaneix, J. Favret, J.-P. Peter, Georges Duby.

Atherton, John. "The Function of Space in Michelet's Writing." Modern Language Notes, 82 (October 1967), 336–46.

Bachelard, Gaston. *L'Air et les songes: Essai sur l'imagination du mouvement.* Paris: Corti, 1943.

——. *L'Eau et les rêves: Essai sur l'imagination de la matière.* Paris: Corti, 1942.

——. *La Poétique de l'espace.* Paris: Presses Universitaires de France, 1957.

——. *La Terre et les rêveries du repos.* Paris: Corti, 1948.

Barthes, Roland. *Michelet par lui-même.* Paris: Seuil, 1954.

——. "La Sorcière." *Essais critiques.* Paris: Seuil, 1964.

Besançon, Alain. "Le Premier Livre de 'La Sorcière.'" *Annales: Economies, Sociétés, Civilisations,* 26 (Jan.–Feb. 1971), 186–204.

Borzeix, Jean-Marie. "L'Unité et l'union, du *Peuple* à *La Bible de l'humanité.*" *Romantisme,* 1–2 (1971), 111–16.

Calo, Jeanne. *La Création de la femme chez Michelet.* Paris: Nizet, 1975.

Carré, Jean-Marie. *Michelet et son temps.* Paris: Perrin, 1926.

Cornuz, Jean-Louis. *Jules Michelet: Un aspect de la pensée religieuse au XIXe siècle.* Geneva: Droz, 1955.

Engel, Claire-Eliane. *La Littérature alpestre: en France et en Angleterre aux XVIIIe et XIXe siècle.* Chambery: Dardel, 1930.

Europe, 51 (Nov.–Dec. 1973). "Michelet" issue. Articles by Paul Viallaneix, Maurice Bouvier-Ajam, Gérard Milhaud, Georges Cogniot, Roger Bellet, André Wurmser, Jacques Madaule, Edward K. Kaplan, Catherine Clément, Linda Orr, Jacques Seebacher, Maria Wodzynska-Walicka, Jean-Louis Cornuz, Istvan Fodor, Marin Bucur, and Miklos Kun.

Gaulmier, Jean. *Michelet.* Paris: Desclée De Brouwer, 1968.

Giraud, Victor. "L'Evolution spirituelle de Michelet." *Revue des deux mondes,* 5 (1927), 218–29.

Goncourt, Edmond and Jules de. *Journal: Mémoires de la vie littéraire, 1851–1896.* Ed. Robert Ricatte. 22 vols. Monaco: Flammarion, 1956–1958. Orig. pub. 1887–1888.

Gossman, Lionel. "The Go-Between: Jules Michelet, 1798–1874." *Modern Language Notes,* 89 (May 1974), 503–41.

Guéhenno, Jean. *L'Evangile éternelle.* Paris: Grasset, 1927.

Halévy, Daniel. *Jules Michelet.* Paris: Hachette, 1928.

Hauser, Henri. "Michelet naturaliste et l'âme française d'aujourd'hui." *Revue du mois,* 19 (Jan.–June 1915), 151–71.

Hertzen, Aleksandr Ivanovich. *From the Other Shore.* Trans. Moura Budbery. *The Russian People and Socialism, An Open Letter to Jules Michelet.* Trans. Richard Wollheim. London: Weidenfeld and Nicolson, 1956.

Johnson, Mary-Elizabeth. *Michelet et le christianisme.* Paris: Nizet, 1955.

Kaplan, Edward Kivie. "Michelet's Poetic Vision: The Structure of his Philosophy of Nature and Man." Diss. Columbia University, 1970.

Michelet cent ans après. Ed. Paul Viallaneix. Grenoble: Presses Universitaires de Grenoble, 1975. Articles by Paul Viallaneix, Linda Orr, Jacques Seebacher, Jean-Pierre Richard, Pierre Malandain, Edward Kaplan, Louis Le Guillou, Simone Bernard-Griffiths, Elisabeth Brisson, A. Govindane, François Papillard, and discussion led by Françoise Gaillard.

Monod, Gabriel. *La Vie et la pensée de Jules Michelet, 1798–1852; Cours professés au Collège de France.* 2 vols. Paris: Champion, 1923.

——. *Jules Michelet.* Paris: Hachette, 1905.

Paris. *Michelet: Sa vie, son oeuvre 1798–1874.* Paris: Archives de France, 1961.

Picon, Gaëtan. "Michelet et la parole historienne." Introduction. *L'Etudiant.* Paris: Seuil, 1970.

Poulet, Georges. "Michelet et le moment d'Eros." *La Nouvelle Revue française,* 30 (October 1967), 610–35.

Refort, Lucien. *L'Art de Michelet dans son oeuvre historique jusqu'en 1867.* Paris: Champion, 1923.

——. *Essai d'introduction à une étude lexicologique de Michelet.* Paris: Champion, 1923.

Revue d'histoire littéraire de la France. 74 (Sept.–Oct. 1974). "Michelet" issue. Articles by Roland Barthes, Michel Serres, Linda Orr, Jacques Seebacher, Frank Bowman, Bernard Leuilliot, Jacques Viard.

Serres, Michel. "La Sorcière." *Hermès (La Communication, I).* Paris: Critique, 1968, 219–32.

Van der Elst, Robert. *Michelet naturaliste: Esquisse de son système de philosophie.* Paris: Delagrave, 1914.

Viallaneix, Paul. *La Voie royale: Essai sur l'idée de peuple dans l'oeuvre de Michelet.* Paris: Flammarion, 1959, rpt. 1971.

——. "Le Héros selon Michelet." *Romantisme,* 1–2 (1971), 102–10.

White, Hayden. *The Historical Imagination in Nineteenth-Century Europe.* Baltimore, Md.: The Johns Hopkins University Press, 1973.

Wilson, Edmund. *To the Finland Station: A Study in the Writing and Acting of History.* New York: Doubleday, 1955.

Index

No reference is made to the four books of natural history, but all other works of Michelet are listed under their titles.

JULES MICHELET

Designed by R. E. Rosenbaum.
Composed by York Composition Company, Inc.,
in 11 point linotype Janson, 2 points leaded,
with display lines in Deepdene.
Printed letterpress from type by York Composition Company
on Warren's Number 66 text, 50 pound basis.
Bound by John H. Dekker & Sons, Inc.
in Joanna book cloth
and stamped in All Purpose foil.

Library of Congress Cataloging in Publication Data
(For library cataloging purposes only)

Orr, Linda, 1943–
Jules Michelet: nature, history, and language.

Bibliography: p.
Includes index.
1. Michelet, Jules, 1798–1874.
DC36.98.M5077 944'.007'2024 [B] 76–13662
ISBN 0-8014-0976-4